The Entrepreneurial Shift

This is a provocative study of how American-led entrepreneurship transformed business education in Europe. Starting with Silicon Valley's high-technology businesses, and examining business schools in France, Germany and the Czech Republic, the book shows how management education shifted in response to an increasingly entrepreneurial business context. Traditionally, training focused on learning about existing models and how to use them to best advantage; there was little room to embrace continuous change. New technologies have been liberating, enhancing variety and change in European business schools. The educational emphasis has turned now to thinking "outside the box" – embracing technological solutions, and creating organizations in which constant transformation is an everyday phenomenon. This study is an important contribution, and will be of interest to academics, students and practitioners who are concerned with how and why business is and should be taught today.

ROBERT R. LOCKE is Emeritus Professor of History in the Department of History at the University of Hawaii at Manoa. He is the author of *The End of the Practical Man* (1984), *Management and Higher Education Since 1940* (1989) and *The Collapse of the American Management Mystique* (1996).

KATJA E. SCHÖNE holds a Master's degree in International Business Studies and a Ph.D. in International Relations.

The Entrepreneurial Shift

Americanization in European High-Technology Management Education

ROBERT R. LOCKE AND KATJA E. SCHÖNE

CAMBRIDGE
UNIVERSITY PRESS

CAMBRIDGE
UNIVERSITY PRESS

University Printing House, Cambridge CB2 8BS, United Kingdom

Cambridge University Press is part of the University of Cambridge.

It furthers the University's mission by disseminating knowledge in the pursuit of education, learning and research at the highest international levels of excellence.

www.cambridge.org
Information on this title: www.cambridge.org/9780521840101

© Robert R. Locke and Katja E. Schöne 2004

This publication is in copyright. Subject to statutory exception and to the provisions of relevant collective licensing agreements, no reproduction of any part may take place without the written permission of Cambridge University Press.

First published 2004
First paperback edition 2011

A catalogue record for this publication is available from the British Library

ISBN 978-0-521-84010-1 Hardback
ISBN 978-1-107-40339-0 Paperback

Cambridge University Press has no responsibility for the persistence or accuracy of URLs for external or third-party internet websites referred to in this publication, and does not guarantee that any content on such websites is, or will remain, accurate or appropriate.

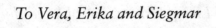

To Vera, Erika and Siegmar

Living history is not like reading it.
History once written has the
illusion of inevitability.

JEAN-PAUL SARTRE

Contents

Illustrations

Acknowledgements

Nobody writes a book without assistance. Since this book is co-authored and each author had at times slightly different agendas, especially in the research phase, the lists of acknowledgements differ.

Robert Locke would like to thank the people in the School of Management, The Queens University, Belfast, for their generous support when the project began in 1999. He wishes especially to thank C. Anne Davies, former Head of the Queen's School of Management, and Professor Paul Jeffcutt for having made an Honorary Visiting Professorship there possible and, during the tenure of the professorship, for funding numerous research and lecturing trips in Europe plus a six-week research stay in Silicon Valley, May–June 2000. Dr. Davies and Mark Braly, of the US Department of Defense, not only participated in many of the interview sessions in Silicon Valley but also arranged for some of them to take place. Robert is very grateful. He would also like to thank people in the Department of Business Economics in the State University, Groningen (the Netherlands), and especially among them Luchien Karsten, for permitting him on numerous visits to use their lecture halls and seminars as a resource for his work. Special thanks are due too to the staff in the French Consulate in San Francisco, for organizing a session with Braly regarding French people in Silicon Valley.

Katja Schöne would like to thank the Stiftung der Deutschen Wirtschaft for its financial support and Alain Fayolle, Joseph Orlinski and people in the ESC Lille for their help in preparing the interviews in France. Both authors, moreover, send special thanks to the interviewees in France, Germany, the Czech Republic and California, for consenting to be interviewed. The book depends so much on their generous cooperation.

Several people have contributed to the actual preparation of the book. Peter J. van Baalen, of Rotterdam University, read an early draft of the manuscript, which was improved subsequently in the light of

x   *Acknowledgements*

his insightful comments. Vanessa Karam has proof-read the work with her usual sharp-eyed acumen. Katy Plowright, our editor, has not only shepherded the book through the acceptance and production process but has added constructively to its organization, thought content and style. We are grateful to all.

The authors also wish to acknowledge the support from family and friends that is so necessary to the fulfillment of a project. Robert Locke thanks Anja, Ivonka, Regina, Luba and Helene for housing him during the writing phase. Katja Schöne thanks her parents, and Sissi and Ulrich, for moral support, and Vera Locke, Robert's wife, for her loving understanding. Robert seconds this sentiment and adds much thanks to Vera for the time she granted him to work on the book. Her love and help, and that of Katja's parents, explain the book's dedication.

Finally, the authors would like to thank each other in this statement of appreciation. They have reached across the generation divide and bridged it in the most rewarding fashion. Neither thought at the beginning of the collaboration that it would be so rewarding personally. It was everything that – and even more than – an intellectual, co-venture should be.

"It was astonishing (and this is not too strong a word), our intellectual journey together, and we are grateful to each other for the intensity of the conversations and the joy of them as we worked our way through the intellectual problems the study presented. We both share equally in the good or bad of what we have done."

ROBERT LOCKE
Görlitz, Germany, and Honolulu, Hawaii

KATJA SCHÖNE
Dresden, Germany

Abbreviations

AIE	Association of Innovative Entrepreneurship
ANVAR	Agence Nationale de Valorisation de la Recherche
ARP	Agentura pro Rozvoj Podnikání (business development agency)
ARPA	Advanced Research Projects Agency
Bac	Baccalauréat
BBA	Bachelor of Business Administration
BIC	Business innovation center
BMBF	Bundesministerium für Bildung und Forschung (Federal Ministry for Education and Research)
BMWI	Bundesministerium für Wirtschaft und Innovation (Federal Ministry for Economics and Innovation)
BWL	Betriebswirtschaftslehre (business economics) – an academic discipline
CEO	Chief executive officer
CERAM	Centre d'Enseignement et de Recherche Appliquée au Management
CIBER	Center for International Business Education and Research
CIDEGEF	Conférence Internationale des Dirigeants des institutions d'Enseignement supérieur et de recherche de Gestion d'Expression Française
CNRS	Centre National de Recherche Scientifique
CREGE	Centre de Recherche Economique et de Gestion d'Entreprise
DEA	Diplôme d'Etudes Appliquées
DESS	Diplôme d'Etudes Supérieures Spécialisées
DEUG	Diplôme d'Etudes Universitaires Générales
DFG	Deutsche Forschungsgemeinschaft (German Research Association)
Doc. Ing.	Doctor Ingenieur

DOD	Department of Defense
EBS	European Business School
EC	Ecole Centrale – a premier French engineering school
ECD	Ecole du Commerce et de la Distribution
EDP	Electronic data processing
EEC	European Economic Community
EM	Ecole de management
ENA	Ecole Nationale d'Administration
ENSAIT	Ecole Nationale Supérieure des Arts et Industries Textiles
ENST	Ecole Nationale Supérieure des Télécommunications
EOE	Experimentally organized economy
ESC	Ecole supérieure de commerce – the generic term for French schools of commerce
ESCP-EAP	Ecole Supérieure de Commerce de Paris-Ecole d'Administration de Paris – a premier French ESC
ESISAR	Ecole Supérieure d'Ingénieurs en Systèmes industriels Avancés Rhône-Alpes
ESMA	Escuela Superior de Marketing
ESSEC	Ecole supérieure des sciences économiques et commerciales – a premier French ESC
FH	Fachhochschule – a sub-university school
FHT	Fachhochschule für Technik
FNEGE	Fondation Nationale d'Education de Gestion d'Entreprises
GIP	Groupement d'intérêt public
HBS	Harvard Business School
HEC	Ecole des Hautes Etudes Commerciales – a premier French ESC
HHL	Handelshochschule Leipzig
HRD	Human resource development
HU	Humboldt Universität
IAE	Institut d'administration d'entreprises
IMT	Innovation management techniques
INSA	Institut National des Sciences Appliquées
INPG	Institut National Polytechnique de Grenoble
INPL	Institut National Polytechnique de Lorraine
INSERM	Institut National de la Santé et de la Recherche Médicale
IPO	Initial public offering
IR	Information revolution
IT	Information technology

IU	International university
IUT	Institut universitaire de technologie
LMU	Ludwig-Maximilians-Universität (Munich)
MBA	Master of Business Administration
MIT	Massachusetts Institute of Technology
MOT	Management of technology
NASA	National Aeronautics and Space Administration
NPVD	New product and venture development (Sloan School of Management)
NYU	New York University
OECD	Organization for Economic Cooperation and Development
OR	Operations research
PARC	Palo Alto Research Center
PEI	Program of Entrepreneurship and Innovation (University of Washington)
PIMENT	Programme d'Initiation au Management de l'Entreprise
RAIC	Regional Advisory and Information Center
R&D	Research and development
RWTH	Rheinisch-Westfälische Technische Hochschule
SAIC	Services d'Activités Industrielles et Commerciales
SARL	Société A Responsabilité Limitée (limited company)
SNCF	Société Nationale des Chemins de Fer
SME	Small and medium-sized enterprise
SPD	Sozialdemokratische Partei Deutschlands
STPA	Science and Technology Parks Association
TGZ	Technologie- und Gründerzentren
TH	Technische Hochschule
TQM	Total quality management
TU	Technische Universität
UCLA	University of California, Los Angeles
UGH	Universität Gesamthochschule
UNESCO	United Nations Educational, Scientific and Cultural Organization
UTC	Université de Technologie Compiègne
VC	Venture capital
WHU	Wissenschaftliche Hochschule für Unternehmensführung
WZL	Werkzeugmaschinealabor
YEO	Young Entrepreneurs' Organization

Introduction

I N this introduction we wish to do three things: first, to discuss the
subject and its importance; second, to look at how we, as historians,
approach "Americanization"; and, finally, to sketch out our scheme
of presentation.

The subject

This book investigates the impact of the information revolution on
the form and content of management education, first in the United
States of America, where IR initially flourished, and then in Europe, to
where it – in varying different degrees – spread. We call the educational
innovation "the entrepreneurial shift."

The importance of the shift

In order to mark the significance of this shift, we seize on Friedrich
Nietzsche's mythopoetic vision of Dionysus and Apollo because their
conflicting attributes sum up, in a powerful and timeless metaphor,
the states of human consciousness that produced the striking transformation the book describes. In his study of *Young Nietzsche*, Carl
Pletsch observed that, for Nietzsche, the Apollonian "is the principle of clearly delineated images, permanence, optimism, individuation,
and rationality. It is striving for clarity." This is the ethos of classical
American corporate management. On the other hand, for Nietzsche,
the Dionysian expresses "the principle of flux, impermanence, suf-
fering, and pessimism . . . an irrational force, impulsive, wild, and
instinctive." This is the creative power behind entrepreneurialism. On
a philosophic plain, while Nietzsche "affiliates Schopenhauer's concept
of the 'idea' or 'representation' with Apollo, he associates Dionysus
with the 'will.'" Accordingly, whereas the Apollonian vision is timeless and "responsible for the constant formulation and reformulation

1

of the forms of knowledge and rationality that order our everyday life, [thereby] concealing the underlying Dionysian reality from ourselves," the Dionysian urge, which is "momentary, exceptional, and counter-intuitive," is "dangerous to any structure of reality." It contains "the death wish and every other destructive instinct as well as the life instinct. It is the maelstrom of every impulse caught in the flux of time." It characterizes precisely the creative/destructive behavior of the great entrepreneur. For this reason, for us as well as for Nietzsche, "the Dionysian is the more profound of the two modes; it can only be ignored at the price of cultural sterility and ultimately [economic] extinction."[1]

Such mythopoeticisms might seem far removed from corporate boardrooms, but they are not. Professor Gunnar Eliasson, of Stockholm's Royal Institute of Technology, although using economic phraseology, conjured up the same imagery of contrast when contemplating recent management change. He concluded from longitudinal surveys of management opinion in the changed economic environment of the late twentieth century that inherited systems of management behavior could no longer govern creatively. When he interviewed managers in fifty US and European firms between 1965 and 1975, he concluded that the predominant characteristics of management behavior for them were "short-term and long-range *planning* and a strong belief in repetitive environments, forecasting and centralized leadership of standardized production (Eliasson, 1976)." But when he interviewed managers in fifty firms between 1985 and 1995, fifteen of which were IT startups, he discovered that "out had gone reliance on detached analytical thinking in executive quarters, in had come experimental behavior . . . the distinction between uncertainty and risk." Eliasson called this second environment that of the "experimentally organized economy." It is experimental because entrepreneurs with several possible options never "know them all; even though they have stumbled upon the absolute best solution, they will never know it because the knowledge base is always insufficient. The business manager will never feel safe, and will have to recognize in his management practice the possibility of coming out as a loser." In this EOE, failure need not be attributed to managerial ineptitude, as it would in a "full information economy," but can come from unavoidable risk. Failure consequently has to be considered

---

[1] All quotes about Nietzsche are from Pletsch (1991), pp. 131–32.

a normal business experience – one from which entrepreneurs learn, as in any experiment (Eliasson, 1997).

In the EOE, then, management behavior has changed from that encountered by Eliasson in firms during his first interviews. Managers not only move from a "full information economy" to one of information "uncertainty," but the kind of knowledge used in entrepreneurial decisions is obtained differently. In the "full information economy," it is gained formally; in the EOE, it is more tacitly acquired skills and innate ability that count. Apollonian management in older firms might learn new methods of governance over time and become intrapreneurial but they would not be leaders in bringing change about. That would require Dionysian "will."

The great events that transformed the American economy in the information revolution of the late twentieth century were brought about primarily by entrepreneurs and intrapreneurs in the Dionysian mode. They sparked the imagination of those who had lived under the control of the corporate managerial hierarchies after World War II, and the management schools that had trained them to be managerial Apollos, to create an education appropriate to the entrepreneurship of the "information age." They strove, therefore, to include the entrepreneurial dimension in management education. This book examines this educational event, and covers the emergence of "entrepreneurship" in American management education and its subsequent impact on such education in three European countries in the high-tech era.

The book's scope

In the title we use the word "European." It is, of course, an exaggeration to equate Europe with France, Germany and the Czech Republic, but we think it is a permissible one. France and Germany, two major European economies, with significant and influential management education establishments, occupy a large enough place on the continent to make their combined educational experiences "European." France, moreover, represents Latin Europe, where its influence has particularly radiated, while Germany has traditionally exercised influence in Central, Northern and Eastern Europe. The Czech Republic's inclusion cannot, of course, be justified on similar grounds. But, we thought, to be European the book had to take into account the "New Europe" after 1990. We could not broaden the scope of the study to include

large numbers of countries. The research complexities evoked by lin-
guistic, social and economic diversity in Eastern Europe made this
too arduous a research task. Nor did we wish to include formerly
peasant-based countries that would have shown little interest in phenomenal Silicon Valley and the American high-tech entrepreneurship
that so much caught the attention of Western Europeans. We wanted
to see how a mature industrial country that had been cut off from the
United States and Western Europe since World War II had been able to
absorb the whole range of American ideas about management education, including the latest ones on entrepreneurship studies. Within the
previous Communist bloc, the Czech Republic stood out. It has been
technically, industrially and educationally the most advanced of these
countries for centuries and, therefore, offered the most fertile soil for
an investigation. In different ways, then, these three country histories
illustrate the changing practices of greater Europe in entrepreneurial
education.

"Americanization"

Since it is the study's focus, something at the outset also needs to be
said about US influence, or "Americanization." It is not so much an
historical phenomenon as a nomenclature that historians and others
have applied to the developments in Europe that have been greatly
affected by events in the United States. Specifically, in the case at hand,
American events are seen to have greatly influenced management and
management education in Europe. Such American influence has a long
history. It began before World War I, when the "scientific management" movement caught Europe's attention. Its chief exponent, the
American engineer Frederick Winslow Taylor, visited and was feted in
Europe; Taylorism became familiar to Europe's industrial managers
and engineers. There was nothing, despite the terminology, particularly "scientific" about Taylor's methods and aims; nor was there
anything exclusively American about them. France had its pioneer in
scientific management in Henry Fayol, Germany in Professor Georg
Schlesinger of the Technical University at Charlottenburg. But scientific
management or Taylorism came to represent a certain rationaliza-
tion of production particularly espoused in America, which permitted
the professional manager to replace the skilled worker as the arbi-
trator of shop-floor procedure: standardization of work through the

implementation of time and motion studies, control through budgeting and standard costing, etc.

Taylorism continued to influence European management after World War I. To it was added the rationalized mass production methods made famous at Henry Ford's new River Rouge plant. In Germany the word "Fordismus" signified mass production. In addition, certain features of American management education attracted attention in Europe during the 1920s. The index of the Harvard Business School, developed to forecast business cycles, was one, until it failed ignominiously to predict the stock market collapse of 1929. The collections of business cases developed as teaching tools at Harvard Business School were another. In France the Paris Chamber of Commerce created a center in 1932, which housed these Harvard-developed American cases for French consultation. But the collapse of market-driven American managerial capitalism in the Great Depression largely ended American influence in inter-war Europe, where each country turned in the 1930s to protectionism, the nationalization of industries, and corporatism to find a way out of the morass.

"Americanization" at the time was not used to describe collectively the influence of American scientific management, mass production or business schools on pre-war European management. But after World War II people increasingly used the word to cover the multiple and multiplying US influences on European management. The immediate post-war period indeed is the classic age of Americanization, and it has been dealt with extensively in the historical literature.[2] But Americanization, to use a phrase of Jonathan Zeitlin in the introduction to his work with Gary Herrigel on the subject, always remains a "contested historical project" (Zeitlin, 2000, p. 18). This means that scholars disagree about the content of Americanization, on how much it has influenced management in Europe, where and when. Still, as these scholars also attest, a consensus has emerged about the content of immediate post-war Americanization; it boils down to the spread of US-propagated, multidivisional, international corporate structures and forms of governance, headed by managerial hierarchies and the managerial philosophies that went with them, and the continued Taylorization of management methods in factories and on the shop floor. This post-war Americanization also embraced a number of educational events that are of direct interest

---

[2] See the citations in Zeitlin (2000) for works on the subject.

to this study because they were designed to promote the creation of a management professional class and educate them to their corporate functions. This education included the fostering of a management press (*L'Expansion*, *Der Manager*, etc.) patterned on American business and management periodicals, the development of in-house corporate management training programs following American corporate examples, and the spawning of management schools with programs that leaned heavily on American institutional models.

If the post-war period can be called the classic age of Americanization, it is historically bounded because subsequently the content of Americanization changed. Some feel that this even happened in the era of "Japanization" – i.e. after what Locke has called the collapse, around 1980, of the American management mystique (Locke, 1996). Locke asserts that a Japanese management mystique replaced the American in the 1980s, but Professor Alfred Kieser of Mannheim University contends that this Japanization really amounted to a further expression of management's international Americanization (Kieser, 2002a). He argues, in effect, that because American management academics and consultants led the Japanization movement in America and in Europe, Japanization was an American version of Japan. Kieser makes a good point. Japanese management by its very nature was inward-looking, firm-centered. It, in contrast to management in the United States, had never developed the capacity to proselytize. When corporate Japan expanded dramatically in the 1960s, 1970s and 1980s, there were no graduate management schools in the country. The only academic business education that existed consisted of a few commercial courses taught by professors who were, like German BWL professors, alienated from praxis, and, unlike the Germans, without a research-driven scientific culture. Since few non-Japanese spoke their tongue, their language also hindered international interaction. American consultants and management academics got the job of spreading knowledge about Japan, then, partially by default but partially, too, by the fact that they had created a powerful teaching and research establishment in the post-war United States. Japan arrived in Europe through an American conduit and what the Americans reported was selective, and often misunderstood or even wrong.

But if Japanization was just another form of Americanization, in this form it not only differed from post-war Americanization but also directly challenged its content. This change in content was described in books such as Kenney and Florida's *Beyond Mass Production: The Japanese System and its Transfer to the US* and Oliver and Wilkinson's *The Japanization of British Industry*,[3] and a host of other works published for American and European audiences.[4]

Still another Americanization, the most recent, arrived with the "information revolution" (*c.* 1975–2000). There is no need in these preliminary remarks to outline the content shift that this Americanization has brought since it is, with special focus on management education, the subject of the book.[5] Suffice it to say that this content shift amounted to changing the emphasis in management education from management per se to entrepreneurship – and to add that all these content shifts over the years make the study of Americanization a "contested historical project."

The historians' approach: contested historical project versus neutral analytical category

The investigation of Americanization as a "contested historical project" can be considered, one French management specialist noted, both as an expression of the historians' effort to "give birth to the forgotten past," ("faire naître l'histoire oubliée") and that of the social scientists' to use longitudinal studies in order to understand "the functions of organizations today and tomorrow" ("le fonctionnement des organizations aujourd'hui et demain"; Marmonier and Thiétart, 1988, p. 163). Because of their scientific ambition, most social scientists when they use historical examples are not content to leave them in an historical form. They abstract "neutral analytical concepts" from the historical record, proceeding from the purely historical level to higher levels of abstraction, where they slough off historical specificities and replace them with "neutral analytical concepts" unbound by time and space. Many works of this type exist. We choose one to illustrate this abstraction process, because it deals with a subject matter similar to ours – i.e. competitive advantages developed in the United States in

---

[3] Kenney and Florida (1993) and Oliver and Wilkinson (1992).
[4] Some examples are Abegglen and Stalk (1985), Fruin (1992), Holland (1989), Nonaka and Takeuchi (1995), Taiichi (1988), Ozaki (1992), Kagone et al. (1981) and Aoki (1990).
[5] See chapter 4 for definitions of Americanization specific to the context of this study.

the "information age." In Michael Best's study *The New Competi-tive Advantage*, the author selects historical production systems (at the Springfield Armory, Ford, Toyota, Canon and Intel) and designs ana-lytically neutral production models for each of them (the Springfield Armory = interchangeability, Ford = single-product flow, Toyota = multi-product flow, Canon = new product development, and Intel = systems integration). Since he is interested in the United States' new competitive advantage, he moves outside the production system of the firm into the region – i.e. he looks at Silicon Valley, which he character-izes with the neutral analytical term "cluster dynamics." Then he com-bines Intel's systems integration with Silicon Valley's cluster dynamics to produce the firm-integrated regional cluster – the neutral category of an "open systems dynamic."

Social scientists argue that it is not their purpose to recreate events, but to use them to formulate the neutral categories that escape history to become general knowledge of interest to scientists and instruments for policy makers. Others, however, including dissenting social scien-tists, doubt the validity of the procedure and its results. David Colan-der, a noted economist, observed that the theory of knowledge justi-fying his subject was "unsound." In their work economists only have in common the methodology of modeling.[6] Gunnar Eliasson, arguing from within the economists' house, also affirms the weakness of their analytical tool kit. A Schumpeterian, he has spent the last twenty years trying to find useful concepts because "the management teacher as well as the economic theorist needs a realistic model (method) to support teaching and thinking." But he concluded in 1997: "Since no realistic theory of dynamic markets exists, no good theory of the firm had been created. The moral, hence, is that so far we have excellent firms, not thanks to, but despite management teaching" (Eliasson, 1997, p. 12). Even the usefulness of modeling has been questioned. Padraig Dixon, a student of economics at Trinity College, Dublin, has concluded that econometric modeling stands on shaky ground.[7]

---

[6] Colander (2002), p. 142; see also Ormerod (1994).
[7] Dixon (1998): "Econometrics . . . is plagued by problems of . . . weak data, ideology affecting the outcome of empirical tests, and misdirected effort. . . Despite all that . . . econometrics could best be considered a type of 'weak testing,' which shows, if nothing else, *some* sort of relationship exists between the variables under discussion."

This is not the place to delve deeply into the troubled epistemology of social science, but, since our methods differ and social scientists so often denigrate them, we want to explain why social science reification is of dubious value for us and for historians in general. First of all, it does violence to historical reality. Anybody who studies history quickly learns how much is lost when social scientists use "neutral analytical concepts." The shock of American corporate executives and their workers in old staple industries (rubber, steel, automobiles, household appliances, cameras, machines tools, etc.) watching their firms crumble during the 1980s, never to be resurrected again, under the onslaught of Japanese competition; the panic visits of Ford executives to Toyota in 1979 to see first-hand the new production methods; the joint venture entered into with Toyota by General Motors in California (New United Motor Manufacturing, Inc. – NUMMI), where the humbled US automobile giant learned how to make cars from the Japanese upstart; the 1980 NBC documentary "If Japan Can, Why Can't We?" – a *cri de coeur* from the Americans revealing a surprising collapse of confidence in the prowess of their corporate management and a new admiration for that of Japan. This all happened. Japanization occurred. The exciting and compelling story of Silicon Valley, where technology-spawned industries produced an information revolution that astonished the world. These events also occurred – but they are not on the radar screen of "neutral analytical concepts," although they were and are a vital part of the lives of the politicians, civil servants, legislators, managers, entrepreneurs, scientists and educators who lived through and created them. The "neutral analytical concepts" of the social sciences seem not only to ignore but even to suppress them.

The reification process also creates parameters that hinder the discussion of cause and effect in history. Some very significant events are historically unique, non-repeatable but powerful causal agents. The cold war, for example, explains the rise of Silicon Valley much more than any economic ideas about the dynamics of markets or theories of the firm. In fact, a counter-factual but logically sound argument can be made that without the cold war (a unique event) the information technology revolution would not have happened at all. It was the willingness of the American people to bear the burden of defense (after Sputnik), a non-economic motivation, that led to IT. As Howard Rheingold puts it, "If necessity is the mother of invention, it must be added that the Defense Department is the father of Technology; from the army's first electronic digital computer in the 1940s to the Air Force research into head-mounted displays in the 1980s, the US military has always been the prime contractor for the most significant innovations in computer technology" (Rheingold, 1991, p. 18). If social science abstractions cannot explain why Silicon Valley came into existence then their value to those explaining historical process can certainly be questioned.

But the most serious charge we two historians level against the method of reification is that it eliminates the subject of Americanization. That is why, perhaps, the historians Zeitlin and Herrigel, in their study of Americanization, state that it was not a "neutral analytical concept." General analytical categories are antithetical to culture-specific nomenclature. Accordingly, Best, although motivated to carry out his study by the recent competitive advantages Americans had achieved in IT, has, in his social scientist guise, had to couch it in neutral analytical concepts so as not to restrict the modelization with regard to time or place. In the process, the late twentieth-century United States disappeared. The same observations can be made about how management scientists handled Japanization. It started out in American reports to be a discussion of Japanese practices – e.g. the Toyota production system – and ended up in neutral analytical concepts – e.g. "lean production."

This book, therefore, turns not to the neutral analytical concepts of social scientists but to the historical actors themselves in order to encounter and reconstruct the most recent phase of Americanization in its entrepreneurship education mode. In doing so, the hope of creating any neutral analytical concepts about the nature of Americanization is sacrificed – which, in any event, for the reasons just given, would have been a very faint hope. And the problematique is taken on of those who study historical personages and events. This includes the need to substantiate the historical generalizations made: the range and validity of evidence, the source critique, the usual rigors of the historian's craft.

The approach differs from that of the deductive social scientist. The historian is much more interested in the actor, in the individual, qualitative, nuanced testimony that reflects life, than in statistics and quantification. He/she relies on interviews more than questionnaires; he/she presents evidence more in the form of historical examples; and he/she arrives at generalizations inductively rather than deductively – that is, begins with a subject area more than a hypothesis and formulates the subject itself more precisely and hypotheses about it while reading extensively into the detailed sources and conducting interviews.

This is precisely how the authors have proceeded in the preparation of this study. The two principal subjects that it examines were not identified until two years of intensive reading about the information revolution and management education had been carried out. Only then did entrepreneurship studies as a distinct topic within management education become the focus of the work. The other subject, the two-phase development of Silicon Valley, did not emerge before months had been spent reading books and articles and doing interviews on the valley, and then its appearance occurred simultaneously with the realization that entrepreneurship studies were the subject of the book. In short, the details were not sought out as examples to support preconceived generalizations but to produce generalizations. Only after sources had been examined in their specificity – to a cumulative point where a new instance added nothing to our understanding of the patterns of behavior and opinion already derived from them – could the research stop and the individual examples be cited to give specificity to historical argument.

This procedure arouses the suspicion of deductive reasoners that the historian might simply select the example that supports his/her preferred generalization and ignore the example that does not. To accept the inductive method and argument by example, therefore, does require considerable trust in the integrity of the researcher, because it is always possible that the intellectually dishonest can choose non-representative historical examples or the lazy can reconstruct historical patterns based on insufficient research. And it is probably more difficult to check on the work of the inductive researcher, because of complex inductive processes, than on that of the quantifier, although social science "objectivity" can be "rigged" too.

The research problem involves more than the professional integrity of the historian. Nobody reading the evidence from the past can claim, however exemplary the historical investigation, that he/she is capable objectively of resurrecting "forgotten history." The subjectivity of observers, both individually and culturally, prevents events from being recreated as they actually were. But there is no need to despair about this. History is a contested project, an ongoing debate about how the past should and could be reconstructed. This book contributes to this debate. The results, if modest, can claim, moreover, to be as "useful" to policy makers as those derived from social scientists.

Scheme of presentation

We begin with a chapter on Silicon Valley and the information revolution. It is not based much on the commentary of historians. But the absence of their comment should not be surprising. They have been more involved in the discussion about the Americanization of European industry and management, and management education after World War II.[8] The Americanization process during the information revolution is so recent that most historians have not discovered it yet. The chapter draws heavily on the historical actors – the entrepreneurs, politicians, civil servants, managers, technologists and professors – who were involved in the IR in Silicon Valley or who reacted to that revolution. The information comes primarily from parliamentary inquiries into Silicon Valley, from books, brochures, magazines and newspaper articles about it, and interviews of randomly found Europeans living in the area. The interviews took place in April and May 2000. Through this evidence the chapter establishes the uniqueness of the Silicon Valley historical experience, how it differed from that of entrepreneurial and corporate America that preceded it, and the impact of this experience on Americans and Europeans, who at times seemed almost mesmerized by their encounter with Silicon Valley.

The chapter's originality lies in the distinction it makes in the phases of the valley's development. Discussions heretofore have treated it primarily as a region of IT. Although this characterization is true, the success model within this IT framework shifted from an essentially technological to an entrepreneurial mode about 1990. The chapter carefully outlines the differences between these two modes of perception, because the subsequent argument about education hinges on this perception change.

Chapter 2 deals with the impact of the Silicon Valley experience on management education within the region and elsewhere in the United

---

[8] For the post-war Americanization of European industry, see, for example, Djelic (1998), Zeitlin and Herrigel (2000) and Kipping and Bjarnar (1998); for the post-war Americanization of business education, see, for example, Locke (1989) and (1998b), Engwall and Gunnarsson (1994), Engwall and Zamagni (1998), Gourvish and Tiratsoo (1998) and Gemelli (1998).

States. Japanization had already forced US business schools to adapt to a new reality; Silicon Valley had a similar effect. That effect is examined in terms of new programs, their contents, and innovative programs of interaction between business praxis and academia, such as the Business Plan Competitions. The focus is on the growth and institutionalization of a new discipline in American business education: entrepreneurship studies. The sources consulted include brochures and flyers issued by schools about their entrepreneurship study programs, books and articles on the development of American entrepreneurship studies in institutions of higher education, and the agencies that supported them.

Chapter 3 prepares the ground for the analysis of the French and German reaction to the new field of entrepreneurship studies. It examines management education systems existing in the two countries from the perspective of the historical forces that drove their development before 1940, and their response after World War II to the first period of Americanization. The chapter is based primarily on secondary sources, which have treated the history of management education in France and Germany rather comprehensively.

Chapters 4 and 5 explore the French and German responses to the new American educational challenge of entrepreneurship studies. The first of the two chapters considers the reaction in terms of the creation of a new academic discipline. It looks in depth at how Germany and France have come to introduce entrepreneurship/technopreneurship as a new field of study. It does this in part through the presentation of the results of systematic interviews with people responsible for or involved in entrepreneurship education in the two countries. The second of these chapters considers the high-tech networking involved in this new educational challenge. Since to be Americanized in this recent phase of Americanization means not only to introduce entrepreneurship as a new academic discipline but also to create instrumentalities promoting new venture creation, changes in the interactions among groups relevant to entrepreneurship are important to "information age" Americanization. These changes are examined in this chapter for both countries.

The French and German interviewees presented in chapter 4 are newly established scholars in entrepreneurship studies. In order to assure their representativeness and the reliability of their responses, they were chosen from a carefully selected pool of experts. We identified the pools with the help of institutions that have tracked the development of entrepreneurship studies in each country since their emergence. For France, it was the Agence Pour la Création d'Entreprises, an agency promoting new venture creation, which has established a database (OPPE – Observatoire de Pratiques Pédagogiques d'Entrepreneuriat) registering all institutions of higher education engaged in entrepreneurial studies, together with their educational offerings, the year of their introduction, the person in charge, etc. For Germany, it was the Förderkreis Gründungs-Forschung, an organization promoting entrepreneurship research, which has also registered institutions of higher education engaged in entrepreneurship studies. Moreover, Schöne's participation in several conferences about entrepreneurship education in France and Germany guaranteed that we did not miss any potential interviewees. These data indicate that the interviews conducted reflect the state of entrepreneurship studies in France and Germany. All interviewees were provided with a standardized, carefully structured questionnaire.

A separate chapter, chapter 6, is dedicated to the Czech case, for the Czech Republic experienced a different historical past. It faced the Americanization that France and Germany encountered in the post-war world, and the new developments of the information age, at the same time, after the collapse of communism. Having encountered the first Americanization much earlier, the French and Germans could more easily differentiate than the Czechs could the first period of Americanization of management education from that of information age entrepreneurialism, and take it in their stride.

In the Czech Republic, since entrepreneurship studies have not yet been developed as a field of study, the experts interviewed have been drawn from a range of contiguous fields, which allowed us to understand the Czech situation and its history. Those interviewed are mainly heads of three types of institutions: holders of small business university chairs; providers of manager education; and people from agencies involved in the promotion of new venture creation and innovation. Schöne, although she could not attend conferences about entrepreneurship education (the field not yet existing), did visit meetings on innovation in the Czech Republic so as not to overlook potential interviewees. As with the German and French interviewees, the Czechs received a standardized, carefully structured questionnaire.

Information gained from the study of other kinds of sources supplemented the interviews. Many of these documents are not cited

in the bibliography because of space considerations (study bulletins, brochures, announcements and flyers, issued by schools about
entrepreneurship study programs in Germany and France). They have
been sifted through with thoroughness and care. Moreover, a host of
books, reports, articles, etc. about the introduction of entrepreneurship studies in these countries are cited in chapters 4 to 6 and in
the bibliography. It would have been impossible, without consulting
documents other than interviews, for the latter to have made much
sense to us, for interviews had to be interpreted within the greater
context of knowledge about entrepreneurship studies, gleaned from
non-interview sources. Because of this combination of data we feel
confident that they reflect the state of entrepreneurship studies in the
three countries very accurately.

The book closes with a chapter of conclusions and policy reflec-
tions. With respect to the latter, since the study will have developed no
neutral analytical categories, it cannot lay out any history-free predic-
tions for change. But no social scientist had laid out a program that
predicted Japanization; none had used any research-derived blueprint
that forecast the creation of the high-tech habitat in Silicon Valley.
Their historical appearance actually caught people mostly by surprise.
Our knowledge of their development is after the event. It is impossible,
therefore, to predict when the next Silicon Valley will appear, where,
and what the revolution it brings will be. Or even if it will be. But we
can examine how people feel at present about the lessons of Silicon
Valley/Americanization in entrepreneurship education and how they
have changed their views of management education from those held in
the past.

1 | *Phenomenal Silicon Valley and the second Americanization*

To those who believed that it is markets that spur technological discovery best, and – because of the cost of R&D – do so in big firms, Silicon Valley proved to be an exception. There big firms, especially before 1970, did drive IT, but outside the parameters of market criteria. Afterwards, increasingly, consumer demand spurred IT development, but entrepreneurial start-ups rather than the traditional, well-known big firms satisfied much of the market. Not many Americans in 1960 anticipated such a turn of events. Hence the learning curve about Silicon Valley has been a steep one.[1] This book is itself an expression of that steep learning curve. Hegel said that the Owl of Minerva takes flight at dusk, meaning that understanding only comes from looking back at events. This study could not have been conceived until Silicon Valley's history had reached a point where it became clear that it could be understood in terms of a two-phase development. This twofold division provides a focus. Part one of this first chapter elaborates on the two phases. Part two concentrates on the character of the entrepreneurship generated during the second phase, which will be the period and subject of principal concern. Part three, the greater part, looks at European reactions to Silicon Valley during both phases, but especially the second, since the core of the work is about the Americanization of entrepreneurship education in France, Germany and the Czech Republic, which happens in the second phase.

The Czechs' response to Silicon Valley is left out of the discussion in this third section. That might seem topically illogical since the reaction

---

[1] Josef Schumpeter, the seminal economist on entrepreneurship, originally stated in 1912 that individual entrepreneurs drove technical change, but he revised his opinion, with the invention of large R&D departments in sizable established firms in the 1940s, to one where the big established firms that could afford long-term R&D drove technological development. See Schumpeter (1996).

of people from the other two countries is discussed. But one major factor militates against the inclusion of the Czechs at this point. France's and Germany's encounter with Silicon Valley occurred during each phase of its development; the Czechs, living in relative ignorance of Silicon Valley until 1990, absorbed both the first and second phase of the valley's influence telescoped into one. The logic of time sequence, therefore, and the awkwardness of discussing Czech experience anachronistically, convinced us that we should discuss the Czechs' reaction in chapter 6, where their belated encounter with a mature American entrepreneurship is also handled.

The two-phase development of Silicon Valley

Before 1970: IT through governmental research

The statement in the introduction (that IT, exploited commercially during explosive post-1970 growth, originated in government-sponsored research) requires elaboration. Not greed, not free market demand, but fear stimulated IT, especially after the Soviet Union exploded atomic bombs and possessed the intercontinental ballistic missiles to deliver them. American taxpayers for long decades paid the enormous costs of superpower rivalry. Most of that money went for conventional weaponry, but millions also went to research in IT. Consequently, one group of scholars noted, "from the explosion of the first Soviet atomic bomb in 1949 until the mid-1960s, the driving force for science policy remained the military-technological competition with the Soviet Union" (Alic et al., 1992, p. 97).

Probably, for this study, the pertinent example of this government-created IT is the personal computer. After Sputnik the government lavishly funded a new organization, ARPA, as part of a crash program to help the United States regain the supposedly lost initiative in science and technology. In 1964 a team of ARPA founders visited Douglas Englebart, whom NASA had already supported in founding an Augmentation Research Center at the Stanford Research Institute. ARPA's people gave him computer equipment plus a million dollars a year to "create the mind amplifying computers," he described in his publications (Rheingold, 1991, p. 81). After four years the Englebart team presented the fruits of their work:

Sitting on a stage with a keyboard, screen, mouse, and the kind of earphone-microphone setup pilots and switchboard operators wear, Englebart navigat[ed] through information space . . . He called up documents from the computer's memory and displayed them on the big screen at the front of the auditorium, collapsed the documents to a series of descriptive one-line headings, clicked a button on his mouse and expanded a heading to reveal a document, typed in a command and summoned a video image and a computer graphic to the screen. He typed in words, deleted them, cut and pasted paragraphs and documents from one place to another . . . The assembled engineers, programmers, and computer scientists had never seen anything like it (Rheingold, 1991, p. 84).

Government projects also created cyberspace networks. It started with SAGE (Semi-Automated Ground Environment), a computer-activated, real-time continental air defense system developed at MIT's Lincoln Laboratory under Air Force contract, continued through ARPANET (a computer network that linked their research centers), and which ARPA researchers gave to the commercial world.

This government-sponsored research produced commercially valued artifacts and technology, but, just as – if not more – importantly, it created a highly sophisticated corps of scientists and engineers that got involved subsequently in commercial IT. By the early 1960s the federal share of the nation's R&D had reached 66 percent, "with defense-space related work accounting for about 85 percent of the federal total." The "huge buildup of US military R&D in the 1950s and 1960s provided a larger stock of scientists and engineers than many other Western countries" (Alic et al., 1992, p. 114). By 1965 the percentage of the US workforce consisting of graduate scientists and engineers was at least three times per capita that of its principal industrial rivals in the free world. Because government-sponsored IT transferred to the commercial firm, the presence of a large group of scientists and engineers working on government projects helped subsequently to develop market-serving private firms.

Joshua Lerner's survey in the 1980s provides indirect evidence of this. It shows that 24.2 percent of the scientists and engineers with defense-related positions in 1982 had shifted to civilian jobs four years later, but it also shows that 26.5 percent of the scientists and engineers who had been in defense-oriented jobs in 1986 had been in non-defense positions four years earlier.[2] There was a considerable flow of skilled people

[2] Lerner (1990), cited in Alic et al., 1992, p. 113.

between defense and private commercial industries in these years in a sustained interrelationship.

The data cited covers scientists and engineers generally, and hence applies only by inference specifically to people in IT. But direct evidence about the transfer of IT scientists and engineers from government into commercial firms can also be cited. Xerox's Palo Alto Research Center, which developed the technology that Steve Jobs copied into Apple's Macintosh, hired "hundreds of ARPA superstars" after 1970. These included Bob Taylor, who had headed ARPA's computer research center, where he "typically monitored fifteen to twenty research projects across the country at a given time" (Smith and Alexander, 1988, p. 78). PARC hired him "primarily to staff the Computer Science Laboratory with his ARPA people." It also hired Ivan Sutherland, who had preceded Taylor as head of ARPA's computer laboratory; Alan Kay and Butler Lampson, who had worked on ARPA funded projects; and a research group, which PARC hired away from Englebart's Augmentation Research Center. Alan Kay claimed that PARC in the early 1970s had seventy-six of the hundred best computer scientists. Taylor commented years later of one of the recruits, Butler Lampson, that "he had the best track record for innovation in computer science than anyone in the world" (Smith and Alexander, 1988, p. 67).

Science and technology competence transferred rather easily between government projects and commercial industry. This, at least, is the judgment of the study by Alic and colleagues: "Technical skills transfer more easily from defense to the commercial firm than managerial ones" (p. 124). But only after 1970 did "venture capital replace the military as the leading source of financing for Silicon Valley start-ups," and Silicon Valley firms were the most commercial, market-oriented in the US at that time (Saxenian, 1994, pp. 17–18). Apparently, then, military procurement officers, lobbyists, politicians and DOD bureaucrats selected and sponsored the brilliant IT research projects that invented the technology of the information revolution.

This conclusion gainsays the point that Erkko Autio and Riikka-Leena Leskelä have made in a recent survey of entrepreneurship: "According to modern theory, economic growth is ultimately driven by the search for new ideas by profit-seeking innovators."[3] Werner Sombart's explanation of modernization comes closer to the mark. He

---

[3] Autio and Leskelä cite Romer, 1990, for this opinion in Reynolds et al., 2001.

argues that "the growth of large-scale nationalistic warfare . . . was [its] . . . root cause, since the demand for more effective weapons of offense and defense stimulated technology and invention."[4] In Silicon Valley in the 1950s "the share of military shipments of semiconductors reached 70 percent [of the market], and it oscillated around 50 percent during the 1960s, with the defense market being concentrated in the higher layers of the technology" (Castells and Hall, 1994, p. 17).

But historians might be satisfied with no development model at all. If American firms were themselves not particularly prescient (not investing heavily in the research and development of products of which in the early phase they could not imagine their market usefulness), neither did DOD bureaucrats and generals perceive the long-term commercial prospects that private firms had missed. If a specific IT were an unexpected dividend, there was no guarantee that such investments would have similar pay-offs in the future, that huge amounts of money spent on defense R&D would somehow have commercial spin-off. Huge defense-sponsored R&D could just as easily have resulted in little commercial transferability. The connection between pre-1970 IT R&D and post-1970 IT commercialization, then, would simply be an accident, a unique historical circumstance.

Post-1970: IT through entrepreneurial start-ups, not big firms

When considering the dynamic of technological change, both the firm and the habitat within which it operates come into play. If the firm is not receptive to the opportunities presented in the environment, it does not prosper; but, if the environment is not conducive to entrepreneurial impulse, the new firm does not appear and grow. Both, and the interaction between them, are part of the Silicon Valley story.

The existing firms

While certain iconic firms epitomize Japanization (e.g. Sony, Toyota, Canon, Komatsu, Honda), so do iconic companies typify the second period of Americanization (e.g. Microsoft, Intel, Oracle, Apple, Yahoo, Sun Microsystems). All of them are recent start-ups, most in Silicon Valley. Absent from the list are the old Fortune 500 companies with

---

[4] Quoted in Brinton, 1950, p. 339.

which Americans, indeed the world, are so familiar. Michael Best's *The New Competitive Advantage* bases his new firm, with enhanced entrepreneurial capacities, on Silicon Valley's Intel (Best, 2001). He calls the Intel model one of systems integration, which old mainstream manufacturers such as Ford lacked. They were organized to promote a single-product flow system of mass production. While it is clear that the production systems of older firms lacked entrepreneurial flexibility, it is not clear, from the analysis, why these great corporations did not foresee and transform themselves into cutting-edge IT entrepreneurs.

Professor Eliasson's idea of an experimentally organized economy usefully suggests that the mode of governance in the old Fortune 500 companies kept them from grasping the entrepreneurial opportunity of post-1970 IT, even when it had been developed in their own companies. Xerox's leadership is the prime example. The corporation's top management all but ignored the computer research done in its Palo Alto Research Center. The firm's chief executives in the 1970s, the years of innovation, had recruited their management teams from finance people at Ford motor company and marketing people at IBM. One of the two CEOs, Archie McCardell, installed a "phased program planning" process for project evaluation, brought with him from Ford when he came to Xerox. He, like the members of his team, believed that "if you sat on something long enough and hard enough . . . you could control the outcome." Smith and Alexander complained that Xerox's top managers were "so risk-averse and numbers-bound that meaningful change seemed impossible. They had become nothing more than bean-counters bound to heartless formulas without factors for enthusiasm, faith, or finesse" (Smith and Alexander, 1988, p. 157). They were not managers who could appreciate the possibilities of the personal computer technology developed at PARC, their own research facility, and who would take the appropriate start-up decisions. The same entrepreneurial stodginess characterized IBM management, which, after delaying the development of the personal computer (clinging to mainframes), outsourced the software that went into their personal computer – once they belatedly did develop it – to two young entrepreneurs, Bill Gates and Paul Allen, of fledgling Microsoft. The software they farmed out, to IBM management's chagrin, turned out to be more important than the hardware, the personal computer, that IBM developed. For these big firms to have missed the personal computer and the software applications it employed was a calamitous systems failure. Managers from the old school, they were unable to function well in the EOE. In Silicon Valley, it turned out, technological development was "based on the foundation of new firms to develop new, high-risk ventures," because "in practice . . . older firms often lacked proper incentives for risk taking and thus had difficulty with radical innovation" (Vitols, 2001, p. 555).

The habitat for IT start-ups

Information about Fortune 500 firms generally charts their poor performance during the Japanese challenge. Myriad statistics confirm industry shutdowns and lay-offs in the early 1980s as big steel, big rubber, and big automobiles reeled from the onslaught.[5] But, as iconic Japanese firms prospered at the expense of American giants that had formerly seemed invincible, start-up entrepreneurialism also flourished in the United States. Evidence about job creation highlights this contrasting performance. Between 1980 and 1997 Fortune 500 companies lost more than 5 million jobs in the United States, while the economy as a whole created 34 million new jobs (Zacharakis et al., 1999). These were real jobs provided by the 600,000 to 800,000 new companies created in the United States annually, amounting to between fourteen and sixteen start-ups for every hundred existing businesses. There was a lot of turmoil. Business failure rates ran at twelve to fourteen for every hundred existing establishments. But the annual gains in establishments amounted to 2 percent. Between 1982 and 1995 about 30 percent of American firms were either new or terminated. Studies show, moreover, that in the United States entrepreneurialism of opportunity greatly outstripped entrepreneurialism of necessity.[6] This high rate of entrepreneurship of opportunity can be seen as the rate at which an economy rejuvenates itself.

Start-up tempos depended on regions. A 1994 study of 382 US labor markets shows that, in manufacturing, the number of start-ups varied extensively from 114 per 10,000 inhabitants in high-activity urbanized

[5] Locke (1996), especially the chapter "The mystique vanishes."
[6] Reynolds et al. (2001) show that, among twenty-nine countries surveyed, the United States ranked at the bottom of those countries where start-ups could be classified as a "necessity," self-employment for survival, and near the top of those countries where start-ups could be called ones of "opportunity, self-employment by personal preference."

districts to 2.4 per 10,000 in the least active rural ones.[7] Regional concentrations, within manufacturing, became more pronounced as some regions developed an expertise in a type of commercial activity, producing a sustained regional advantage for some type of work. The best-known examples of this are Silicon Valley and Boston's Route 128. The degree to which these two regions dominated high IT can be divined from a few figures. William Bygrave has observed that fewer than 20,000 of the 600,000 to 800,000 annual US start-ups (in 2000) were financed by venture capitalists. Among those receiving venture capital, 53 percent by 1981 were in these two regions, and the percentage of venture capital devoted to them increased over the years; so did the total amounts of venture capital invested, rising from $4.3 billion in 1986 to $13 billion in 1997 (Reynolds et al., 2001, p. 24). The venture-capital-financed firms made an extraordinary contribution to the nation's well-being. A study by Wharton Econometric Forecasting Associates has concluded that the companies backed by venture capitalists "created 4.3 million new jobs and generated $736 billion in revenues in the year 2000. The relatively small number of these firms accounted for 3.3 percent of total jobs in the US and 7.4 percent of GDP. Within that group, Silicon Valley and Boston Route 128 start-ups made the major contribution."

The dynamism sprang not from the established firm but from the entrepreneur's interaction with a regional habitat. In the case of Silicon Valley that interaction was seminal. Books and articles written in the early 1980s attributed this creativity to the Valley's counter-culture: Steve Jobs, the backpacking trekker in search of spiritual fulfillment in India; Steve Woziack, the brilliant, slovenly, eccentric drop-out; the hackers, bearded misfits, obsessive, sharing – at war, if not with corporate America, at least with its image. The eccentricities explained this risk-taking society. But by the mid-1980s a serious evaluation of regional dynamism began to crowd out counter-cultural explanations.

Entrepreneurship in Silicon Valley in its second phase

A look from the inside

Although rigorous hard-data scientists considered regional analysis "soft" science, studies by Harvard Business School's Michael Porter

[7] Reynolds et al., 1994, p. 449, cited in Reynolds et al., 2001.

gave them a cachet of respectability.[8] Michael Best's book on *The New Competitive Advantage* consciously followed Porter's lead. AnnaLee Saxenian's work also drew attention to regional dynamics, specifically focusing on Silicon Valley. Her academic affiliations reveal this geographic orientation: Associate Professor, University of California, Berkeley, City and Regional Planning. She forms part of a Silicon Valley group that publishes on habitat analysis. Their work includes the book *The Silicon Valley Edge*, a collection of articles that emphasizes hi-tech regionalism;[9] it appeared in 2000.

The book argues that the sustained success of Silicon Valley is not due to "its scientific advances or technological breakthroughs, [but] the edge [that] derives from a complex 'habitat' or environment that is tuned to turn ideas into products and take them rapidly to markets by creating new firms." It can do this because, as AnnaLee Saxenian puts it in *Regional Advantage, Culture and Competition in Silicon Valley and Route 128*, "Silicon Valley has a regional network-based industrial system that promotes collective learning and flexible adjustment among specialist producers of a complex of related technologies . . . The functional boundaries within firms are porous in a network system, as are the boundaries between firms themselves and between firms and local institutions such as trade associations and universities" (Saxenian, 1994). Professor William F. Miller, the group's unofficial leader, lists eleven criteria that generate efficacy in a high-technology habitat:

1. Knowledge intensity;
2. Quality of workforce;
3. Mobile workforce;
4. Rewards risk taking;
5. Open business environment;
6. Community collaborations;
7. Developed venture capital;
8. University interaction;
9. Quality of life;
10. Government involvement;
11. Indigenous companies (Miller, 2000).

The topics gain specificity when combined with subcategories that add content to their abstraction. Scores of items can, in fact, be

---

[8] Porter, 1990, and 1998.
[9] Lee et al., 2000b, and Saxenian, 2000. See also Saxenian, 1994, and 1989.

classified under each of the eleven points the authors of *The Silicon Valley Edge* have identified. Technopôles, industrial parks, patenting laws, start-ups and entrepreneurial study programs (university interaction); angel investors and venture capitalists (developed venture capital); immigration policies and job protection policies (workforce mobility); taxation policies on start-ups, stock option policies and bankruptcy laws (rewards risk taking); civic entrepreneurs and non-profit alliances with businesses (community action); business incubators (open business environment); and many others that highlight the intricacies of a high-tech habitat. For our book, however, one of the factors in particular needs to be stressed: the triple helix, which fits under category eight, university interaction.

The triple helix

Famous publicly funded state-run research institutes exist in the United States. But the US government allots most of its research budgets to laboratories in public and private universities and to private firms. The government permits researchers on its projects, who work in these laboratories, to retain individual intellectual property rights to their discoveries and the law permits universities to grant licenses to commercial firms to exploit the discoveries that government-funded researchers make in university laboratories. The university and the researchers share in the dividends garnered from this government-paid research. If the research results in a start-up firm, the university can allow it to exploit university-held patents in exchange for stock in the new company, and the university professors are not only allowed to leave academic positions to work temporarily for the firm, with rights to return to their university positions, but, while remaining in their university positions, they are permitted to sit on the firm's board of directors and/or to work as a consultant. The system is elitist; in 1997 seven great US universities took in 60 percent of the royalties from firms exploiting their discoveries (among them the University of California at Berkeley, $178 million, and Stanford, $40 million). But it resulted in ten times more transfer of patents to firms than were transferred from laboratories run by the federal government.

There is much anecdotal evidence about this symbiosis between university research and private firms in Silicon Valley. "At Stanford," William F. Miller writes, "as well as at the University of California

at Berkeley, there are lively interactions between industry professionals and executives with faculty and students through many seminars
and conferences. At our Stanford seminars dealing with high-tech
entrepreneurial activities, at least half of the attendees will be from
industry" (Lee et al., 2000a). Michel Ferrary, visiting Stanford from
the French business school ESSEC from 1999 to 2000, was surprised
to find professors, students, industrialists and venture capitalists min-
gling freely at Palo Alto functions (Ferrary, 2000). Some rather spectacular entrepreneurship stemming from university graduates involved in
this interchange can be cited just for Stanford's Computer Science
Department (Andy Bechtolsheim, a founder of Sun Microsystems;
John Hennessey, a founder of MIPS Technologies, Inc.; Jim Clark, a
founder of Silicon Graphics and Netscape; Jerry Kaplan, a founder
of Tecknowledge, Go and Onsale; Forrest Basket, technical officer at
Xerox PARC, Sun Microsystems and SGI; Scip Stritter, a founder of
MIPS; Len Bosack, a founder of Cisco Systems; and David Cheriton,
a founder of Granite Market Value). The combined worth of these
companies in 2000 amounted to about $90 billion.

MIT's graduates affected IT entrepreneurialism even more spectac-
ularly. Boston Bank's study of the school's graduates provides con-
vincing evidence of this start-up intensity (Moscovitch et al., 1997).
Four thousand companies founded by MIT graduates, mainly in manufacturing, employed some 1,100,000 people and had annual sales of
around $232 billion. They had about 8,500 plants and offices, at least
one located in each of the fifty states, and were thus a national industrial force. But, among the fifty, five states had the most employees, and,
of the five, California (162,000) and Massachusetts (125,000) had the
most. Four hundred and sixty-seven MIT graduates had firms headquartered in California, with approximately $86 billion in sales. MIT
graduates founded 1,065 firms in Massachusetts with some $53 bil-
lion in sales. Clearly, the value-added performance of the Californian
firms founded by MIT graduates exceeded the performance of those in
Massachusetts, probably because the former were more high-tech. If
companies in high-tech, high-growth industries (software, electronics
and biotechnology), which amount to 66 percent of the MIT-founded
firms, are isolated from the others, their concentration in California and
Massachusetts is even greater: 70 percent of electronic and 68 percent
of software firms.

These two regions also brought about significant innovations in high-tech finance. Since regular banks and financial institutions were risk averse, particularly when unproven new technologies were involved, Silicon Valley itself fostered the venture capital and angel financial networks required for entrepreneurial start-ups. Not initially, as the first venture capital firm started in Boston right after World War II, but by the mid-1980s major financial institutions had moved into the venture capital market in the valley. Silicon Valley's own social network created a self-support system of finance, reinvesting part of their wealth in fostering the next generation of entrepreneurs (Castells and Hall, 1994, p. 19). By 1981 "of the $1.4 billion in total venture investments, 15 percent went to Massachusetts-based companies and 38 percent went to California" (Saxenian, 1994, p. 184). The angels and venture capitalists that supported IT start-ups knew the technology of their investments well. AnnaLee Saxenian comments about those in Silicon Valley: "They brought technical skills, operating experience, and networks of industry contacts – as well as cash – to the ventures they funded." This closeness to local technology networks, she feels, explains venture capital and angel investment performance. To support this view she quotes a former Wall Street executive: "In New York, the money is generally managed by professional or financial promoter types. Out here [Silicon Valley] the venture capitalists tend to be entrepreneurs who created and built a company and then sold out. When problems occur with any of their investments, they can step into the business and help out." Tacit knowledge about IT learned in Silicon Valley made up more of venture capital competence than knowledge of traditional financial and investment techniques. Founders of high-technology firms, who could have formidable scientific and technical but few business skills, needed them. As the venture capitalist firms matured in the valley, they liked to think they "played a key role in networking to find suitable new managers . . . and to impose new management structures on firm-founders reluctant to share authority" (Vitols, 2001, p. 555).

Neutral analytical categories again

Thus, the triple helix (the entwining of government-sponsored research in a fruitful relationship with universities and start-up firms) situated in an open community of highly motivated and qualified people produced the IT habitat of late twentieth-century northern California. Not surprisingly, people in regions all over the United States, but particularly where industries suffered from Japanese competition in the 1980s, in order to restore prosperity sought to follow the Silicon Valley example. A burgeoning literature exists on regional renewal: in the old rust belt districts and on the Atlantic seaboard (New York City's Silicon Alley) as well as in new regions – i.e. Austin, Texas; Portland, Oregon; Seattle, Washington; and Boise, Idaho. Since they came later, these regions clearly emulated the Silicon Valley precedent.[10] Problems arise, however, when Boston's Route 128 is placed in this group of followers. It, not Silicon Valley, was the United States' first IT district. In a normal sequence of events, Silicon Valley should not be the mother lode of IT, but those laurels should fall to Route 128. And in the realm of university interaction the Boston Bank's survey of the MIT entrepreneurs seems to confirm this judgment. Best seems to think so. "Few [universities]," he states, "are associated with the development of entrepreneurial firms and regional growth dynamics, like those linked to MIT" (Best, 2001, p. 158). But Silicon Valley did not just follow Route 128 in IT. The history of followers and leaders is more complicated. While Silicon Valley thrived in the late 1970s, Route 128 went into decline. In *The New Competitive Advantage* Best himself explains Route 128's fall:

The predominant organization structure of leading 128 companies was top-down, design was centralized and production capabilities were neither lean nor agile. They were not organizations designed to integrate technology management with production to pursue emerging market opportunities on a regional basis. [The firms] were not adaptive to market and technology shifts (p. 127).

What pertained to firms characterized this entire high-tech region.

AnnaLee Saxenian, in her 1994 study, is not impressed by the link between MIT and Massachusetts' start-ups when compared to the links between universities and start-ups in Silicon Valley. The creation of high-tech start-ups required entrepreneurs and a receptive habitat as much as it did the presence of a great research and teaching university

---

[10] Whereas venture capitalists invested around $2 billion in New York City's Silicon Alley in 1999, they invested some $13 billion in Silicon Valley.

such as MIT. Boston Bank's MIT survey confirms the importance of habitat to entrepreneurship because, aside from the need for a first-class research university, "quality of life, proximity to markets, and access to skilled professionals" ranked highest in the decision of MIT graduates about where to locate their firms. That is why so many of these graduates, as the survey shows, located start-ups in Silicon Valley: superiority of habitat. Accordingly, Route 128's weakness, as Best states, "was exposed by the emergence of the focus and networks open systems in the . . . model of Silicon Valley." Route 128's salvation came when people there – the original IT pioneers – learned in and from California about how to refocus on regional networking and open systems. Between 1989 and 1996, when the reorientation occurred, the number of MIT graduates' start-up firms in Massachusetts increased from 639, with some 190,000 employees, to the already mentioned 1,065 firms, with around 353,000. By the mid-1990s, then, this reinvigoration of Route 128 could be counted among Silicon Valley's signal achievements.

Local globalism

Silicon Valley's products permitted people to overcome the boundaries of space. A person could – and did – live in one place while working anywhere or everywhere in cyberspace. All this was unprecedented. Silicon Valley technology did not just facilitate globalization; it *was* globalization. The medium became the territory. Paradoxically, to participate in IT creation required a presence in Silicon Valley, to stay on top of the latest ideas, to get financing, find experienced public relations firms to launch IPOs, to network in this very special local habitat in every way. Major firms that had been left behind started up research centers in Palo Alto or Menlo Park, and venture capitalists located on Sand Hill Road, in order to stay abreast of – and, hopefully, get a leg-up on – rapidly onrushing technological events.

Silicon Valley became a global village. The first visitors arrived when the valley's semiconductor industries emerged as an important part of the US space and defense build-up. Charles de Gaulle visited in 1960 and big foreign firms in the 1970s went there to join the information revolution. In 1975 Philips took over Signetics, the American firm which in 1961 had itself spun off from the first big semiconductor firm, Fairchild; in 1977 Siemens bought Litronix Corp.; in 1978 the Japanese firm NEC snapped up Electronic Arrays; and in 1979 the French firm Schlumberger acquired Fairchild Semiconductors itself.

But the real influx of people followed on the development in the 1980s of that special aspect of IT called interactivity. Interactivity is the IT sector where the actors interact in real time, personally and directly in cyberspace, with people and things. It sprang from the personal computer, standardized software applications and the Internet, which eliminated the monopoly control of experts over operations and made them the province of everybody. With the multiplication of business opportunities that the technologies of interactivity brought, Silicon Valley acted like a magnet to newcomers.

Saxenian tells part of this story, using 1990 US census data, in her work on Chinese and Indian emigrant entrepreneurs (Saxenian, 2000). Whether they came to study technology in US universities or after completing their studies at home, or both, they founded companies. At the turn of the twenty-first century the Asian immigrant entrepreneurs were founding 17 percent of Silicon Valley's high-tech start-ups each year. Almost simultaneously, IT centers developed in their homelands – in Taiwan, in Singapore, in Bangalore – incited through the Silicon Valley connection. The extent to which Europeans participated has not been studied systematically. They began to participate in what Frenchmen called the "ruée d'or" (gold rush) in the mid-1980s. Jean-Louis Gassée, who arrived at Apple then, is one of the few early pioneers. But the great influx is recent – something that happened in the 1990s. Numbers are not easy to determine; estimates provided by the French consulate in San Francisco vary widely, from 10,000 to 40,000 Frenchmen in San Francisco and Silicon Valley, which – even if the smaller number is used – is still a lot of French scientific and engineering talent living in northern California.[11] Rumors about German visitors put their number even higher – twice that of the French. The British arrived in great numbers too, although they were less easy to identify because they blended more rapidly with the Americans. Every European country had a presence.

And they organized. The French formed the DBF, a French-speaking association that gathers for wine and cheese at a selected but different Silicon Valley venue each month to hear a guest speaker, who might be a successful French entrepreneur, or a visiting member of parliament or

[11] Ledru, 2000, and Raud, 2000.

a minister. For, after the individuals arrived privately in Silicon Valley and the news got out, the various high-powered government and parliamentary missions and officials began to come, to evaluate the brain drain and satisfy their curiosity. The Germans created their own club, Deutschland-USA, headquartered in Mountain View, California, and a Web site filled with news about high-tech goings-on of interest to the German expatriate community and those back in the fatherland. And the German-American Chamber of Commerce established a special Web site, "Silicon Valley for Germans," which provides business-to-business news and networking services.

Europeans take in Silicon Valley

In order to understand reactions to Silicon Valley, the state of European management mentality after a four-decade post-war confrontation with US management has to be taken into consideration. Most interested scholars are familiar with the organizational and managerial model that Americans presented to post-war Europe. The success of US core corporations and the well-being of individual Americans seemed to be inextricably interlaced after the war. Five hundred corporations (*c.* 1950) produced half of the nation's industrial output, employed 12 percent of the nation's non-farm workers and dominated the economy. These corporations were run by managerial hierarchies in pyramidal organizations in which workers were the doers and management the thinkers, in command. Professor Eliasson discovered this management at work in his first interviews (conducted between 1969 and 1975), with their short-term and long-range planning methods and their belief in a repetitive environment, which permitted forecasting and centralized leadership of standardized production in an Apollonian world.

Americans offered European leaders money and expertise after 1945 to help their economies recover and prosper. And the skills of corporate America were useful. Post-war French management had to renovate gas and electricity grids, roads and railroads, and telephone services. It tackled industrial innovation in the big programs projects in airplane construction, atomic power and other heavily capitalized industries. West Germany faced similar problems, although it did so with a development ideology less imbued with Colbertism.

There is no need to rehash the arguments about the success of this "Americanization" after the war. For France, Luc Boltanski's 1987 book *The Making of a Class: Cadres in French Society* probably best depicts it, if most favorably: the productivity missions to the United States, the creation of a management press, the reform of business education and a host of other accomplishments that instructed French government officials, businessmen and educators about the American ways of management and organization (Boltanski, 1987). Numerous books also cover the Americanization story in West Germany.

Others dispute the importance of this American influence on European management. Historians talk of continuities when evaluating French recovery. Richard F. Kuisel observes that the innovation and management of France's post-war economy was not a recent vintage, just learned from America, but something that came out of the ministries after World War I (Kuisel, 1981). Some point out that the operational research and industrial planning techniques used, if heavily influenced by Americans, had roots in France. The engineer-economists from the Ecole Polytechnique, who worked for the ministries, could trace the origins of their methods to forebears in the nineteenth century. Their work inspired the "modernization" plans permitting France to garner some Nobel Prizes in economics along the way.[12] Jean Bouvier writes similarly about "the reforms of the credit system introduced after the Second World War" (Bouvier, 1984, p. 80). They emerged from the disputes and proposals of the 1930s. These disputes and proposals, he writes, "with their hesitations and mediocre results, [might seem] an epoch removed from our own day and age," but they were integral to France's post-war modernization. Germany had similar if different managerial and organization traditions, which resisted American influence, on which it successfully depended (Hartmann, 1963).

By the mid-1970s, the French and German elites could congratulate themselves on the success of their managerial efforts. German industry was even recognized in the United States for the originality, quality and solidity of its achievements (Locke, 1996). France rebuilt and then aggressively expanded its economic infrastructure and developed thriving new industries. The results, in numbers, Bela Balassa observed in 1981, were quite impressive: "Between 1958 and 1973, the annual average rate of growth of GNP averaged 5.5 percent. . . . France showed the best economic performance among the EEC countries" (Balassa, 1981). France, more than Germany, which relied more heavily on the

----

[12] Etner, 1978, Drèze, 1964, and Nelson, 1963.

Americans, even entered IT. In 1966 the government championed the creation of a French computer company to rival IBM, the Compagnie Internationale pour l'Informatique. In the 1980s it presented an action program to develop French microchip and personal computer manufacturing, to "make France the third power in technology in the year 2000" (Trégouët, 1998, p. 157). With these accomplishments, if a management challenge existed in the minds of Europeans by the early 1980s it did not come from the United States but from Japan.

And indeed, from the mid-1980s to the mid-1990s European confidence – like that of the Americans – was shaken by the performance of Japanese manufacturing. *The Machine that Changed the World*, which described Toyota's lean production system, probably drew most attention (Womack et al., 1990). Volkswagen had co-sponsored the MIT project that produced the study, and the resulting book, which was translated into many languages, became a best-seller. *Süddeutsche Zeitung* ran a series of articles in 1994 on lean production that brought the message to a broader public. Even more importantly, the Germans, French and other Europeans set about reforming their production systems along Japanese lines. The Steinbeis-Transferzentrum TQU Akademie, founded in 1986 by Professor Dr. Jürgen P. Bläsing, carried on a campaign to introduce total quality management into German industry. It worked closely with German, Austrian, Swiss and American quality control societies, and with hundreds of clients in their implementation. Professor Horst Wildemann's group, which learned about Japanese production methods in the United States, worked tirelessly and quite successfully, with American consultants, to introduce just-in-time, group work, continuous improvement and other aspects of lean production into German firms, including the biggest (e.g. Volkswagen).[13] In France, Sweden and elsewhere in Europe, where certain industries felt hard-pressed (automobiles, machine tools, electronics, precision instruments and optics), the German experience was repeated.

Thus two factors complicate any discussion about European reaction to Silicon Valley. One is the two phases of Silicon Valley development, which divide roughly between pre- and post-interactivity. If 1970 is taken as a culmination year for the first phase, 2000 can be considered

---

[13] A list of his publications, and a discussion of his work, can be found in Locke, 1996.

the culmination year for the mature second phase – that of interactivity. The period between is one of gradual transition, the watershed period between the two phases being in the late 1980s and early 1990s. The second factor is the Japanese challenge, which burst on the scene in the mid-1980s just before the ramification of interactivity fully captured the imagination of those living outside the United States. The Japanese production system clearly challenged the management and organizational structures that had emerged in European firms during the post-war period of Americanization. But this challenge is different from and had little to do with the challenge that Silicon Valley in its second phase posed to Europeans in the 1990s. Indeed, as interactive IT gained people's attention, the Japanese factor rapidly receded from European purview.

First-phase reaction: the technological habitat

During Silicon Valley's first phase people focused on (1) information technology transfer and (2) the management and organization of firms. Technology transfer led to a heavy emphasis in the late 1970s and the 1980s on the creation of technopôles and science parks. In a twenty-year period France established 39 of these "industrial-university" campuses, which welcomed some 2,322 enterprises, with 57,880 employees. Regional governments interested in job creation got heavily involved (de Kerorguen, 1994). The same thing happened in West Germany, where the Fraunhofer Institutes worked closely with industry on technology transfer. In the 1980s, moreover, local and regional governments in partnership with the national government opened forty science parks and centers for new enterprises throughout the Federal Republic of Germany (Sternberg, 1988). Sternberg's analysis of the West German science parks and centers for new enterprises emphasizes technology transfer and job creation. Nothing is said in it about entrepreneurship; the word does not appear in the text, nor is the idea even broached that Germany established these parks to foster more of a high-tech entrepreneurial culture in the country.

An article by Helmut Nuhn, "Technologische Innovation und industrielle Entwicklung – Silicon Valley, Modelle zukünftiger Regionalentwicklung?" (Technological Innovation and Industrial Development – Silicon Valley, Model for Future Regional Development?), also looks back at the first phase of Silicon Valley, but with the post-1980

Japanese challenge in mind. Nuhn's study counts among many that Europeans carried out in the 1980s in an era of de-industrialization and regional decline, pinpointing prosperous regions that could serve as guides to industrial renewal – e.g. on regionally based networks of small firms specializing in shoes, textile, and leather goods in Italy, on the coexistence of small and medium-sized makers of machine tools, textile machines and automobile components with great firms in the state of Baden-Württemberg, Germany, and on similar regions of flexible industrial clusters in certain regions of Sweden, Denmark and Spain (Nuhn, 1989). In his study, Nuhn dwells on the pioneers in Silicon Valley, Professor Terman, who founded the Stanford Research Institute, and the industrial park where Terman's students, Hewlett and Packard (partially financed with the professor's money), located their firm. And he also singles out Shockley, the Nobel Prize winner at the Bell laboratories, who, with his associates, founded the semiconductor industry.

But, despite the talk of pioneers, Nuhn's is a traditional regional development study that emphasizes the financial role of big eastern banks, and the growth-maturity model of development where the semiconductor industry concentrates in order to find economies of scale, moves out of the valley in search of cheaper sites and labor, and ends up in crisis in the mid-1980s. He concludes that it would be an "unreasonable regional policy to concentrate on high-tech firms; it would be much better to transfer technology to new production processes and products in existing firms, through the restructuring and renewal of their production facilities" (Nuhn, 1989, p. 264). In others words, Nuhn was much more interested in confronting the Japanese challenge to existing German staple industries (automobiles, cameras, machine tools, rubber, precision mechanics and electric appliances) than in meeting Silicon Valley's in uncharted technologies. So he answers his question "Silicon Valley, Model for Future Regional Development?" with a clear "no."

Similar views prevailed in France. The French had always been sensitive to the "défi américain" during the first phase of Silicon Valley's development because of their preoccupations with national independence and defense. They made considerable efforts, beginning in the 1960s, to develop a computer industry and information systems (Minitel). But, as Senator Réné Trégouët's inquiry retrospectively reports (*Les pyramides du pouvoir aux réseaux du savoir*), every attempt to promote a national computer manufacturer had ended in

heavy losses in France, as the costs of production and distribution outstripped sales income (Trégouët, 1998). After trying to find solutions
by bringing Olivetti into a consortium with St-Gobain and Machine
Bull, the French government nationalized Bull. This venture failed,
after ten years of deficits (1982 to 1992). Result: at the beginning of
the 1990s no French firm was seriously involved in the manufacture of
computers. An attempt to equip schools with information age technology also proved disappointing: the quality of the computer software
was so poor that the computers were not used more than three hours
a month in 60 percent of the schools. In the secondary schools, after
four years of computerization (1988 to 1992), only 15–20 percent of
the teachers used the machines in their classes. "In all," the inquiry
concludes, after two decades of effort "these [government] attempts
cost the French taxpayers F40 billion [in subsidies] with very paltry
results" (Laffitte, 1997, p. 213). From a French perspective, then, the
reports make gloomy reading.[14]

These facts pertain primarily to the IT of the first Silicon Valley
phase, when the efforts at technological transfer sparked by the valley's greatly admired science park relied on big firms. Between 1973
and 1989 Sophia Antipolis, the "first European technopôle," attracted
large national and international firms and public and private research
laboratories to its premises. "At this time," a group of scholars at its
business school CERAM later observed, "the creation of new firms
was not at the heart of the immediate preoccupations of the park's
promoters" (Albert et al., 1999, p. 7).

Questions about the "governance of existing firms," a second focus
late in Silicon Valley's first phase, preoccupied the French more than the
Germans. The Germans, through co-determination and group-work
experiences, had a much more intense intra-firm consultation culture
than the French. The German problem in this period of Japanese challenge really boiled down to the recognition and adoption of policies
that facilitated the implementation of total quality production in their

---

[14] The following French reports and investigations have been consulted here:
  Allègre et al., 1997; Assises de l'Innovation, 1998; Berne, 1994; Colletis
  and Levet, 1997; CPR-Group, 1998; Crespin et al., 1996; Gandois, 1997;
  Joyandet et al., 1997; Kahn, 1999; Laffitte, 1997; Lorentz, 1998; Majoie,
  1998; Martin, 1997; Martin-Lalande, 1997; Meyer, 1999; Meyer and
  Brown, 1999; Sérusclat, 1997; Térouanne et al., 1998; and Trégouët,
  1998.

plants. The co-determination regime in big German corporations facilitated the transfer process much better than the top-down hierarchical
management structures existing in American and French corporations.
German manufacturing management worked hard, efficiently and successfully at the introduction of "lean production" into their facilities
(Locke, 1996).

Concern about firm governance in France, in the late 1980s and early
1990s, went much deeper than in Germany. Jean-Louis Barsoux and
Peter Lawrence in their study of French management observe that "the
notion of the all-seeing, all-knowing boss is fairly widespread in France.
This makes it difficult for the bosses themselves to ask the advice of
their subordinates since . . . the *patron* is supposed to have a monopoly
of ideas and solutions" (Barsoux and Lawrence, 1990, p. 148).

This distancing of the CEO from his staff is even more pronounced between
the management cadre and the lower order. In the French firm there is low
emphasis on dialogue, teamwork and confrontation of opinions, all essential to "lean production," high on formal, interpersonal relations, isolation,
punctuated by formal meetings in which the junior manager rarely speaks
up. Written communications, expressed in highly codified frameworks, are
stressed with authority moving from the top down (Barsoux and Lawrence,
1990, p. 78).

Most French people still believed at the beginning of the 1980s that
their system had served the nation well. After Japan, they knew it was
anathema to the triumphant lean production regime.

Those visiting and studying Silicon Valley found similar reasons to
question French management in firm governance. "All hierarchies are
shaken," one report states; "each has access to the same information, the power hierarchy changes its nature, its modalities of expertise
have to evolve" (Joyandet et al., 1997, p. 28). This report, listing the
changes required in French enterprise organization and management,
cites an article in *The California Management Review* from 1992,
which presents the attributes of the "classic enterprise" and those of
the "new flexible model" of the firm (shown in table 1.1).

But these comments about the new flexible model, although published in California, were neither particularly American nor especially
original. Similar points had been made throughout the 1980s about the
flexibility of the much-admired Japanese firms. The emergence of the

Table 1.1 *Attributes of the classic enterprise and the new flexible model*

Classic enterprise	New flexible model
One center	Multiple centers
Independent activity	Independent units
Vertical integration	Multiple alliances
Uniform structure	Diverse structures
Enterprise culture	Cosmopolitan culture
Accent on efficiency	Accent on flexibility

Source: Joyandet et al., 1997, p. 28.

new flexible model is associated as much with the quality revolution in Japan as with Silicon Valley.

Europe's reaction to the second phase: Silicon Valley's entrepreneurial habitat

Silicon Valley by 1989, with some 330,000 high-tech workers, including 6,000 Ph.D.s, in 2,000 high-tech firms, 3,000 manufacturing electronic firms and 3,000 firms providing necessary producer services, was being "hailed worldwide as an heroic model of innovation in the service of unprecedented growth" (Castells and Hall, 1994, p. 12).

Only especially prescient people anticipated that the valley then stood on the threshold of greater growth in the 1990s of a kind that would transform people's views about what California's economic prowess meant. The sources that evinced this singularly new opinion grew with the immigrants and visitors who arrived to participate in that future. Much of their reaction is on the Internet, which Silicon Valley did so much to create, and it is a source used in our research. The copiously Internet-posted material consulted is supplemented by information derived from interviews that Locke conducted with his associates during a trip to the valley in April–May 2000.[15] Reports,

---

[15] The interviewees are: Doug Henton, of Collaborative Economics: strategic advisors to Civic Entrepreneurs, a Palo Alto firm (at Palo Alto, April 5, 2000); AnnaLee Saxenian, Department of City and Regional Planning, University of California at Berkeley (at Stanford, April 13, 2000); William F. Miller, Stanford Graduate School of Business (at Stanford, April 5,

books and brochures, written by bureaucrats, politicians and heads of committees and parliamentary commissions (many of which are also available on the World Wide Web), extend and add bulk to our sources covering Silicon Valley in its second phase.

Saxenian, who is very much preoccupied with this entrepreneurial second phase, has observed that Silicon Valley was rather "an historically special case than a regional prototype" (Nuhn, 1989, p. 49). The sources confirm this view: that people in the 1990s seemed to have "rediscovered" Silicon Valley, despite its having drawn attention for thirty years. She and the other newcomers had found something new, for the technologies ceased to be their central preoccupation, being replaced by the "entrepreneurialness" of the valley itself. William F. Miller has noted that Silicon Valley can be depicted as a series of S-curves, where a dominant technology after reaching its maturity is unfalteringly succeeded by another, thereby sustaining the prosperity of the valley over decades, from the commercial exploitation of the integrated circuit (1960–69), to semiconductor- and microprocessor-spawned personal computer firms (1970–85), to burgeoning software and Internet companies (1985–2000), to the biotech and e-commerce start-ups and beyond (Miller, 2000). People in the second interactivity phase began to perceive the valley in terms of the region's entrepreneurial capacity always to jump from the end of one S-curve (an exploited technology) onto the beginning of the next S-curve – the new expanding one – thereby sustaining high-tech IT growth. The

2000); Sean O'Riain, Department of Sociology, University of California at Davis (Berkeley, April 24, 2000); Marina Gorbis, Institute for the Future, Menlo Park (Menlo Park, April 26, 2000); Stéphane Raud, Attaché for Science and Technology at the French consulate in San Francisco (April 4, 2000); Ludovic Ledru, on assignment to the French consulate in San Francisco to do a report for the Ministry of Foreign Affairs on French people in IT in Silicon Valley (at the consulate, April 4, 2000); Michel Ferrary, Assistant Professor at ESSEC, visiting the Department of Sociology at Stanford University and doing a study of French venture capitalists (at Stanford, April 6, 2000); Alain Baritault, French IT journalist living in Palo Alto (at Palo Alto, April 20, 2000); and corporate executives with firms located in San Francisco and Silicon Valley: Sylvain Dufour (at San Francisco, April 26, 2000); Jean-Louis Gassée (at Menlo Park, April 26, 2000); Julien Nguyen (Redwood City, April 20, 2000); Jérôme Calvo (at Palo Alto, April 27, 2000); and Lucy Cohen-Harris (at San Francisco, April 10, 2000).

entrepreneurialism itself, not the technologies, became the subject. This excitement about the entrepreneurialism in Silicon Valley led to academic redefinitions of the field. Alain Fayolle has observed that, in the 1990s, American researchers began to define entrepreneurship as a "process, which takes place in different environments and under different configurations, which introduces change in the economic system through innovation, by individuals who generate or respond to economic opportunities and who create value both for themselves and for society" (Fayolle, 2001, p. 55). The new definition expressed a dynamic Silicon Valley entrepreneurial ideal.

The reorientation presented language difficulties to foreign visitors emerging from the first technological phase. The word "entrepreneur" is French, but the French did not have an equivalent for the popular American term "entrepreneurship," so, just as they had had to invent and popularize words for "management" and "manager" during their post-war encounter with Americanization, they had to cope similarly with the new circumstance. The term "entrepreneurship" was translated into French. The result, *entrepreneuriat*, seems awkward and "unFrench" and has had difficulty gaining currency. Words for other aspects of the new and startling entrepreneurial culture had to be invented. "Start-up," which trips off the American tongue so easily, was taken over. The Germans also adopted a German word, *Existenzgründung*, but it contains a connotation of commitment in it that goes beyond the rather ephemeral American "start-up." And *Existenzgründung* belies the Silicon Valley idea of "easy come, easy go," of the acceptance of risk and failure as a normal part of business life. Usually, therefore, the French and Germans avoided the language problem by using the American "start-up." They also had to search around for other language equivalents for words that Americans used in their high-tech entrepreneurship, such as "incubator" which they sometimes translated as *Brutkasten* or *pépinière*, or just left in the American original. In short, the Europeans began to talk about Silicon Valley after 1990 less in technological terms than as a new entrepreneurial culture – one, as their language struggles indicate, that clashed with their own.

When commenting about Silicon Valley's entrepreneurialism, the remarks of European peripatetics are the most colorful. Internet articles urged the French and Germans to go west and visit the El Dorado. People who did usually experienced a business culture shock. Anja

Dilk, in a report entitled "Kulturcrash im Silicon Valley – Deutsch-Amerikanische Grenzerfahrungen," describes how Thomas Neubert reacted when sent out by his Munich firm in 1991 to find start-up ideas for investment:

The start-uppers do not work in a brightly lighted office-land as would be expected in Neubert's Munich firm. They wear no stylish suits like their German colleagues. The digital pioneers in the Valley, bent over their computers in little, gray workstations, wear jeans, T-shirts, and tennis shoes. No hint of the German business world here. Neubert: 'This was a very different work culture, a completely different world – really depressing' (Dilk, 2002, pp. 1–2).

But the perplexed Neubert did not rush back home. He stayed to found a business in Silicon Valley and to understand and appreciate, like other Germans and Frenchmen, its environment. *Manager Magazin*, in a 1999 article entitled "Go west, Germans," spelled out the opportunities in this unfamiliar entrepreneurial culture (Gärtner, 1999), and the same sort of exhortations appeared on other national Web sites.

Some, emphasizing the culture clash, decided that Silicon Valley's culture was too alien to their own to be fit for emulation. But most commentaries, despite the culture differences, insisted that, if they could not create an entrepreneurial culture at home identical to that in Silicon Valley, they could not ignore change since without it they could not participate adequately in the information age and the new economy. In the late 1990s, the French suddenly and painfully realized that an even greater technological gap had opened up, and a most significant one since the technology made up the sinews of entrepreneurial interactivity. Not only was France behind the United States in IT; it lagged, according to the Trégouët report, behind its European partners in Silicon Valley's second-phase technologies. In 1995 French investment in IT amounted to only 1.6 percent of GDP, compared to 1.7 percent in Germany 2.35 percent in the United Kingdom and 2.8 percent in the United States. In 1996 the ownership of personal computers per household reached 14.4 percent in France, 20 percent in the United Kingdom, 30 percent in Germany and 35 percent in the United States. During the same years (1995–96) software output grew by 4–5 percent in France, 10 percent in Germany and 15 percent in the United Kingdom. The French had especially neglected Internet and multimedia applications, and refrained from individual usage of software and hardware. The Trégouët report concludes: "Our country is only just ahead of the Czech Republic, Hungary, Spain and Italy in terms of the number of computers per 1,000 inhabitants hooked into the Internet. It is not only far behind the USA and Scandinavia but also behind our principal European partners, Great Britain and Germany, as well as Ireland, Belgium, and Holland" (Trégouët, 1998, p. 1). In May 1997 a London conference of Eureka members (Germany, Japan, the United States, the United Kingdom, and France) presented the results of a survey of firms and consumers in its countries. It placed France last in several categories of IT usage and Germany next to last. In all these usages the United States was far ahead.[16]

The Trégouët report, citing an NOP research group survey, concludes – not surprisingly with these numbers – that "France's delay with regard to her entry into the information society is incontestable and, besides, not contested" (p. 1). As for the consequences of such a gap, the French pondered them well. The Kahn report notes that "IT had produced one-third of American growth in the past four years. IT's contribution to French growth in 1998 was 0.5 percent" (Kahn, 1999, p. 3). In other words, high unemployment in slow-growth France and Germany and low unemployment in high-growth America could be attributed almost exclusively to the presence or absence of an entrepreneurial IT sector. The Laffitte report adds that "France's late entry into the information society risks having nefarious consequences in that which concerns new products and services, and, because of their absence, on our economic situation and the radiance of our language and culture" (Kahn, 1999, p. 3).

German commentators were more subdued and less chauvinistic than the French, but they were alarmed. In 1992 Heinrich Henzler and Lothar Späth published a book with the provocative title *Sind die Deutschen noch zu Retten?* (*Can the Germans still Be Saved?*), which catalogues a list of German industrial woes (Henzler and Späth, 1992). Much of the book deals with the Japanese challenge to big German firms, but it also deals with Silicon Valley's entrepreneurialism. Germans observed that, with few exceptions, the country's industry had

---

[16] NOP Research Group interviewed management and consumers groups; cited in Trégouët, 1998. The usages measured were modems, Internet access, e-mail, video conferences, individual usage, Web sites and CD-ROM.

made and was making little contribution to information business and industry, and they stressed the absence of start-ups.

In this regard the Global Entrepreneurship Monitor proved especially instructive. A research group, operating on the assumption that the rate of entrepreneurial start-ups could vary from country to country, set out on a comparative study in 1997.[17] The 1999 survey, the first, covered ten countries, the 2000 twenty-one and the 2001 twenty-two, including France and Germany every year. The results are particularly unfavorable for both, as in a Total Entrepreneurial Activities index they rank below average for European countries and far below the North Americans.[18] The reports look at entrepreneurship in general, but there is no reason to believe that German and French ranking would be higher if the focus was on high-tech start-ups. Indeed, engineers in both countries avoided creating their own enterprises, favoring instead career paths in big companies. This occurred especially in France with engineers from the prestigious schools. Whereas graduates from MIT, Stanford and the University of California were entrepreneurial spark plugs in high-tech Silicon Valley, those from the Ecole Polytechnique and the Ecole Centrale de Paris preferred working for large corporations. Most engineering start-ups, in a not very enterprising culture, graduated from *arts et métiers* schools, whose careers within big firm managerial hierarchies, in any event, would be less promising (Fayolle, 1999a).

This was the new entrepreneurial challenge from Silicon Valley that these Europeans perceived. The perception is important, because this book is less concerned with the American achievement than with how the Germans, the French and the Czechs borrowed from Silicon Valley, and a valley-influenced United States, in order to meet the perceived challenge. Nonetheless, the Americans in their own success self-analysis contributed to the European evaluation of it. For instance, the authors of *The Silicon Valley Edge* outlined a habitat model, which we have

[17] Initially the group included people at Babson College and the London Business School, with support from the Kauffman Center for Entrepreneurial Leadership, but it was joined by other sponsors, such as IBM, and national groups studying their own countries (at Cologne University for Germany, at the Lyon Business School for France).

[18] Global Entrepreneurship Monitor reports exist for each year, and there are reports in German and French prepared by their national teams. They are available on the World Wide Web.

sketched, that was meant to guide people in their search for regional high-tech start-up sustainability. Europeans living and visiting Silicon Valley, in seeking explanations for its dynamism, touched – if unsystematically – on similar themes.

European commentators said little about the origins of the entrepreneurial spirit in individual Americans. But they frequently spoke and wrote about its presence in Americans and its absence in their compatriots. Denis Payre, the president of a very successful French IT firm, who had worked at Oracle, complained that the "values of French society do not recognize the entrepreneur."[19] He was vague about the cause, ascribing it mostly to the evil influences of a welfare state. Croissance Plus, a French group supporting entrepreneurship, attributed its rarity to an absence of incentives. Specifically, it advocated the adoption of the American policy of stock options. In Silicon Valley, stock options enabled start-ups to attract exceptionally well-qualified people without an immediate outlay of cash and much-needed start-up capital, or the payment of the inflated salaries that would be necessary to entice good people away from other companies (CPR-Group, 1998, p. 2). The Croissance Plus Report favored allowing "stock options in firms less than seven years old, involved in new technologies." This required a change in tax laws, which discouraged the use of stock options in France, since the state taxed the stock options heavily when they were realized. This complaint moved reformers in each country to urge its government to propose the removal of legal obstacles to a stock options reward system And it led to European participation in the Global Entrepreneurship Monitor's comparative studies into the state of entrepreneurship in their societies.

Observers, especially those starting a business in Silicon Valley, spoke less about incentives than about how the valley's environment supported the start-up process. Stories abound about the comparative availability of venture capital. Stephen Krempl complained that German high-tech inventors faced a daunting task bringing their ideas to the market in the early 1990s in Germany:

Who is not fifty and graying can spare himself a trip to the bank and to venture capitalists . . . It borders on absurdity that a German start-up must first place ads in American journals like *Wired* or *PC World* in order suddenly to get calls from Dortmund, Düsseldorf, or Munich . . . The entrepreneurs

[19] The remarks of Denis Payre are in Assises de l' Innovation, 1998, p. 8.

are too slow and have not discovered the value of the "win-win" situation; the venture capitalists are too inexperienced and do not know the power of marketing; the press is incompetent . . . (Krempl, 1999, pp. 1–3).

French people in France and in the Silicon Valley expatriate community discussed the finance question the most. They complained about the absence of venture capitalists in France, often attributing their own decisions to start a business in Silicon Valley to their presence there. Michel Ferrary observed that France lacked habitats where successful entrepreneurs in IT who understood the commercial value of a research idea could support the innovative start-ups with cash and expertise (Ferrary, 2000). The reports stressed that the French banking structures, with weak ties to industry and a legal framework that discouraged "all innovation," offered no useful alternative. Observers in both countries emphasized that the problem was especially acute at the very beginning and in the latter stages of the start-up process, when making the firm public. They lamented the lack of angels and angel networks, which did so much to get projects off the ground in Silicon Valley. At the mature stage, when venture capital was available, there was no opportunity to make the firm public.

People realized that European stock markets could not play the role that NASDAQ played in Silicon Valley entrepreneurship. They campaigned for the creation of European equivalents. They held up this relationship as a "Modell für Deutschland" (Jutta Rubach & Partner, 1999). The hoopla about the founding of Germany's Neuer Markt emphasized the Silicon Valley connection. At a celebratory "Silicon Valley Congress," in Dresden, bankers, venture capitalists and professors from both countries met to exchange "tips and discoveries." The press release pointed out: "In Silicon Valley consultants and finance managers as well as professional investors regularly deal with the most difficult tasks. From this division of labor German Gründer can learn something" (Earlybird, 1999).

The Europeans did not limit their appreciation of the Silicon Valley start-up environment to the finance provision. Sylvain Dufour, CEO of Pagoo.com (a Silicon Valley start-up), thought that public relations firms were as critical to a successful start-up as venture capitalists because of the role they play in promoting IPOs on the stock exchange. Dufour commented that Silicon Valley high-tech firms tend to outsource everything from janitorial services to their own management

(Dufour, 2000). That they can do so depends on the excellence of the habitat, and, as Julien Nguyen, a polytechnician and co-founder of PlanetWeb.com noted, all these support services in Silicon Valley are "extraordinarily good" (Nguyen, 2000). The expertise extant in the habitat has a formal knowledge component but also one based largely on tacit skills acquired through community experience. French and German commentators could not find similar services in their countries. Law, accounting, public relations, building maintenance and other services existed but they were not attuned to the specific needs of high-tech start-ups. In their interviews, start-up entrepreneurs in California noted how Silicon Valley's range of community services met their needs perfectly and those at home did, and could, not.

Finally, the Europeans emphasized the differences in research intensity and university interaction. Of the French interviewed in Silicon Valley, none involved in the government inquiries thought the French environment deficient in a scientific-educational sense. Those whom Locke interviewed, mostly engineers trained in France, found they compared favorably with their American counterparts. They were, for example, better programmers, with more imagination and product inventiveness. Investigative reports said the same thing. The mission on technology and innovation (1997) pointed out that the publications of French scientific laboratories were very respectable; those in fields important to IT, such as mathematics, were quite strong, comprising 7.2 percent of world publications in the subject (Allègre et al., 1997). And the Germans could also point to solid science in the Max Planck Institutes and other research establishments.

The problems arose when it came to connecting this research with the entrepreneurial economy. The French reports in particular emphasized that the nation's research system kept apart the elements that the American triple helix (the term caught their attention) brought together. Unlike in the United States, publicly funded research in France primarily occurs in state-owned and-operated laboratories. The researchers there until very recently were forbidden to engage in commercial activity – that is, to work as consultants or join a firm with rights to return (if they wished) to their former state laboratory job, or sit on the boards of private firms. Attempts to remedy the problem failed, for a law of 1982, which authorized the creation of GIPs to bring scientists and entrepreneurs together, did not end the culture of isolation between the two. By the late 1990s only ten GIPs had been established;

Suzanne Berger, a French scientist at MIT, told the Trégouët mission in 1997 of the continuing "isolation of our [French] groups, and most particularly those in firms" (Trégouët, 1998, p. 29). Because the state streamed public funds into its own research laboratories, it neglected research in institutions of higher education. But, had it put the money there, the results might not have improved.

French critics affirmed that, among educational institutions, the *grandes écoles* had the greatest contact with industry. But this contact had not been exploited entrepreneurially. Michel Ferrary described the response when he attempted to foster networking between finance and industry and the engineering students at the EC. The student engineers did not discuss projects with professors, who stood aloof; neither, because of their suspicion of the finance sector, did they talk about any projects with venture capitalists (Ferrary, 2000). The Trégouët report noted that French corporate managers refrain from this networking. In French firms managers cling to Taylorism, to cost-cutting, to "the organization of activities founded on optimization and return on investment," with techniques that French managers and students of management found thriving when they visited America after World War II. Such an outlook during the "re-engineering" movement of the early 1990s prompted French management to stress lay-offs and entrenchment rather than "profound modification of work methods, changes in hierarchies, and new approaches to clients" (Trégouët, 1998, p. 148). And, according to Suzanne Berger, this type of management discouraged the emphasis on innovation that created the sort of research entrepreneurial networks existing in Silicon Valley.

If these Europeans in the late 1990s evaluated the Silicon Valley start-up environment in such a positive light, their critique also emphasized the obstacles to the creation of such an environment back home. They stressed the need for legislation to enhance entrepreneurial incentives – e.g. stock options, tax relief and initiatives to foster venture capital creation and investment. They emphasized reform in the equity markets, which did indeed lead to the establishment of the Neuer Markt and the Nouveau Marché. And they favored reform legislation that would permit academic researchers, like their Silicon Valley colleagues, to engage actively in the founding and operation of companies.

Among obstacles to entrepreneurship, the French critics during Silicon Valley's second phase especially singled out the baneful influence of the state. William F. Miller and his colleagues ranked government involvement among the eleven high-tech habitat features. These Silicon Valley residents certainly understood the important role that government played in the triple helix, but they thought low direct government involvement essential to the rapid transfer of technology to market-serving start-up commercial firms. Although this view contradicted the previously highly admired French "étatism," alarm about backwardness in IT in France in the age of interactivity emboldened anti-Colbertists. Anticipating Miller's argument, they now blamed their country's shortcomings on the state. In the Trégouët report, that most stringent critic of France's bureaucratic phenomenon, Michel Crozier, is quoted, along with many other sociologists, scientists, businessmen and legislators, as saying: "In France, the model of success remains the hierarchical statist model." Sabine Chalvon-Demersay, a sociologist, said: "Yesterday's unquestioned, hierarchical, vertical power faces today's power organized in consensual and horizontal networks." Senator Trégouët said: "These elites are a society of arrogance . . . often caught in flagrant offenses of inefficiency and incompetence . . . a defiant society vis-à-vis the market and our capacities to innovate." The last quote refers specifically to the long train of failed government initiatives in IT. Even Minitel, which state telecommunication engineers successfully promoted, had reached a "cul-de-sac" (Crespin et al., 1996, p. 6). Compared to the Internet, Minitel was too expensive, it was restricted to France in an era of globalization, and it lacked multimedia capacities. And it had little capacity to spur entrepreneurship. Since its efforts were so insufficient, moderate critics wanted "the State to renounce its traditional mode of action of relying on *grands programmes*" (Crespin et al., 1996, p. 6). The more radical wished, following the supposed American example, for the state to get out of the IT habitat altogether.

Germany had no Colbertist state to attack, but entrepreneurs there felt strongly – to use the title of one book on the subject – about how *Bureaucracy Puts Brakes on Start-ups* (*Gründungsbremse Bürokratie*). This report, based on the work of a panel founded by the Deutsche Ausgleichsbank, concluded that, of a "hundred start-ups, sixteen were delayed by the requirements of public administration. Every fifth start-up had to wait a year for authorization, in the service sector every fourth start-up had to wait one year" (Skambracks, 1999, p. 52). Numerous official specifications, the complicated rendition of legal texts and repeated demands for additional documents burdened the process.

Conclusion

This body of contemporary evidence not only in itself expresses Silicon Valley globalization, but it discusses its nature. We are not interested in the accuracy of the critiques expressed but in the state of awareness itself and its scope. The Europeans' evidence did not address comprehensively every issue that American-based experts, such as Miller and his group, had raised. Americans in their analysis of IT habitats emphasized more than Europeans the importance of civic entrepreneurs and partnership between non-profit and profit organizations as key elements in Silicon Valley's success. But the French and Germans singled out the elements that made Silicon Valley – and, through it, other American centers – exceptional in their ability to foster IT entrepreneurship: the triple helix that spawned IT commercially; the building of readily exploitable financial and service networks that facilitated the transfer of ideas into successful start-up firms; and, in general, the benefits to eager entrepreneurs that accrue from working in an open society.

To use such "neutral analytical concepts" to show the complexity of the Europeans' reaction to phenomenal Silicon Valley does not mean that there was, for them, anything neutral about the experience. The urgency of their remarks and their themes clearly reveal a preoccupation with an American-generated challenge. For this reason they were engaged in an "historically contested project," which could prompt them to reject American examples – however much they might have admired them – as unsuitable for the organizational and managerial cultures of their own countries.

Americanization implies that this would in fact be the case. And the evidence that accumulates suggests that it has been the case. The Neuer Markt and Nouveau Marché have not worked to service start-ups in the same way as NASDAQ. Nor have they gained investor confidence. The way that venture capital markets has developed differs; the roles of established banks (in Germany) and of the state (in France), as providers of venture capital, have deviated considerably from American practice, even after reform. But the extent to which Americanization transpired or was rejected in the three countries during the information age can be determined only when European reaction and receptivity are examined very carefully. It is beyond the scope of this book to take on this wide-ranging task. Its focus is more modest: to concentrate on the second Americanization as it relates to entrepreneurship education in France, Germany and the Czech Republic. Although a science and technology focus on university interaction had existed in Silicon Valley from the start, our prime concern about the entrepreneurial culture of universities dates from the post-1990 appreciations of the valley's role in the start-up dynamic. Before directly delving into this subject, however, chapter 2 prepares the ground by examining how Silicon Valley's IT revolution affected management education in the United States.

2 | *American management education: adding the entrepreneurial dimension*

THIS chapter deals with the evolution of entrepreneurship studies in the United States. Since Americans hold an instrumental rather than a consumption view of education, institutions of higher education inevitably got busy studying start-ups. But the motivation was twofold. People were interested – on the one hand – in how to go about starting a firm and – on the other – in entrepreneurship as an academic field of study. Before high-tech entrepreneurship itself became an important topic, the engineers and applied scientists involved in technology transfer and Japanese production methods almost ignored the subject. Then, in the 1990s, engineering and applied science faculties got interested in the process of starting firms, but they were – with some important exceptions – not preoccupied with entrepreneurship as a study field. Engineers and scientists had been attracted to the academic study of management subjects when, after World War II, US engineering schools developed the field of operations research. But OR had rigor; it required mathematically based modeling. Entrepreneurship, without the scientific credentials of OR, could not easily carve out a niche in the pedagogies of science and engineering. This left the study of entrepreneurship to others: principally those interested in management. This chapter looks primarily at entrepreneurship where it gained a place in academic business and management study programs, but it also considers the spillover of entrepreneurship studies into science and engineering in the most recent high-tech stage of development.

Since in historical subjects sequence is important, the chapter begins with a brief survey of American management education after World War II, because the state of academic management studies before entrepreneurship studies developed has as much to say about how they developed as the state of the demand for them in the economy and society. The second part of the chapter examines the new discipline's evolution within the parameters set by the established institutions of business, management and engineering education. The section

51

analyzes entrepreneurship curricula, research and – of special interest to entrepreneurship programs – outreach into the community. It carefully distinguishes entrepreneurship studies in general from those in high technology in particular, because the latter and their emulation in Europe are the chief concern of the book.

American management education after World War II

The rise of academic management education

Americans invented management, and they also invented management education. Since people who run businesses have always been trained and educated in some way, to say that Americans invented management education has a special meaning: the academic setting. This study limits its scope to that meaning. Business schools, graduate schools of management and schools of industrial administration are an American creation, and they became a significant export item. The academic institutionalization of management education separates it from management praxis and, consequently, entails a perhaps inevitable friction between the two. The friction, although ever-present, waxes and wanes in intensity depending on time and circumstance. American management education, like American management, therefore, must be approached not as a "neutral analytical concept" but as a contested historical project if its changing content and societal fit is to be understood in the information age.

Before management education came management, but before the twentieth century there was no "management." It originated in the United States as – to use Heinz Hartmann's words – "a fourth production factor," a "strategic variable for the development of the firm" (Hartmann, 1963, p. 149). Most Americans accepted the resulting managerial estate to be more rational actors in the firm than other employees, the better objectively to handle the firm optimally from the perspective of stockholders and – some even believed – employees. But this management idea, of management as a self-standing function, has rarely been adopted in start-ups or small firms where ownership and leadership have been inseparable. Rather, the concept of a professional management corps grew with the increasing size of corporations in the dramatic expansion of markets within a continental nation. Growth began after the civil war (1861–65), accelerating thereupon into the twentieth century. The changing ratio between the numbers of managers and employees within corporations magnified the size of the managerial class. Between 1948 and 1960, David M. Gordon reports, "the rates of supervisory to non-supervisory employees increased nearly 75 percent – from roughly thirteen supervisory employees per hundred non-supervisory to more than twenty-three" (Gordon, 1994, pp. 56–57).

Management education in the United States served this corporate clientele. By 1949 some 370,000, mostly undergraduates, were studying business subjects at 617 American college and universities – double the number of engineering students. The schools awarded 72,128 business baccalaureates that year. Thereupon the era of the MBA began: 4,814 degrees in 1960, around 23,400 in 1970, 49,000 in 1980 and 70,000 in 1990. Curriculum content also evolved. Pre-1945 students engaged in little more than commercial studies. But after the war schools seriously upgraded study content.

The war itself had brought change because it intensified intercourse between science and management. The early success of British OR enticed Americans, with their superior resources, to try their hand at it. Statistical methods helped solve production problems, and mathematical equations eliminated transportation bottlenecks. In production and transportation good examples of successful wartime OR can be found. The cold war resuscitated OR after brief post-war neglect and brought even greater intensity in its military applications. Among defense-based management applications it was undoubtedly linear programming that drew the most attention. George B. Dantzig and his associates at the Rand Corporation developed it for the United States Air Force (USAF) in 1947; afterwards scientists used linear programming techniques in numerous operations (e.g. traffic control in the Berlin airlift and maximizing bombing effectiveness in the Korean War). Economists, attracted to it, claimed that linear programming was a special case of marginal analysis, perfectly compatible with neoclassical economic theory, and useful in decision making (Dorfman et al., 1958).

Science in management automatically brought about the adoption and expansion of its methods where science takes place. This occurred outside universities in "think-tanks," such as the Rand Corporation and governmental research institutes. But university involvement in this management research, because of the triple helix, became commonplace during the cold war. The Case Institute of Technology in

Cleveland founded the first OR department. It did so at the instigation of the Chesapeake and Ohio Railroad and in response to USAF requests (funding research on airplane design). This institute organized a national conference on OR in November 1951, to which 150 people came from all over the country.[1] Several other universities also established OR programs (Carnegie Tech, UCLA, Ohio State University, the University of Pennsylvania, etc.). Of them, by the mid-1950s, Ohio State University and Case especially were recruiting industrial clients. Private consultancy firms worked with the universities (Booz, Allen, and Hamilton alone counseled clients about operations research in its fifty-two offices).

OR developed primarily in engineering schools and departments in the 1940s. The Operations Research Society of America claimed that thirty schools offered these studies in 1959 (Operations Research Society of America, 1959). But, for scientific rigor to move into management studies fully, knowledge of its tools – the requisite mathematical and science mapping skills – had to be brought to students in business schools. In the early 1950s they were still vocation-oriented undergraduate institutions. Schlossman, Sedlack and Wechsler describe how a determined group of reformers at the Ford Foundation, in league with business school professors, took up the task of reform.[2] Business schools toughened admission requirements in mathematics and introduced mathematical models and statistics into behavioral science, traditional functional management (marketing, finance, etc.), general management, and decisions science courses. Success came in the spectacular growth of MBA programs and the creation of elite graduate business schools, which quickly became famous for their achievements in management science. After a decade of reform Herbert A. Simon, of Carnegie Tech, "declared himself positively exhilarated by the progress we have made . . . towards creating a viable science of management and an art based on that science" (Sass, 1982, p. 303). The reform of education after World War II, proceeding first in the schools of technology and then in the business schools, had enabled, as Locke concluded, "American institutions of higher education to become, twenty years after . . . [the war], centers of research and teaching in scientific

---

[1] Locke, 1989, chapter entitled "The new paradigm."
[2] Schlossmann et al., 1987, in Locke, 1998b.

management, wherein the scientific treatment of management itself held pride of place" (Locke, 1998b, xxi).

The wedding between science and management that occurred in the 1960s proved to be a powerful force in American business school education. Decades after the post-war reforms, in 1997, Professor Eliasson could remark: "The bulk of subjects on the teaching agenda of business schools, like investment calculation and financial economics, rests on the assumption of a [formal knowledge] model" (Eliasson, 1997, p. 6). The formal knowledge model permitted research in the best American business schools to gain respectability in the academic scientific community that had eluded pre-war business subjects. It became the yardstick when judging the acceptability into academia of a new subject in business studies. Moreover, students educated under the system found favor in business and industry. Jeremy Hope and Tony Hope observed in 1997 that, in a survey of 402 US firms, 97 percent reported using a formal budgeting program, focusing time on measured variables considered critical to management control (Hope and Hope, 1997, p. 151). George Ritzer, in a book entitled *The McDonaldization of Society*, echoes this judgment. He describes how the end of the twentieth century saw the triumph of Taylorism, not its disappearance, in the American firm (Ritzer, 1995). Hope and Hope affirm that MBA education entirely satisfied this demand: "The main thrust of their written materials remains the hierarchical, production-driven models where the priorities are volume and scale, the management mentality is one of contract and control, and the way to compete is to lower unit costs by all means possible" (Hope and Hope, 1997, p. 222). If 97 percent of American corporate management still use top-down control systems, business schools apparently have a market for MBAs educated in the curricula that brought them academic prestige after the war.

Counter-currents: epistemological doubts and cultural vectors

Three counter-currents in the last quarter of the twentieth century have challenged the "scientific" paradigm that established itself in American management education after the war. Two of them will be dealt with summarily because they are somewhat tangential to the subject of this book. The third will be treated extensively in the second part of the chapter because it is its heart.

Epistemological doubts

The first counter-current divided science from management. People in praxis had always been skeptical, but doubts arose in academia itself. The *Methodenstreit* this entails has deep roots in academia. In 1883 the Austrian marginalist Karl Menger defended the methods of the classical school of economists in a carefully argued book, *Untersuchungen über die Methode der Sozialwissenschaften*. The German historical school made this defense necessary because it had claimed that the deductive logic employed in classical economics produced universalistic economic principles, little grounded in economic experience. But the ahistorical school – e.g. Menger – replied that this was the very point of a formal science. The German neoclassical economist Erich Schneider somewhat later stated their idea succinctly:

Theoretical propositions are always conditional propositions of the form: if A, then B. If this or that assumption is fulfilled, then this or that relationship is valid. The theoretical propositions always have the character of logical necessity and are according to the assumptions made either right or wrong. A theoretical proposition, like a dogma, cannot be denied. The most that can be said is that a theoretically correct proposition is not relevant because its assumptions do not apply to the present situation. That does not mean the proposition is wrong. It only means that the proposition does not apply to present circumstances (ist nicht aktuell) (Vogt, 1980, p. 37).

The deductive economists added that the inductive historical school, with its ad hoc empirical methods, would never produce a science of economics. Gustav Schmoller, the leader of the historical school, conceded as much (Schmoller, 1904, p. 107). The historical school lost this battle.

If the historical school created history, not science, the formal science of neoclassical economists still struggled with problems of applicability. The powerful tools that econometricians and OR scientists used during and after World War II seemed to overcome this problem. By the late 1970s, however, the academic doubting recommenced. Articles in the *Operational Research Quarterly*, as Locke analyzed them, increasingly called into question the mathematical models for being *nicht aktuell*.[3] This critique proved particularly devastating to OR when one of its most prominent advocates, Russel Ackoff, joined the doubters (Ackoff, 1977).

[3] Locke, 1989, chapter entitled "The new paradigm revisited."

The epistemology of science began to crumble. A major book, *The Turning Point* by Fritjof Capra, challenged the Cartesian-Newtonian assumptions upon which management science had been built (Capra, 1982). And the critics took aim at the economic and management sciences themselves. Donald D. McCloskey, a former cliometrician, attacked the principles of economics on epistemological grounds (McCloskey, 1983). W. Grant Astley's influential essay "Subjectivity, sophistry, and symbolism in management science" narrowed the discussion to the field of management. In the article he expressed the growing epistemological doubts that undermined the faith in science that Herbert A. Simon had expressed seventeen years before.[4] Astley asserted that academic research, if questionable science, still helped management praxis in the sense that it created an "ideology," a language of shared concepts and values that made management work. The belief in management as "ideology" marks the invasion of postmodernism into its province.[5] This outlook offered only a feeble cultural justification for the management function and the allegedly scientific educational system behind it. It deviated radically from the triumphant post-war modernist view, which had validated the rise of a managerial class, educated "scientifically" in business schools, on the grounds that it could, as a result of this education, objectively and efficiently govern – as Michael Fores said – "relations between human beings and their world" (Fores, 1996, p. 110).

Cultural vectors
The second counter-current carried cultural factors into management studies. From the mid-1960s the American Graduate School of International Management (Thunderbird) integrated foreign languages, history, comparative courses in the humanities, foreign internships and exchange studies into its Arizona program. But this constituted an educational exception at the time, since Americans conceived of management primarily as a "neutral analytical concept," to be taught and researched in universalist/ahistorical/acultural modes. With the emergence of the Japanese challenge people began to emphasize management's cultural origins. The number of books and articles on the subject

[4] Astley, 1984, reprinted in Locke, 1998b.
[5] See, for example, the collection of articles reprinted in Calás and Smircich, 1997.

that appeared between 1979 and 1995 are legion; some became best-sellers.[6]

Business and management schools responded after Japan's emergence, establishing special institutes and adding elective courses and programs with cultural dimensions. Some reflected regional interests. Hawaii's Pacific-Asian Management Institute (which offers MBAs with a focus on Japan and China), the University of Texas (Austin) with a Mexican focus, and the joint Asian/MBA programs at Cornell, Michigan, the University of California at Berkeley and the University of Pennsylvania are examples. Other business school programs had a global reach. The Joseph H. Lauder Institute of Management and International Studies founded at Wharton in 1983 best illustrates this tendency. It gives a joint MBA/MA degree to a linguistically skilled, highly qualified, international group of students each electing to concentrate in one of a number of cultural regions. The 1988 Trade Act, which authorized the US Department of Education to aid financially in the creation of sixteen Centers for International Business Education and Research, brought government support to this cultural bent. The CIBER program soon expanded from sixteen to twenty and then to twenty-six schools, stressing languages, regional studies, foreign business internships and study exchange programs.

For the few Americans who sought to build their science on solid epistemological foundations, postmodern attacks were disturbing. But American scientists are essentially pragmatic beings. If a better – i.e. more useful – idea comes along, they accommodate it even if it undermines previously held fundamental beliefs. They sleep peacefully without any epistemology at all.[7] Management studies, moreover, have generally been held not to be sciences but technologies – methods to reach goals efficiently. The stated goal had usually been to serve praxis; or, at

---

[6] See, for example: Tanner and Athos, 1981; Ouchi, 1981; Abegglen and Stalk, 1985; Halberstam, 1986; Thurow, 1985; Vogel, 1979; and Womack et al., 1990.

[7] David C. McClelland, comparing Americans to Germans, writes that "the American advances an idea somewhat tentatively as a hypothesis which he may defend more or less vigorously, but he is ordinarily quite willing to adjust it if someone else comes along with a better idea – because ideas are not so crucial to him as they are to the serious German, who is often trying to establish the firm and unshakable moral basis for existence" (McClelland, 1964, p. 86).

least, that was officially the case. Actually, management scientists in the postmodern era are quite content to have praxis believe – or pretend to believe, since it provides the endowments – that academic management education serves a useful function, if no more than to propagate the ideology of managerial capitalism.

Culture helped American management education to become globally more aware. But it did not significantly alter the main thrust of business education. Culture studies took place primarily in fringe institutes of business schools and through elective courses. The core of business studies remained culturally neutral and universalistic in assumption. The business schools themselves were content to study the traditional subjects in their MBA core (marketing, finance, etc.) using pedagogy bereft of a solid epistemology or instrumentality at its base. And to do "scientific" research. To be accepted into American management academia at the end of the twentieth century, entrepreneurship studies had ostensibly to meet standards that most existing management fields did not themselves meet: to teach codified forms of knowledge justified through scientific research. That was (is) academic management education's fiction of the day.

Coping with entrepreneurship in American business education

Entrepreneurship in the doorway to academia

Americans have always been entrepreneurial. It is not in their soul, but is almost an inevitable result when ambitious people are let loose on a rich, unexploited continent where the indigenous groups cannot stop their own conquest. Multiplying barber-shops, hardware stores and beauty parlors on main streets eventually drew the attention of America's new management educators, but they discussed them in small business rather than entrepreneurial terms. Only when entrepreneurship brought the proliferation of start-ups that quickly matured into global enterprises, a concomitant transformation of people's personal and business lives in a new technological environment, and vastly increased employment and national wealth did the management educators really take notice. This produced entrepreneurship studies, the third counter-current. It amounted to a counter-current because academia in established management disciplines resisted its intrusion into the management education domain.

The intrusion of entrepreneurship studies into academia was conditioned by the degree to which people thought knowledge about it could be codified. Initially academia and praxis believed entrepreneurship could not be a field of knowledge. Entrepreneurs were born, not taught; the information about them was non-codifiable. Business schools almost ignored entrepreneurship. They were management schools. Therefore, up to 1970, "entrepreneurship was a 'dirty word' in academia . . . Professors interested in the subject were threatened with weak recommendations for promotion and tenure" (Dunn and Short, 2001). Professor Eliasson's comments about the experimentally organized economy that replaced the era of Apollonian certitude seem at first glance to confirm rather than gainsay this judgment, for he spoke of managerial skills in the new world of "incomplete knowledge" as being tacitly acquired on the job, not those codified and learned in classrooms. But Eliasson also spoke of managers in Schumpeter's sense of the driven, creative individual. In the EOE managers had become entrepreneurs, whether working inside the firm, in intrapreneurship, or in the economy. The distinction between manager and entrepreneur is critical and profound because it deals with the essence of man. This is why we choose Nietzsche's poetic vision of Dionysus and Apollo to dramatize the significance of the subject in the introduction.

People who discuss the great entrepreneur usually do so in Dionysian terms, of anti-intuitive will, of creative destruction, of the exceptional individual. Indeed, during the radical industrial transformation of the past two decades, Schumpeter's demonic idea of the creative-destructive entrepreneur has been cited so much by so many that it has been turned into a cliché. People characterize corporate managers, on the other hand, in Apollonian terms: knowledge-based behavior in a rational order. Small wonder that management scientists ignored entrepreneurship in the academy. It did not fit into the Apollonian world of knowledge they had been constructing there during most of the last century. This resistance has been particularly successful so long as the individual remained the focus of entrepreneurialism. Imparting codified management knowledge to students would never turn them into entrepreneurs because will more than knowledge defined them. But Silicon Valley changed the vision. No longer could entrepreneurial achievement be explained just in terms of exceptional individuals. Exceptional individuals they had to be, but explanations now had to include the issue of entrepreneurial embeddedness in a high-technology habitat.

Establishing a new discipline: curricula, research and outreach

Although the phenomenon of Dionysus remained elusive, American academic researchers now had a much greater field of knowledge to analyze and to propagate. But entrepreneurial studies to seek acceptance had to go through a development process, which in American academic management education meant three things. They had (1) to develop widely adopted curricula, (2) to become a serious research field and (3) to establish outreach from academia into the community. Each accomplishment will be considered in turn.

Curricula

The obstacles to the development of curricula resembled those that would hinder entrepreneurial research (the next topic). Poets, writers and (perhaps) scholars might describe the Dionysian man, but nobody could explain how to become one. Since business studies ostensibly had a utilitarian purpose, to prepare students for managerial careers, entrepreneurship studies that restricted themselves to Dionysian individuals could not develop into a respectable academic discipline with proper curricula. But undergraduate and graduate curricula could and did develop as embedded entrepreneurship. At first the subject had to win the approval of faculty teaching core management courses. They would naturally insist initially that nothing special needed be done in their management subjects to accommodate entrepreneurship. Sara Sarasvathy's study of entrepreneurial decision making, as opposed to customary management decision making, illustrates how mistaken this assumption could be (Eifertsen, 2001).

She interviewed twenty-seven founders of companies valued between $200 million and $6.5 billion. Contrary to conventional teaching, she found that successful entrepreneurs did not try to predict how a market would respond to a product or service. Instead, they would launch into an unpredictable market and focus on what they could control – i.e. securing prior commitments from stakeholders and strategic partners. She called this "effective reasoning," because it inverted the traditional reasoning taught in business school classrooms, which prompted people to develop the perfect market or financial plan at the outset of

Table 2.1 *Small business management entrepreneurship courses in the United States*

Development of course offerings in small business management (SBM) and entrepreneurship (ENT)					
1979–82		1982–86		1979–86	
SBM	ENT	SBM	ENT	SBM	ENT
2-year schools +20 (12%)	+13 (144%)	+48 (25%)	+17 (188%)	+68 (40%)	+31 (344%)
4-year schools +45 (35%)	+17 (69%)	+106 (60%)	+90 (214%)	+151 (116%)	+107 (428%)

Source: Solomon and Fernald, 1991.

their venture. In college courses market research is among the first steps students are told to take. But "only four of the twenty-seven [entrepreneurs] in the study said they would even consider using any of the traditional market research methods. They didn't believe in them. Many . . . in the study tried to sell an idea before they had a prototype" (Eifertsen, 2001). Marketing, finance and other fields had to make space for entrepreneurship in their courses, or alter their subjects to make them part of the curriculum on entrepreneurship, for the field to progress.

A step toward recognition came with the separation of entrepreneurship from small business studies. Although American four-year colleges and two-year community colleges began to offer courses specifically designed for small, family-owned business after World War II, few entrepreneurship courses per se existed until the mid-1980s. Then things changed. The educational surveys of the Small Business Administration reveal the growth in course offerings and a rather sudden strong shift in orientation from small business to entrepreneurship halfway through the decade.

Top business schools' offerings follow a similar pattern. Professor Miles Mace taught "starting a new venture" first at the Harvard Business School in the late 1940s. Professor Richard Morris taught a course called "new ventures" at MIT in 1961. Business schools at the University of Southern California in 1971 and Carnegie Mellon University in 1972 introduced courses on entrepreneurship, and Babson College entered the field in 1981. *Success* magazine's 1999 ranking of twenty-five "best" business schools with these studies shows that their interest in entrepreneurship education quickened after 1980. Almost half of the schools did not even have a course in entrepreneurship before that decade.[8]

The move into entrepreneurship education registered in the surveys of the 1980s accelerated in the early 1990s. Academic study of entrepreneurship "took off" with what Professor Jeffrey Timmons of Babson College called "the silent revolution" of start-up ventures (Dunn and Short, 2001). Estimates of the numbers of institutions involved vary considerably. Carolyn Brown states that, in 1985, 85 schools offered courses in entrepreneurship; in 1999, 170. Donna Fenn and Michael Warshaw in *The Profit Minded Professor* claim that number to have been about 400 in 2000 (Fenn and Warshaw, 2000, p. 2). Numbers could vary because of different definitions about what constituted an educational program. Vesper and Gardner, in their survey of entrepreneurship studies (1999), made the following the basis for inclusion: having three or more for-credit courses aimed at an undergraduate or graduate degree. Although this definition eliminated many schools, 104 schools met their criterion, 75 percent of them US colleges and universities. The Small Business Administration's survey of American universities and colleges, conducted in 1997–98, gave the most spectacular results: some 200 endowed professorships in entrepreneurship, 310,000 students taught, in 1,400 institutions (Katz, 1998, p. 46).

Limited by a paucity of materials, entrepreneurship started as a single course. Its standard components were: concept of entrepreneurship; characteristics of an entrepreneur; value of entrepreneurship; and building a business (assessing opportunities, market and self ability, developing an idea, finding the capital, starting up the business and managing a business). Thereupon, a course became courses and, then, turned into entrepreneurship programs. Vesper and Gartner report the "frequency count of entrepreneurship courses," in the identified

---

[8] The twenty-five business schools were located at the Universities of South Carolina, Pennsylvania, California (Berkeley and Los Angeles), Arizona*, Louisville*, Texas (Austin), Illinois (Chicago Circle), Washington, Maryland*, Colorado*, De Paul University*, Saint Louis University*, Case Western University*, Rensselaer Polytechnic Institute*, Stanford University, Northwestern University, Ball State University*, Brigham Young University*, Cornell University*, MIT, Columbia University, San Diego State University, Babson College and Harvard University. The asterisks signify post-1980 creations. Survey cited in Debourse et al., 1999.

Table 2.2 *Entrepreneurship courses in the United States, 1999*

Course	Total	Undergraduate	Graduate	Both	Unsure
	Number of schools offering particular courses				
Entrepreneurship, start-up	120	16	35	63	6
Venture finance	83	19	45	16	3
Venture plan writing	42	7	12	12	2
Venture marketing	35	4	22	8	1
Technology transfer	30	4	21	5	0
Product development	19	0	18	1	0
Opportunity finding/screening	24	2	12	8	2
International venturing	21	6	11	1	3
Innovation evaluation	19	4	15	0	0
Law for entrepreneurs	18	3	12	2	1
Creative thinking	16	4	10	2	0
Entrepreneurship research	12	2	9	1	0
Entry via acquisition	11	0	10	1	0
Franchise development	10	3	3	4	0
Venturing in arts, software, etc.	9	2	6	1	0
New product marketing	8	1	6	1	0
E'ship for bankers, biologists, etc.	7	1	2	4	0
E'ship for non-business majors	6	3	1	2	0
New venture laboratory	5	1	4	0	0
Entrepreneurial economy	4	1	3	0	0
Social entrepreneurship	3	0	2	1	0
Sociology of entrepreneurship	3	0	1	1	0
TOTALS	504	83	269	134	18
Percent	100%	16%	53%	27%	4%

Source: Vesper and Gartner, 1999.

schools. It shows that schools offered three times more courses at the graduate level and that, among them, schools reserved by far the largest number of special courses for graduate students.

This means that big graduate management schools had the more elaborate curricula. A couple of examples illustrate this point. The Sterns School of Business at New York University offered graduate students three entrepreneurial tracks: finance, management and marketing.

The core courses:
Patterns of entrepreneurship;
Entrepreneurship and management in small business;
Entrepreneurial finance;
Planning and starting a new business; and
Entrepreneurial consulting practicum.

Key and related entrepreneurship courses:
Venture capital financing;
Entrepreneurial management in the corporation;
Restructuring firms and industries;
Brand planning for new and existing products; and
Competitive management from technology.

At the other example, the Stanford Graduate School of Business, students could take:
Private equity investing seminars;
Investment management and entrepreneurial finance;
Social entrepreneurship;
Human resources in entrepreneurial companies;
Integrated design for marketing and manufacturing;
Legal challenges in entrepreneurship;
Entrepreneurship: formation of new ventures;
Entrepreneurship and venture capital;
High-tech entrepreneurship;
Strategy in entrepreneurial ventures; and
Evaluating entrepreneurial opportunities.

The rapid growth in US start-ups fueled this curriculum development. It did so first by stimulating unprecedented student demand. In the "past," Kevin Farrell wrote in *Venture* magazine (1974), "most business schools would offer electives in small business or in managing the family business." Ten years later he wrote: "Students now are demanding courses that teach practical skills for starting and growing businesses" (Farrell, 1984). In 1994 1,248 students sought places in four entrepreneurship classes at the University of Chicago's Graduate School of Business; the same year one-third of the students at

Northwestern's Kellogg Business School expressed interest in courses in entrepreneurship; at Stanford's business school, the number of seats in elective courses in entrepreneurship grew from 294, in the 1992/93 academic year, to 1,000 in 2000. Ninety percent of Stanford MBA students enroll in at least one of the twelve courses dealing with the entrepreneurial process.[9]

Secondly, a thriving business community directly supported new academic programs. The steadiest and most generous supporter over the past quarter-century has been the Ewing Marion Kauffman Foundation. The Kauffman Center for Entrepreneurial Leadership, at the local, regional, national and international level, sponsored curriculum development and student involvement projects, organized enterprise creation competitions, seminars and lectures on various aspects of entrepreneurship, financed courses and programs on the subject, funded research programs, and generally acted as a clearing house for the collection and dissemination of books, articles, brochures and electronic media products on entrepreneurship. Numerous local and national foundations participated as well, as is their wont in American management education. American firms and business people have not been bashful about attaching their names to buildings, and business school administrators have readily solicited the monies that building dedications occasioned. The names of America's graduate schools of business and management offer plenteous testimonials to this. In the 1990s generous benefactors started funding centers and institutes of entrepreneurial studies, usually lodged in business schools but sometimes located in schools of engineering or jointly housed in schools of business and engineering. Jerôme Katz's research shows that, as the decade began, a center of entrepreneurship, with a budget on average of around $2,000,000, opened every month, and the numbers intensified toward the decade's end (Robinson and Haynes, 1990, p. 41). Here, with starting date, is a representative sample of business-sponsored centers:

Babson College's Blank Center of Entrepreneurship (1998); Baylor University's Blaugh Center of Entrepreneurship (1995); Carnegie Mellon University's Jones Center for Entrepreneurship (1990); Chapman College's Weatherby Center for Entrepreneurship (1995); Georgia

[9] See the Web site for the Center of Entrepreneurship at Stanford University at www.Stanford.edu.

Institute of Technology's Price Center of Entrepreneurship (1994); Indiana State University's Johnson Center for Entrepreneurship and Innovation (1998); Miami University's Page Center for Entrepreneurship (1994); New York University's Berkley Center for Entrepreneurial Studies (1997); Northwestern University's Heizen Center for Entrepreneurial Studies (1997); Saint Louis University's Smurfit Center for Entrepreneurial Studies (1990); Tulane University's Rosenblum Institute for Entrepreneurship (1991); University of California at Berkeley's Lester Center for Entrepreneurship and Innovation (1990); University of Virginia's Batten Center for Entrepreneurial Leadership (1996); and UCLA's Price Center for Entrepreneurial Studies (1995).

Centers of entrepreneurship brought study programs together. There was more money for more professors and more courses. And the entrepreneurs had input in their operations, since they sat with academics on governing boards or committees. The best centers in effect brought entrepreneurship education to fruition. They sponsored research in the field, developed the teaching of entrepreneurship within the greater university, promoted an entrepreneurial culture among students, upgraded the expertise of the professors in their field, coordinated the initiatives and activities initiated by members of the entrepreneurial milieu, established bridges between the university, business and government, projected an image for excellence in entrepreneurship studies for networks of universities, and participated actively in the community by organizing post-experience seminars on entrepreneurship for consultants and businessmen.

But the work of the centers of entrepreneurship does not end this story of educational development. No curriculum could take on life in America without the necessary reading materials, texts and audiovisual aids; and publishers furnished them. In 1996 Katz and Green identified over four dozen textbooks used by instructors in classes on entrepreneurship (Katz and Green, 1996). There were casebooks that provided lengthy examples of successful start-ups; conventional texts that offered a variety of study topics with definitions, examples and applications; business planning texts that focused on developing a business plan; and industry-specific texts that looked at developing a small business within that industry. A search of "books in print," using the terms "entrepreneur," "small business," "family business," "start-up business" and "new venture," resulted in a list of over 625 different books for use as texts in college courses (Katz and Green, 1996). In the

United States Dryden, Harvard, Irwin and ITP published several texts, including most of the leading ones, in terms of market share. There were also lots of "wraparounds," videos of successful entrepreneurs and entrepreneurial cases, computer programs for building financial statements and other elements of a business plan, text banks, transparencies and study guides.[10]

In most colleges and universities, located in small cities and rural settings, the studies cover non-tech start-ups of the sort that many Americans dream of owning (a pizza parlor, a service station, a clothing store, etc.). But, within all of this, high-technology entrepreneurialism held an important place. Studies flourished at the centers of American high-tech prowess. Entrepreneurship education at MIT grew rapidly. In the 1997–98 academic year, more than 930 MIT students enrolled in entrepreneurship courses, a 221 percent increase from 1996–97. At MIT's Sloan School of Management a concentration in entrepreneurship for MBAs is available in the new product and venture development track. NPVD, one of six career management tracks offered in the MBA, assembles a series of courses from a number of disciplines, carefully selected to provide students with the special range of skills and insights in finance, strategy, management, product development and other areas required to start up and guide the growth of new ventures. The NPVD track 1997–98 was the second largest at Sloan, and the most popular track for first-year MBA students.

Undergraduate and graduate students could profit from an MIT policy that allowed anyone to take any subject, regardless of major, assuming that appropriate prerequisites had been met, instructor permission obtained, and space was available. Thus, engineering and science students could target business subjects and Sloan management students could enroll in some engineering and media lab subjects. In the 2001 academic year the courses offered were: "preliminary venture analysis and personal entrepreneurial strategy"; "the nuts and bolts of business plans"; "starting and building a technology-based company"; "marketing: an introduction for engineering entrepreneurs" (not for credit); and "selling yourself and your ideas" (not for credit). The "not for credit" designation indicated engineering's skepticism about entrepreneurship as an academic discipline, but the presence of the engineering students in these courses showed their desire to

[10] Charts in Katz and Green, 1996, list the works.

Table 2.3 *MIT enrollment in entrepreneurship*

Course enrollment in entrepreneurship by year at MIT's Sloan School of Management

Course	1995–96	96–97	97–98	98–99	99–00	00–01
New enterprise	70	107	270	180	161	249
Entrepreneurship laboratory	20	60	138	150	174	117
Entrepreneurship w/o borders			70	55	55	60
Entrepreneurial marketing				60	49	118
Entrepreneurs in the next economy					125	87
Entrepreneurial finance					47	115
Global entrepreneurship laboratory						38
Independent activities period	128	170	283	418	369	458
All others	70	180	165	186	106	233
Totals	288	517	926	1,043	1,086	1,475

Source: MIT Center for Entrepreneurship, Web Site.

be entrepreneurs. To sustain and expand its entrepreneurial tradition, MIT established an entrepreneurship center with seed money from the Kauffman Foundation's Center for Entrepreneurial Leadership, the Coleman Foundation and the Lemelson Foundation.

The Harvard Business School programs need to be included in Massachusetts's high-tech entrepreneurship studies. In 1946 it and MIT helped found in partnership the first venture capital firm, American Research and Development (ARD). Although a broad-spectrum business educator, Harvard retained an interest in high-tech ventures thereafter. MIT was nearby, but it also turned to high-tech Silicon Valley, HBS building a "California Research Center," in Menlo Park at 3,000 Sand Hill Road. There, on-site researchers, caseworkers and Harvard faculty members on extended visits could develop materials for HBS courses that would "expose our students to this unique place" (HBS, 2002, pp. 71–72). This action demonstrated Harvard's understanding of the seminal role that Silicon Valley has played in high technology.

At Stanford, the Graduate School of Business offered courses and seminars on entrepreneurship. Its Center for Entrepreneurial Studies funded a major investigation of "over 175 high-tech start-ups in Silicon Valley." And its students could enroll in a special high-tech venture program sponsored by MIT. Stanford University's School of Engineering began its own formalized high-tech educational foray into entrepreneurship in 1997 with the creation of the Stanford Technology Ventures Program, which functions as a start-up study center within the school. It offers the following courses to engineers: "management of technology ventures"; "global entrepreneurial marketing: industrial engineering"; "technology venture formation"; "introduction to entrepreneurship"; "entrepreneurial finance"; "strategy in technology-based firms"; and an "industry through leaders seminar series."[11]

These programs serve the two principal high-tech regions of America and, since they are national educational institutions, the entire country. Numerous, more regional high-tech programs emerged, too. The Stevens Institute of Technology in 1999 transformed the entire school into an educational and entrepreneurial environment for "technogenesis." The term summed up the institute's goal: to focus "the process of interdisciplinary research resulting in inventions from basic scientific ideas, the engineering, development and commercialization of the ideas in Stevens-connected companies, and most importantly the [furthering of a] distinctive educational environment for all students 'rooted in technogenesis'" (Clark, 2002). The Georgia Institute of Technology's courses included: "commercialization of biomedical technology"; "new product development"; and "innovation." At the Rensselaer Polytechnic Institute students in the MBA Entrepreneurship Concentration took required courses on the "principles of technological entrepreneurship" and "new ventures," and elective courses on "invention, innovation, and entrepreneurship" and "management of technological innovation." These first-rate engineering schools could be expected to have a high-tech emphasis in their entrepreneurial studies.

---

[11] Harvard Business School, 2002, pp. 147–49 (Stanford School of Engineering).

But famous business schools other than Harvard or Stanford did too. Wharton developed entrepreneurship studies courses in "technology and innovation," "management of technology" and "high-technology entrepreneurship." The University of Washington had its graduate students take four high-tech entrepreneurship courses and attend a high-tech entrepreneurship speakers' series in its Program of Entrepreneurship and Innovation. In 1998 more than a third of MBAs enrolled in the PEI core.

These examples clearly indicate how the curricula in high-tech entrepreneurship expanded in the 1990s. And this is far from being a comprehensive survey.

Research

One major American research publication and a host of others provide details about research in entrepreneurship. Babson College's Center for Entrepreneurship combined with the Kauffman Center for Entrepreneurial Leadership in 1981 to sponsor the publication of research papers in a periodical entitled *Frontiers of Entrepreneurship Research*. The yearly survey lists the title and author(s) of research papers on entrepreneurship, grouped under a topical index of the editors' choice. Scrutiny of the number of topics contained in the indices each year shows how the complexity of research has increased over time.

Table 2.4 *The development of topical areas in entrepreneurship research*

Topical areas (TAs) in entrepreneurship research																			
Year	81	82	83	84	85	86	87	88	89	90	91	92	93	94	95	96	97	98	99	00
TAs	7	9	8	8	9	10	18	16	11	24	18	18	13	12	14	21	22	29	37	37

Source: *Frontiers of Entrepreneurship Research* (1981–2000)

The number of topical areas in the indices averaged eight the first five years (1981–85), 14.4 the next five years (1986–90) and 14.6 the succeeding five (1991–95), then jumped sharply to average 30 topics each index for the last five years (1996–2000). Between 1981 and 2000 the number of research topics grew more than fivefold. Numbers alone, then, indicate how enriched entrepreneurial research became over twenty years.

A comparison between the actual topical areas, under which papers were classified, in 1981 and in 2000 makes the growing maturity of the field even clearer.

In 1981, editors classified thirty-nine research papers under seven topics:

1 Surveys of entrepreneurs;
2 Entrepreneurs in other countries;
3 Venture capital;
4 Government and entrepreneurship;
5 Experiments in company formation;
6 Individual entrepreneurial experiences; and
7 Theorizing about entrepreneurship.

In 2000, 147 research papers appear under 37 topical classifications:

1 Entrepreneurial personal characteristics: general;
2 Entrepreneurial personal characteristics: motivations, intentions, and objectives;
3 Entrepreneurial personal characteristics: decision making and cognitive style;
4 Entrepreneurial social characteristics: social capital and social networks;
5 Entrepreneurial social characteristics: ethnicity;
6 New business formation: societal conceptions of entrepreneurship;
7 New business formation: context, geographic and other;
8 New business formation: start-up process;
9 New business formation: opportunity search and recognition, general;
10 New business formation: opportunity search and recognition, technological;
11 New firm financing: equity, searching for funds;
12 New firm financing: equity, angel-entrepreneur relationships;
13 New firm financing: equity, angels, informal investor systems;
14 New firm financing: equity, formal venture capital;
15 New firm financing: equity, decision making;
16 New firm financing: equity, entrepreneur-investor-sponsor relationships;
17 New firm financing: debts, banks, financial structure;
18 New firm financing: equity, initial public offerings, market performance;

19 New firm financing: long-term impact on new firms;
20 Venture capital firms: assessing investment success;
21 Venture capital firms: industry development;
22 New firms: internationalization;
23 New firms: strategic alliances;
24 New firms: franchising;
25 New firms: issues in family-owned firms;
26 New firms: economic sector and performance;
27 New firms: management structure and performance;
28 New firms: human resource management;
29 New firms: high technology, general;
30 New firms: high technology, Internet, e-commerce;
31 New firms: high technology adoption;
32 New firms: growth and survival, longitudinal research;
33 New firms: growth and management;
34 New firms: growth and strategy;
35 Corporate entrepreneurship, new ventures;
36 Societal contributions of entrepreneurship; and
37 Education, training and entrepreneurship.

Clearly, in these twenty years topics that deal with entrepreneurs' individual characteristics multiplied; those stemming from the embeddedness of entrepreneurship grew even more.

A second source, a *Compendium of Entrepreneurship Programs* compiled in 2000, also sheds light on entrepreneurship research. The 128 schools responding to the survey, which the *Compendium* launched, often listed recent faculty publications. The survey provides information about publication outlets and consequently about the growth of the scholarly apparatus needed for a discipline to be recognized.

The entrepreneurship researchers in the *Compendium* published in forty journals. Some did so in established general management journals (*Harvard Business Review, Administrative Science Quarterly, Journal of Applied Behavioral Science, Journal of Small Business Management, Journal of Management Studies, Academy of Management Review*, etc.). They also published in journals not devoted uniquely to entrepreneurship but to small business (*Journal of Small Business Management, Journal of Small Business Strategy, American Journal of Small Business*, etc.). But, to grow, a research discipline had to foment its own book and periodical press. The Americans did this during one decade (1985–1995), founding on average almost two new journals a year.[12] Some attained greater scholarly reputation than others. The *Journal of Business Venturing*, co-sponsored by academics at the Sterns Business School (New York University) and Wharton Business School (University of Pennsylvania), became perhaps the most respected in its field; Babson College's *Frontiers of Entrepreneurship Research* can also be placed in the top rank. Other business schools, with entrepreneurship programs, sponsored research journals. The American publishers Dryden, Harvard University Press, Irwin and ITP welcomed research on entrepreneurship. JAI issued ten volumes in a series entitled "Advances in Entrepreneurship, Innovation & Economic Growth" within several years.

The two sources just cited reveal the field's growing research complexity in general, but they also provide information about high-tech entrepreneurship's contribution to this complexity as a subdivision in the field. The 1981 edition of *Frontiers of Entrepreneurial Research* had no high-tech section in its topical index. Of its thirty-nine articles, only one dealt with a high-tech subject ("Patterns of acquisition in Silicon Valley," by Albert V. Bruno and Arnold C. Cooper). The 1982 edition added a high-tech-related topic to its index ("Spin-offs from universities") but the 1983 edition had none, although there were several articles about high-tech start-ups under the topic "venture funding." The 1984 edition had several high-tech-related topical headings in its index ("venture capital," "technologically innovative venture" and "spin-offs and incubators"). In the editions between 1985 and 1995 the high-tech-related topical headings never fell below four. At the end of the decade the number rose to seven in the 1999 edition and then became six in the 2000 edition. To perceive how research complexity in high-tech entrepreneurship grew between 1981 and the century's

---

[12] With year of founding, they were the *Journal of Product Innovation Management* (1990), *Entrepreneurship Theory and Practice* (1976), *Frontiers of Entrepreneurship Research* (1981), *Journal of Business Venturing* (1985), *Family Business Review* (1987), *Entrepreneurship and Regional Development* (1988), *Journal of Business and Entrepreneurship* (1988), *Journal of High-Technology Management Research* (1989), *Journal of Management Systems* (1990), *Journal of Enterprising Culture* (1992), *International Journal of Entrepreneurial Behaviour & Research* (1994), *Academy of Entrepreneurship Journal* (1995), *Journal of Developmental Entrepreneurship* (1995) and *The Entrepreneurial Executive* (1995).

end, consider the following high-tech topics classified in the 2000 edition: "new business formation: search and recognition, technological"; "venture capital firms, industrial development"; "new firms: high technology, general"; "new firms: high technology, Internet, e-commerce"; "new firms: high technology adoption"; and "new business formation: opportunity, search and recognition: technological." A selection of articles listed under these topics is in the footnote.[13] Many papers on high-tech start-ups also appeared in the edition under other topic headings.[14] Even though "more than 80 percent of the most innovative and fastest-growing companies are considered non-tech, a disproportionate amount of academic research went into the study of high-tech entrepreneurship" (YEO, 2000, p. 8).

Finally, the *Compendium of Entrepreneurship Programs* furnishes information for the surveyed schools about their scope of research interests. The research subjects included: "ethic entrepreneurship"; "entrepreneurial education"; "entrepreneurial teams in rapidly growing new ventures"; "entrepreneurial finance"; "the business gestation process"; "resource acquisition in new ventures"; "strategic alliance formation"; "international entrepreneurship"; "high-tech entrepreneurship"; "venture capital"; "initial public offerings"; "entrepreneurial governance"; "high growth strategies"; "technological opportunities in research/business incubators"; "global start-ups and entrepreneurship"; "factors relating to starting a business"; "innovation and opportunity recognition"; "entrepreneurship and organizational culture"; "theories of complexity and entrepreneurial behavior"; "academic entrepreneurship"; "entrepreneur/banker interaction"; "knowledge intensity"; "Internet marketing"; "entrepreneurial resource acquisition"; "network support for small business"; "strategic use of information"; "assessment of legal environment for start-up firm"; "technology-based new ventures"; "technology-based alliances between entrepreneurial and large firms"; "organizational factors and risk taking"; "cross-cultural opportunity recognition";

---

[13] Among the papers: Kickul and Gundry, 2000; Sawyer and McGee, 2000; Florin and Schulze, 2000; Hynes et al., 2000; Teach and Schwartz, 2000; Cohen and Meyer, 2000; Philips, 2000; Prasad and Naidu, 2000; and Hewitt-Dundas, 2000.

[14] Howorth and Wilson, 2000; Nambisan, 2000; McCline and Bhat, 2000; Stearns and Allen, 2000; Mason and Harrison, 2000; and Autio and Sapienza, 2000.

"informal investors"; "technology transfer"; "new venture growth"; "entrepreneurial networking"; and "team entrepreneurship." The research topics ranged over the entrepreneurial habitat, with those covering high-tech entrepreneurship cropping up more frequently than non-tech on schools' research agendas. Beginning in 1990 some 125 research articles appeared on entrepreneurship, and the numbers increased each year thereafter (Robinson and Haynes, 1990).

Thus entrepreneurship developed in the United States into a "mainstream" research field. This does not mean that it necessarily became useful to practicing entrepreneurs. Stumpf and Shirley point out that "most venture managers are not interested in applying the concepts and models learned in school to their dynamic business situation" (Stumpf and Shirley, 1994, p. 10). Nor are scholars particularly interested in their research being useful to the start-up entrepreneur. A survey of fifty entrepreneurship scholars concluded that they "reject the need to explicitly link scholarship with applicability" (Rosenberg and Jones, 1994, p. 11). But, if the purpose of research is to develop the tools and explore the subcategories of a discipline, academic America in a few short years had done that. Was it enough?

Isabelle Danjou, in a survey of primarily US research publications on entrepreneurship, observes that scholars have approached the subject from three angles: the entrepreneur; entrepreneurial action; and the entrepreneurial context (Danjou, 2000). Although work on all three facets can be found before and after 1980, researchers in the early period concentrated on the entrepreneur, on personality traits and motivation. Only in the wake of William B. Gartner's 1988 article did people begin to study "what the entrepreneur does" instead of "who the entrepreneur is" (Gartner, 1988). The date is significant, because "what the entrepreneur does" had become a burning issue for people seeking to turn their "big ideas" into successful start-ups. And the entrepreneurial context, as the first chapter demonstrates, also took on special significance to researchers because the entrepreneurial process was so much dependent on context. Societal demand in recent years, then, has enriched the research palette of entrepreneurship studies, the externalities of which – books, journals, research centers, research topics and other infrastructure – have been treated here.

But academics raised in the scientific tradition are uneasy with these results. Entrepreneurship studies, as Bygrave and Hofer phrase it, "suffer from the lack of a substantial theoretical base."[15] Nor have the research avenues pursued provided sure results with regard to instrumentality. Research into personality traits has not produced knowledge that allows us to predict who is going to be an entrepreneur. The personality traits identified turn out to be cultural variables.[16] Because research models suppose personality to be static, the important question to the educator – how schools can help transform individuals into entrepreneurs (savoir être) – has been left aside in research. Research into entrepreneurial process has not given more useful educational results. Since it leaves out the entrepreneur (the Dionysian man), the research has not only been unable to predict what actions will lead to entrepreneurial success but has also "run the risk of totally falsifying the entrepreneurial process" (Danjou, 2000). Studies about entrepreneurial context have proved its importance in entrepreneurship, but they have not provided predictive knowledge about how to construct a habitat that will spawn successful high-tech entrepreneurial firms.

Such incertitude would not upset Dionysian man because he knows that permanence and certitude are illusory. But it does confound the Apollonian view of reality that supposes full information, solid theory and predictability. Since academic researchers assume the Apollonian outlook, they have had either to condemn entrepreneurial studies as inherently non-scientific (their early viewpoint) or to claim, as they now do, that they are not yet sufficiently mature. But this stage view of social science epistemology – from youth, through adolescence, to maturity – is historically incorrect. Economics is the oldest social science, but it has never quailed more from epistemological and methodological angst than today. Research in entrepreneurship should not, because of its brevity, suffer any more or less from such doubts. The problem lies not with the discipline but with social scientists who cling to a scientific paradigm that has lost its verisimilitude. At the turn of the twenty-first century what *can* be said is that research in entrepreneurship, under the impulse of the United States' pragmatic imagination, even though eclectic, uncoordinated and disjointed, has been sustained and remarkable.

[15] Bygrave and Hofer, 1991, quoted in Danjou, 2000.
[16] Thus Tuunanen's evidence that the need for "personal recognition" is not a universal trait of the entrepreneur, since it is stronger in American entrepreneurs than Finnish; Tuunanen, 1997.

Outreach

Although academic researchers have evinced limited interest in designing their projects with applicability in mind, those promoting entrepreneurship have stressed community-university interaction. Perhaps they have no choice since they do not have the luxury of researchers who claim to be building a science. Academic-community interaction is an essential part of what they do. They take in students, send them through courses and seminars, and release them – hopefully better equipped – into the entrepreneurial work-world. Both business and the centers of entrepreneurial studies are proactive in their interrelationship. The stream of endowed chairs of entrepreneurship and the financial support to centers of entrepreneurship prove this. So do the contributions from various foundations such as the Kauffman, which places students in internships in entrepreneurial firms and funds the annual Kauffman Conference for Entrepreneurship Centers.[17] Firms themselves also make direct grants to programs, such as General Electric's $375,000 for a three-year study to develop curricula for an entrepreneurship and emerging enterprises program at Syracuse University. And local entrepreneurs sit on the governing boards of the centers, teach as guest lecturers and join with students in the entrepreneurship clubs, which are multiplying in colleges and universities along with entrepreneurial study programs.

On their side, the schools and centers have always been proactive themselves. Professors in entrepreneurship courses frequently have practical experience. Ninety percent of the professors in the twenty-five "best" business school entrepreneurship study programs, surveyed in *Success* magazine, had created or owned a firm; 100 percent had in ten of the schools. Entrepreneurship courses adopted a teaching strategy of "learning by doing" – e.g. doing projects in a start-up process or making a business plan. Entrepreneurs acted as tutors. And the schools reached out beyond the classroom. Entrepreneurial centers at Columbia University, the University of Pennsylvania (Wharton) and the University of Georgia coordinated entrepreneurial training programs at various locations in their respective states (New York, Pennsylvania and Georgia). The University of Illinois (Chicago Circle), with support

---

[17] The information on outreach is taken from the *Compendium of Entrepreneurship Programs* and from the Web sites of various schools and foundations.

from the Coleman Foundation, organized regional study conferences in entrepreneurship. Many centers got involved with business incubators to assist start-up firms. Some business schools had their own (Texas [Austin], Rennsselaer, Case Western, Stanford, San Diego State, etc.). They organized "boot camps," where aspiring entrepreneurs received a short but intensive preparation for their tasks. But probably the most successful outreach came in the 1990s with the business plan competitions. Babson College and the Moot Corps at Texas (Austin) conducted the first single-campus business plan competition in 1984. Two years later the first national business plan competition took place, organized by Tim Messon, University of Miami. Thereafter, business plan competitions multiplied. The famous business schools (Harvard, Wharton, Sterns, Michigan, etc.) created their own. But so did less well-known schools, often as host institutions for international or national business plan competitions (such as the University of Hawaii at Manoa and the University of Texas at Austin). These competitions draw hundreds of participants, whose plans, prepared with council from the business schools, are judged by panels of academics and entrepreneurs. The prizes: prestige and up to $50,000. The competitions create a lot of excitement in the community, with press releases and newspaper and television coverage.

Although these outreach outlets encompass high-tech entrepreneurship, generally they promote non-tech entrepreneurialism. Since it is this study's preoccupation, however, some instances will be cited of institutions that have used the same outlets to service high-tech start-ups. One example is the business plan competition at Stanford, BASES (Business Associates for Stanford Engineering Students) – the major club for engineers interested in entrepreneurship. It has an annual business plan competition, open to all Stanford students. MIT runs an annual entrepreneurship competition, with $50,000 going to each of the three top places. The jury is composed of business angels, venture capitalists, entrepreneurs and professional service people. In nine years thirty-two companies sprang from the competition. At the University of Texas, the business school runs a technology transfer competition in partnership with the university's Mechanical Engineering Department. And, to conclude with examples in internship programs, MIT's entrepreneurship lab, taught at its Sloan Business School, arranges internships in high-tech companies in the Boston/Route 128 region. The number of participating companies in 1999 was eighty-one. At the

University of North Carolina the business school uses the Kauffman Entrepreneurial Fellowship Program to put interns into entrepreneurial firms selected by the Technological Development Agency.

Conclusion

US management education has transformed itself in the past twenty-five years by expanding into research, teaching and community involvement programs in entrepreneurship. Will the future build on the past? The answer to the question depends on how one interprets the past with regard to the future. Entrepreneurship studies did not so much promote the surge in entrepreneurship as benefit from that surge. Today some doubt the continued ebullience of this entrepreneurial source – the start-up economy – and the future of entrepreneurship study programs. But only soothsayers and gypsy fortune-tellers know for sure. The rest of us can guess and make judgments based on the past. From it there is good reason to believe that the insertion of entrepreneurial studies into the American high-tech habitat has enriched its entrepreneurial capability. That, at least, seems to be a consensus emerging from people who have been through entrepreneurial studies. To the question "can you learn to start a business?" Nicole Torres, of the non-academic *Entrepreneur's Start-Up Magazine*, replies rhetorically: "Yes . . . In fact, it would almost seem necessary, as hardly anyone knows what to do from the start" (Torres, 2001). Christopher Pohl, an MBA student at Pepperdine University, after writing a business plan, remarked: "At first my plan was 'garbage,' [but] because of the MBA program, where people have the incentive to critique, it molded quickly and became a well-thought-out business plan" (Torres, 2001).

To some extent such comment begs the great question "are entrepreneurs born or made?" Nobody suggests or should suggest that the innate qualities of Nietzsche's Dionysian man – charisma, curiosity, boldness, decision capacity, leadership and, at times, ruthlessness – present in great entrepreneurs can be learned in classrooms and seminars. But entrepreneurship in a high-tech habitat requires a knowledge that arms this Dionysian man (or woman) with the tools necessary to success. Hence, in the future if not the past, the presence of entrepreneurial study programs in American schools and their interaction with the high-tech community may be important for sustaining entrepreneurialism. The conditional mood is used advisedly in this book because the subject treated is a "contested historical project," not a "neutral analytical concept." At this point in time, therefore, Katz's conclusion about the development of entrepreneurship studies in the United States seems appropriate:

Among American entrepreneurship academics, their administrators, program alumni, and supporters, among the American entrepreneurship media, and among American entrepreneurs, the value and presumed success of tertiary entrepreneurship education is a belief held with passion, bolstered by star graduates, media coverage, and increasing endowments from entrepreneurs. The resulting infrastructure has become the world's largest for textbooks, Web site simulations, trade books, dedicated academic journals, and published research. The field of entrepreneurship today is founded on a rapidly growing base of academic research and direct policy involvement (Katz, 1998, p. 64).

And Katz's conclusion is also a good jumping-off point for a discussion of the growth of entrepreneurship education in Europe. As the last chapter emphasized, nothing happens of significance in the United States without Europeans taking notice. Hence their reaction to Silicon Valley and hence, as the next chapters will show, their reaction to the new developments in management education in the United States.

3 | Adjusting higher education in France and Germany to a post-1945 world

THIS book now turns to Europe. Before considering how the United States influenced the development of entrepreneurship studies in France, Germany and the Czech Republic, however, something must be said about the reform of French and German commercial and engineering education after World War II. Educational conceptions about man and society that went back at least two hundred years anchored the institutions that underwent reform. D. Eleanor Westney, writing about the Westernization of Japan during the Meiji era (1868–1912), notes that "general attitudinal patterns" resist pressure to change more than specific organizational structures and functions (Westney, 1987, p. 219). This is only partially true, however, because "general attitudinal patterns" give life to an educational edifice that permits it to resist institutional change, especially when change undermines the "general attitudinal patterns." Prior to evaluating American influence on higher education in the information age, it behooves us to consider how peculiar the French and German systems were in their origin and in their evolution through post-war reform.

This chapter, therefore, is background. It evaluates the European educational heritage, presenting it primarily as an alternative to the American – or, rather, as alternatives, for the systems differed from each other in the two countries almost as much as they did from the American. Again, historical sequence is important, since the educational systems that existed prior to the quickened interest in entrepreneurship evoked by phenomenal Silicon Valley determined to a great extent the desire and capacity to accept American views of entrepreneurship and the education integral to it. The first part of this chapter sketches the history up to 1940, the second part describes the reforms of the inherited institutions after World War II, and the third part explains the limits of the post-war reforms of French and German academic management education with reference to the United States. The next chapter deals with the introduction of entrepreneurship studies into France and

Germany, while chapter 5 discusses the French and German networking activities for start-ups. Chapter 6 focuses on the quite different experience of the Czech Republic. Although the Czechs had German-influenced educational heritages, their system did not undergo the same American-influenced reforms after 1945. Since interaction educationally was deferred until after 1990, it is best discussed in chapter 6.

The educational heritage

All higher education in modern Europe was elitist in tradition, in that access to it was open only to a few. Beyond this similarity the institutions of France and Germany differed profoundly. Here the focus is on engineering and commercial education, because the heritage in them, and especially the latter, most affected how the entrepreneurial shift occurred in the two countries at the end of the twentieth century.

France and its elitist system of higher education

France in the early nineteenth century already had a bifurcated educational system consisting of *grandes écoles* and university faculties. There was an educational division of labor between the two. University faculties left engineering education to the *grandes écoles*. In the late nineteenth century the system evolved. In the non-university sector of French higher education, private *écoles supérieures de commerce* joined the state engineering schools. Together they form what were, and are still referred to unofficially as, the *grandes écoles*. The commerce graduates did not rival those of the *grandes écoles* of engineering before World War II, but they would see their star continually rising in management circles in the second half of the twentieth century. They are a significant part of the French story. Also, in the late nineteenth century the university got involved in specialist engineering education. Industry increasingly prized these engineering graduates from universities for their specialist skills, but the leadership elite continued to be drawn from the traditional *grandes écoles* of engineering.

This different appreciation of university engineers and *grandes écoles* engineers constitutes an enduring attitudinal pattern in France. It expressed itself in contrasting pedagogies for different career paths. Vincent Degot's article, published in 1980, explains how the educational experience of engineers from the *grandes écoles* and specialist engineers suited divergent career schemes:

The *grandes écoles* aim to produce "generalists" by providing students with the abstract scientific training that will rapidly enable them to grasp the techniques involved without going into the details of application. It may be seen, therefore, that graduates of the lesser schools are intended to hold posts in which they will be in contact with the workers, and hence most effective. Meanwhile, [those] of the *grandes écoles* are fated to rise higher, in order to be able to give full proof of their competence (Degot, 1980, p. 172).

Elite management in what the French called *la grande industrie* and the state technical ministries graduated from the école polytechnique or the école centrale, and the equally famous écoles d'applications (mines, roads & bridges, etc.) that so many of the top engineers attended. The French treasured intelligence over specialist knowledge in this leadership group. This is why the competitive entrance examinations (*concours*) were so important for admittance into the schools. They stressed *culture générale* – i.e. mathematics, French, foreign languages and philosophy, and, in the oral examination, presence, bearing and quick-wittedness. Whereas students by the end of the nineteenth century could study in university engineering faculties after completing their secondary education, those seeking to enter the *grandes écoles* of engineering spent two or three years, after their secondary education, in preparatory classes (prépas) that specialized in getting candidates through the dreaded *concours* for *grandes écoles*.

People in the *grandes écoles de commerce*, which appeared later in the nineteenth century, gradually imbibed the "general attitudinal pattern" of the social elitists in the already established *grandes écoles* of engineering. And the commercial school's pedagogy suffered. Although they were dubbed *supérieures* (advanced) schools of commerce they did not dispense an advanced education in the subject. In the *grandes écoles de commerce* prior to World War II no permanent faculty, no graduate research programs, no serious undergraduate-level management study curricula existed. Students took a series of commercial courses (accounting, commercial law, commercial correspondence, merchandizing, physics, mathematics, etc.) taught by visiting instructors (*vacataires*) brought in from university faculties, the government bureaucracy and/or business. Since very little useful management education took place, then, why should a prospective manager attend?

The answer is that entry, not subsequent study, was the chief point of going to the *grandes écoles de commerce*. For the most famous among them (HEC, the Ecole Supérieure de Commerce de Paris, and ESSEC) this was doubly true. French business leaders and educators did not believe that academic study had much to do with business. Since no serious higher education occurred in the schools, the *grandes écoles de commerce* simply selected out, through an entry *concours*, an intellectual and social elite from the general population. They provided – following the standard of the *grandes écoles* of engineering – social and intellectual screening at entry as much as post-entry education.

German higher education: Wissenschaft *reigns supreme*

In Germany the universities at the beginning of the nineteenth century also left commercial and engineering education aside. But there were no German equivalents of France's prestigious *grandes écoles*. Engineers and merchants were trained on the job and in trade schools. During the century some of these trade schools rose steadily in status and turned themselves near the century's end into institutions of higher education – that is, the engineering and the commercial schools joined the traditional universities in the German-language area to become *Hochschulen*. Originally, the institutes of engineering (*Technische Hochschulen*) and institutes of commercial studies (*Handelshochschulen*) remained separated from the universities. But, as new universities appeared, older universities added new engineering and commerce faculties, and engineering and commercial *Hochschulen* incorporated new faculties to become universities, the educational distinction between universities – as non-utilitarian places of study – and engineering and commercial *Hochschulen* blurred. This development is important. Since universities had the right to confer doctorates, the creation, within their precincts, of new engineering and commerce faculties permitted them to issue doctorates in these fields. This was not as important for engineers, whose institutes had received the right to confer the degree Dr.-Ing. in 1900, as for the *Handelshochschulen*, which had no such right. Faculties of business economics (BWL) in two new universities, Cologne and Frankfurt am Main, provided the doctorates and *Habilitationen* for those who occupied the chairs in Germany's new field of business economics.

Life in technical and commercial studies became somewhat schizophrenic. The business of German universities was to teach, but even more importantly they had the greater calling to engage in scientific research (*Wissenschaft*). Both, ideally, were inseparable, for the best teaching went on during the creation of knowledge in research laboratories or libraries. To participate in the university's *Wissenschaft* community, those in technical and commercial studies had to conform to this *Wissenschaft* ideal, by establishing research institutes, libraries and laboratories, and building graduate degree programs, with an appropriate faculty that published its work in scholarly journals and books. They had to accept the canons of science and scholarship. On the other hand, because commerce and industry are everyday economic activities, these schools' faculties could not easily divorce themselves from the demands of praxis. It was very hard to serve both science and praxis, and in this regard German engineering and commercial *Hochschulen* made different historical choices.

Unlike in France, German firms did not want their management elites pre-selected by the school system. They believed in specialized knowledge. Peter Lawrence describes the qualification diversity and reverence for sapiential as opposed to book forms of learning that make the German work-world one wherein recognition and promotion depend more on demonstrated job performance (*Leistung*) than academic diplomas (Lawrence, 1980, p. 165 ff), *Fachkenntnisse* (know-how in one's specialty) being the paramount qualification (the term is not pejorative in a German context, as it is in a French). Correspondingly, Vincent Degot would not consider the *Technische Hochschulen*, since they produced specialist engineers, to be the equivalent of the French *grandes écoles* of engineering.

As they rose to prominence, German engineering schools managed – while concentrating on scientific research – to keep a close relationship with industry. *Wissenschaft* – knowledge creation through research – was the ideal, but in its pursuit technical *Hochschulen* never lost contact with people in praxis. Their graduates were prized, especially in high-tech industries, as were their professors, because of their research expertise and practical experience (a professor of engineering needed to have worked at least five years to hold a chair).

Handelshochschulen, like the German *Technische Hochschulen*, did not have high entry requirements comparable to the *concours* of the *grandes écoles de commerce*, but they had much more serious study programs. Every student learned a basic element (*Grundstudium*), then specialized in one of the many subjects in business economics – i.e. accounting, banking, insurance, etc. The study content increased in complexity, and the time to finish a first degree (*Dipl.-Kaufl.*) lengthened during the twentieth century, from three years in 1920, to four in 1940, and to five just after World War II. The students did not study management per se but the specialized knowledge that served management. After graduation, *Dipl.-Kaufleute*, like *Dipl.-Ingenieure*, moved into business and industry, according to their specialties, at entry-level positions, wherefrom they competed with everybody else in an organization for advancement into higher posts. German specialist education in *Betriebswirtschaftslehre*, like the education in the technical *Hochschulen*, suited the habits and mores of German business and industry quite well. Those who wanted to teach could, after completing the requirements for a degree in business economics, take additional courses in pedagogy to obtain a teaching diploma (*Dipl.-Handelslehrer*), which permitted them to work in commercial colleges.

Professors of business economics assumed a different stance from professors of engineering in their relations with people in praxis. Even before World War I German academics in commerce studies (BWL) entered into an intense debate as to whether their new field was a *Kunstlehre* (a study of skills) or a *Wissenschaft* (a scientific discipline) – Locke, 1984. The debate was important because, if judged a *Kunstlehre*, BWL would not have a future as a university discipline. Just as people in French *écoles supérieures de commerce* strove to emulate admired institutions, the *grandes écoles* of engineering, the Germans strove to emulate theirs, universities-*Hochschulen*. This meant that BWL had to be a *Wissenschaft* and gain full acceptance within the German university community. *Wissenschaft* won the debate over *Kunstlehre*, with the important implication for BWL that relations with praxis suffered. Unlike in German technical *Hochschulen*, where academic requirements could be overlooked (especially the need for the *Habilitation*) when experienced people moved from industry into professors' chairs, in BWL faculties professors had to have all the academic credentials to hold their chairs. They had to write doctoral dissertations and *Habilitationsschriften*, which their academic supervisors judged on the basis of their scientific merit; they had to conduct research as professors that contributed to the development of business science; and they had to supervise the education of graduate students, from whom

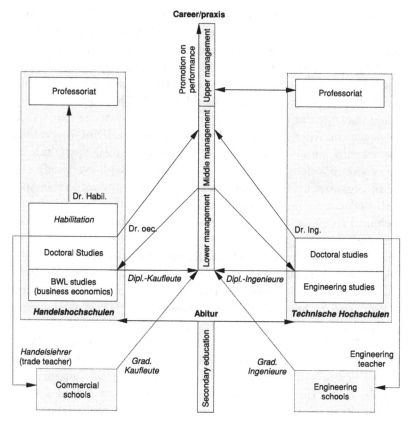

Figure 3.1 German commercial and engineering education before 1940

the ranks of future BWL professors could be recruited. Not much time could be devoted to praxis. The *Wissenschaft* outlook took hold of BWL between 1900 and 1940.

Resumé of chief differences pre-1940 of French and German engineering and commercial studies

Figures 3.1 and 3.2 summarize the educational differences just sketched. They do not pretend to present the systems of higher education in each country in their entirety; they do not even completely present the parts of their programs that pertain to industry and commerce. They serve only as didactic devices intended to clarify the

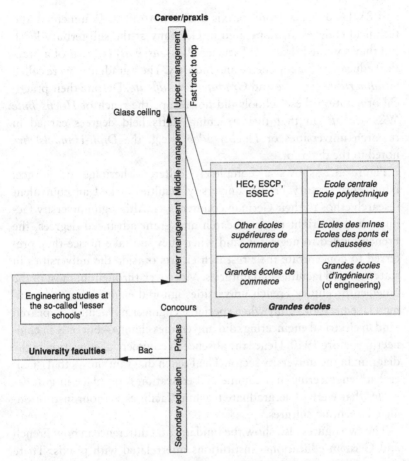

Figure 3.2 French commercial and engineering education before 1940

different ways that French and German engineering and commercial educational institutions interrelated with each other and with praxis in each country in the mid-twentieth century.

The fundamental educational difference stems from the place that research held in higher technical and business education. The diagrams show that, in Germany, these university faculties and *Hochschulen* produced first degree holders (*Dipl.-Ing.* and *Dipl.-Kaufl.*) who streamed into praxis, and graduate research degree holders who worked in industry but also sustained the development of the discipline in academic institutions. German academic engineering's closeness to, and BWL's distance from, praxis is also portrayed. Commercial and technical colleges also operated in Germany at the sub-tertiary level, but they shunned theory-led science (*Wissenschaft*) in favor of a practical education for commerce and industry. Their graduates were called *Graduierte-Ingenieure* and *Graduierte-Kaufleute*. Despite their practical orientation these schools did not escape the reach of *Hochschule Wissenschaft*, in that their teaching staffs held degrees earned in research universities or *Hochschulen* – e.g. the *Dipl.-Handelslehre* noted in the diagram.

Figure 3.2 shows a completely different heritage in France. Nineteenth-century French university faculties lacked an equivalent research ethos to their German counterparts. Although university faculties had the right to do research and grant advanced degrees, the French tended to neglect it, and when they did take notice they preferred to concentrate their research efforts outside the universities in state-fostered facilities and libraries. Moreover, throughout most of the nineteenth century French universities ignored engineering and commercial education. Only when specialist engineering faculties appeared (and in electrical engineering) did universities change – but only in engineering before 1940. Hence the absence of commercial education in the diagram in the university sector. The French diagram shows that "generalist" engineering and commercial education took place in *grandes écoles* that were undergraduate teaching facilities without institutionalized scientific cultures.

The two figures also show the fundamental difference in how French and German educational institutions interrelated with praxis. There was a close cooperation between German technical *Hochschulen* and industry in research matters. But graduates from engineering schools – the *Dipl.-Ing.* – received no special fast-track treatment in their careers. They entered in low-level specialist positions along with *Graduierte-Ingenieure*, and competed with them and practically trained engineers for advancement. In France, the graduates from the *grandes écoles* of engineering did receive special treatment in their careers in the state technical services (*les grands corps d'état*) and *la grande industrie*. The university engineers entered specialist careers, which, the diagram indicates, ended at a glass ceiling before the top positions could be secured. These were monopolized by *grandes écoles* generalists.

The graduates from the *écoles supérieures de commerce* frequently worked in family businesses or in top management in the few big commercial and merchant firms that existed in France before World War II. In Germany, the *Dipl.-Kaufleute* held specialists' positions in banks, merchant houses and the commercial side of industrial firms. They, as in France, were overshadowed at the top by engineers and, unlike in France, by lawyers. For both German engineers and business graduates the acquisition of a Ph.D. could be career enhancing. Therefore, after entering the work-world, the ambitious either worked on a Ph.D. or a Dr.-Ing. part-time or took time out to do so full-time and then returned to praxis. Such a possibility was not available to graduates of French *grandes écoles*, had they desired it, because of the absence of a scientific culture in their system.

If French and German education was dissimilar, it was also different from the American. This was already true before the great expansion of American management education after World War II, and its scientization, described in the last chapter. Since business and management studies are the focus here, the main points of divergence between them in the three countries are of interest. Business schools exist primarily on American university campuses. Although in the middle of the twentieth century they still taught commercial subjects, they existed within a university culture that had taken on the spirit of German *Wissenschaft*. Their professors were, therefore, always under pressure in the best universities to establish themselves in research disciplines as well as to serve the needs of praxis. This distinguished American commercial studies in 1950 from French. American business studies shared a research vision with the Germans but remained closer to praxis and less systematic academically. Kurt Schmaltz, a business economist, pointed out the difference in 1930 when analyzing German and American business periodicals:

If one compares the science as a whole with the development in the United States, it appears remarkable that there is no comprehensive designation. A German studying the American literature is astonished at the strong independence of the various branches of the science of business administration, such as accounting, cost accounting, finance, selling, and marketing . . . A German is not satisfied unless he can fit his special field in as part of a definite system and clearly work out in every way possible the boundaries of the different fields. This rigorously systematic method of work I have not been able to find in the American literature of Business Administration (Schmaltz, 1930, p. 231).

German academic economists issued their first *Dictionary of Business Economics* in the 1920s (*Handwörterbuch für Betriebswirtschaftslehre*), which embodied this integrative ideal, and academic business economists have continued to update the dictionary ever since.

The goal of such work might be integrative but it ended up also being exclusive. Because Americans were much more pragmatic about their studies, they would cross boundaries without qualms if the crossing helped solve business problems. And they were ready to leave business administration a hodgepodge incapable of being systematically integrated. New subjects could not find acceptance so easily in German faculties of business economics because some way had to be found for them to be included in a structured academic discipline. And once the discipline gained maturity this was not easy. German academic custom worked against the adoption of new fields. Academic business economists formed very much a club, with their own association and annual meetings (Locke, 1985). A new subject in BWL could not be created until chairs had been set up, which required ministerial approval, and suitable people appointed to them. But suitable people could not be found in new subjects under the system because, to be eligible, they would have had to acquire the appropriate degrees and scientific training in fields that did not yet exist. In American business schools it was relatively easy to create new fields when the students demanded them and monies to pay for them flowed in from private endowments. And the professors could be recruited from praxis, with a minimum academic requirement, or from other academic disciplines.

Reform after World War II

The period after World War II was one of great reform in French and German business and management education. The Americans had a lot to do with it, both directly, through people and programs, and indirectly, because of admired educational examples.

Reforms in the French grandes écoles of engineering, grandes écoles de Commerce and universities

Grandes écoles of engineering
French engineering education expanded significantly, especially in the university sector. A private sector of engineering schools also grew.

The primarily state-supported *grandes écoles* of engineering, however, kept their premier rank. Before the war some of their graduates had developed a study tradition in management science, the *ingénieur-economists*, that, when it surfaced after the war, played a major management role in the reconstruction of France.[1] The *ingénieur-economists*, under the leadership of Maurice Allais, his associates and students, rivaled the Americans after the war in OR projects specifically in the newly nationalized industries (SNCF, Eléctricité de France, Gaz de France). Allais, who won the Nobel Prize in economics, declared that France was ahead of the United States in operations research. And they introduced teaching and research in industrial administration at the *écoles des mines* and at the *écoles des ponts and chaussées*, working closely, because of the position engineers held in the technical ministries and industry, with practicing managers. OR in the *grandes écoles* of engineering branched out from OR into other aspects of management science. Professor Claude Riveline, head of management studies at the *Ecole de Mines de Paris*, observed in a 1983 interview that his students and staff worked closely with industry. All he had to do to establish useful contacts (he told the interviewer) was to exploit the X network. He reached for a thick volume on his desk, which contained the names of all the living graduates of the *Ecole Polytechnique*, listed alphabetically but also by place of work, with telephone numbers. A quick call could put him in contact with top cadres in firms and ministries, where the cooperation could easily and quickly be arranged.[2]

In short, although the technical and scientific aspects of engineering dominated studies in the *grandes écoles* of engineering, management studies in them gained status. But this is as it should have been for schools that educated France's leadership. After the war, no longer could engineers just rely on their intelligence and experience to guide them in their managerial functions. They needed greater knowledge of management techniques and methods, and post-war reforms provided some of it.

Grandes écoles de commerce

Although it took some time, these schools also learned that something had to be done about their study programs and the quality of their teaching staff if they were to meet the educational needs of business

[1] Drèze, 1964.   [2] Riveline, 1983.

and industry in an American-dominated environment. Since it is a prestige school, which has great influence in French commercial education, the reforms undertaken at the Ecole des Hautes Etudes Commerciales can furnish the example. After several staff members visited the United States, HEC transformed itself into a business school *à l'Américaine*, beginning in 1957. In that year the undergraduate curriculum dropped the old commercial and science courses; students in the first year now spent their time in general studies and in an introduction to management course. In the second year they engaged in more advanced management studies and did an analysis of the nature of the firm. During the third they undertook a special management project in conjunction with a firm. The year 1968 brought computer programming. The innovators also reformed teaching methods and hired permanent faculty with proper credentials in management studies. Marc Meuleau, HEC's historian, has remarked,

In fact, the reform of 1957 amounted to the adoption of American management education . . . The school took up most of the methods it had discovered in the 1950s and the inauguration of its new installations at Jouy-en-Josas (1963) was done in the presence of the American ambassador. The organization of studies at Columbia University in 1956 – 40 percent lectures, 20 percent case studies, 20 percent discussions after lectures, 20 percent seminars where students make reports that are criticized by their classmates – could be found at the school c. 1965–67. It also agreed to accept engineers seeking management education, a common business school practice in the United States.[3]

The other *grandes écoles de commerce*, particularly the most prestigious rivals of HEC, introduced similar American-style reforms. The lesser schools adapted more slowly, but they could not escape the fallout from the American-induced management education revolution.

The universities
More profound changes in France occurred in the universities. Expansion into management education did not come quickly or easily. The first significant reform occurred with the separation of economics from law. Before the war economics had been taught in faculties of law in France. There, economics professors primarily wrote institutional

[3] Meuleau, 1988, p. 48.

history and works about commercial law. They little appreciated neo-classical economics; they lacked the requisite mathematical knowledge that had become part of the modern Anglo-Saxon economist's tool kit. That changed when the economists got their own faculties. Another change happened in the 1950s with the creation of the *instituts d'administration des entreprises*. They were places for post-experience management training – the first in French universities. Gaston Berger initiated this reform movement. He was assisted by a number of enthusiastic young people, including Pierre Tabatoni, who – after visiting the United States – became a tireless advocate of management education in France. He returned to the United States repeatedly, where he taught occasionally in the business school at Northwestern University, cementing his contacts with American management academics.

After a slow start, the student uprisings in 1968 finally hastened reform. It led to the introduction of management and economics degrees at every level of a totally restructured university system. Students could now take a diploma in management at an IUT, two-year community colleges (Bac+2), a DEUG in management (Bac+4), a master's in the subject (Bac+5) and a doctorate. The magnitude of the reform can be appraised from the number of diplomas issued in economics/management twenty years after the introduction of the degrees.

The *grandes écoles de commerce et gestion* (the word "management" – i.e. *gestion* – was added to their names), which had also grown considerably in number during these decades, granted some 19,000 diplomas the same year – less than half of the 40,000 university degrees at the Bac+4 and Bac+5 levels (see table 3.1).

Doctorates in management were very important because without them the field could not develop as an academic discipline. Because they had no academically qualified management teachers at hand, to fill the lacuna, initially the directors of the National Management Education Foundation, which a group of French businessmen, industrialists, bureaucrats and educators had set up in 1968, sent graduate students to North America for academic training. FNEGE worked out special programs with business schools at Northwestern, the University of Texas (Austin) and Sherbrooke (Canada). Usually a student spent some time in a preparatory study program and in meetings before leaving France; then about 30 percent of the students entered three-year management doctoral programs in the United States and Canada, while the others

Table 3.1 *University degrees in economics and management in France*

Number of diplomas, 1994	
DEUG economics/management	9,500
DEUG AES (law and administration)	7,500
Maîtrise: economic and social administration	11,500
Maîtrise: economics	9,000
Maîtrise: economics and management	4,500
Maîtrise: management and sciences	2,000
Maîtrise: accounting and financial management	850
Maîtrise: science and techniques of management	600
Magistère: management and economics	700
DESS: management	6,500
DESS: economics	700
DEA: management	700
DEA: economics	1,500

Source: Mortier, 1996.

took either a one-year course individually or a one-year course created by a host school especially for the French. Between 1969 and 1972 210 French academics underwent this American management education. Upon their return, they moved into academic management teaching positions in France.

In the meantime the French struggled to add management studies to their doctoral programs. Some universities (Paris-Dauphine, the Economic University, is the outstanding example) became centers of research in management sciences. Through them, supported by publishing outlets (e.g. Dunod) and newly created scholarly journals (e.g. FNEGE's *Revue française de gestion*), France, for the first time, developed a serious academic research program in management studies. Professors of economics – ironically, since they had had the same battle with professors of law – fought the attempt to make management a field separate from economics, but finally, in the late 1970s, management became a research field in its own right. The number of management doctorates earned in 1994 shows (table 3.1) that French universities had quickly attained self-sufficiency in educating their *professoriat* in the management field.

Reforms in German engineering education and Betriebswirtschaftslehre

Engineering education

Since the German economic miracle had re-established the economy by the early 1950s, German engineering education quickly restored itself as well. Reform in German engineering education, however, is of interest only in so far as it involved management education. And management education did not draw much attention from engineers after the war. *Technische Hochschulen* stressed *Fachkentnisse* and specialization in research. In the 1950s, when the graduates of the *grandes écoles* of engineering developed OR studies in France, academic German engineering scarcely noticed the subject. Not until the mid-1960s did the German engineering schools get seriously involved in OR, and the interest was always comparatively modest. The German Operational Research Society remained tiny compared to its American, British and French counterparts. Nor did German engineers pay much attention to management studies per se. The professors and the practicing engineers held a deep-seated belief that no such thing as "management" existed. One managed something – a shoe factory, a machine shop or a brass foundry. Management was not generic, something to be studied in itself; it was specific to place. Hence, the engineer's conviction that knowledge of management could best be learned on the job stymied efforts to create management studies in technical institutes.

Engineers in Germany, however, did not close their minds to learning about new management techniques. Various non-academic teaching groups offered short courses on a variety of subjects. There were courses on TWI (training within industry), which Americans had used to improve the efficiency of their factory workers during the war; courses on various aspects of human resource management; there was even a two-day course on "telephone English" for those who had to negotiate with foreign firms. Later, engineers, on short release time, could take courses on group work or on the establishment of quality circles, or how to implement just-in-time production processes. Various engineering associations sponsored these courses, as did groups such as the *Wuppertaler Kreis*, specifically organized to teach people in industry. The training of engineers in matters of management, therefore, was hardly neglected.

But German engineers drew a distinction between an education that made students, *berufsfähig* (capable of work) and training that made them *berufsfertig* (ready for work). The latter they left to the non-academic training courses and to training on the job, the former to the universities. Acquiring the capacity to manage was not something engineers could be taught in *Hochschulen*. Much reform occurred in non-academic management training programs for engineers after the war, but it did not extend to the *Technische Hochschulen*, which distrusted management as a scientific discipline.

Betriebswirtschaftslehre

The importance of business economics to our study cannot be overstated. Commercial studies in German academia began to flourish about the same time as Americans were founding business schools. The oldest *Handelshochschule*, Leipzig, started in 1898; many other foundings followed in the next twenty years. By the end of World War I German professors had stopped calling their study a commercial science (*Handelswissenschaft*) in favor of the more comprehensive business economics (*Betriebswirtschaftslehre*). Professors in BWL left "training" to the non-academics – to the businesses, trade associations and privately funded teaching groups that taught the latest techniques in short courses to active managers. In this regard German BWL faculties differed from American business schools, which offered a plethora of short-term, part-time courses to working managers. The German BWL professors believed, rather, that their task was to give students in BWL a *Denkschulung*, a schooling of the mind, in order to make them *berufsfähig*, and to advance knowledge in their discipline through scientific research. Such lofty views did not stop students from enrolling in business economics. Four times as many of them got diplomas in BWL as in economics – over 50,000 a year – by the mid-1960s. But, as the universities were re-established at the end of the occupation (1950), reform of their study programs in business economics proceeded slowly.

Post-war Germans had to start by reaching back into the past for guidance. In 1965 a German business magazine calculated that, of seventy-eight *Ordinarien* professors in BWL, at least thirty-six had completed their education before the war, and most of the others had been educated partly before the war or in the immediate post-war period by professors rooted in the pre-war tradition (*Der Volkswirt – Wirtschafts- und Finanz-Zeitung*, 1965). If that tradition conceived of business economics as an integrated field with carefully delineated scientific sub-fields, the practical results had, notwithstanding, been somewhat deceiving. Whereas in the United States functional fields flourished and multiplied alongside each other, in Germany accounting had come to overshadow all others completely. German BWL in 1950 concentrated on accounting or accounting-oriented business technologies in its education.

When German universities gathered their faculties together, the business economists, as an article in *Der Volkswirt* suggests, were pre-war educational relics. This incarnated past slowed change for years in German university BWL faculties and commerce institutes. In 1967 G. Brinkmann, in a survey of students in Nordrhein-Westfalen, concluded that the new business technologies (operations research, electronic data processing and personnel management – *Menschenführung-Sozialpsychologie*) "were only cursorily taught or were not taught" in German business faculties (Brinkmann, 1967, p. 119). However, all students took accounting as a preliminary requirement (*Propädeutikum*), and an obligatory subject in their final examinations was *Allgemeine Betriebswirtschaftslehre* (general business economics), which remained accounting bound. All business students were also examined on two functional subjects, selected from a list of options. But this exercise of choice did not lead to major changes. Peter Mertens's 1973 study of business majors at Göttingen and Hamburg shows, for instance, that only 16 percent chose operations research as an examination elective. Moreover, OR was the only new subject (after World War II) among the six most frequently selected examination options. The other choices were quite traditional: commerce, auditing, taxation, industrial administration and banking. The fact that so many students chose auditing and taxation (which are accounting subjects), industrial administration (in which cost accounting customarily is very important), banking and commerce (in which financial accounting is stressed) indicates how extensively the content of pre-war business administration had been projected into the post-war period (Mertens, 1973).

German business economics, therefore, lagged behind rapidly progressing American management studies immediately after the war. Before 1940 US business schools already excelled in marketing and finance. During and just after the war they made similar advances in organization theory and personnel. These and the traditional fields of business knowledge (accounting, marketing, finance, etc.) were fundamentally affected by auxiliary sciences (applied mathematics, statistics, electronic data processing, psychology, sociology and economics). And business schools reoriented from functional fields of knowledge to management as such. Decision making, leadership, group dynamics and related topics became the focus of attention in management education. These innovations did not originate particularly within US schools, but came to them from an environment stimulated by the cold war.

The evidence should not be misunderstood. Because accounting dominated traditional German business economics and most of the newer functional disciplines developed in the United States, and because there is always a time lag in the transfer of know-how, older techniques continued to predominate for a while. Moreover, although *Betriebswirtschaftslehre* could absorb scientific innovation, certain aspects of the tradition worked against speedy adoption. One was that "Schmaltz factor" – the difficulty of assimilating new fields into an already integrated body of business science. Inasmuch as the onrush of new fields eventually made their rejection impossible, the ideal of an integrative science hindered the absorption of diverse new fields into BWL. The control until the late 1960s that the full professors (*Ordinarien*) had over the creation of new professorships and curriculum changes also acted as a brake on the field's adaptation. The full professors' power was transferred to the university faculties in the mid-1960s, thereby giving all academic teaching staff voting rights on new appointments, but academics still monopolized candidate selection. And the state ministries, which had to integrate new sub-fields into their overall teaching plan and to fund new professorships, also delayed change.

Perhaps more significantly, the pre-war separation between BWL academics and businessmen/industrialists grew larger. The *Wissenschaft* paradigm drove a wedge between them. The exchange of views that took place at a meeting in 1965 between a concerned German businessman, Hans Dichgans, and a group of twenty BWL professors reveals the barrier. Locke transcribed the interchange:

A member of the Bundestag, Dichgans had complained that German academic business economics was not willing to be judged on how well it served business. "Everything must the more serve an abstract idea of higher science. Our young professors have less and less contact with praxis." Dichgans recommended that more professors work for extended periods in business and industry, and that their students prepare for business rather than academic careers . . . To the suggestion that more professors acquire practical experience, Professor Wolfgang Kilger . . . replied that for both academics and practicing managers the crucial years in a career occurred between age thirty and forty. A young professor had to devote his efforts to academic science to advance his discipline (and his career) – so there was not much time to work in business. To Dichgans's suggestion that the *Habilitationsschrift* be eliminated as a requirement for a professorship, they also objected. One professor observed that a man who had worked for years as an accountant was ill-suited to teach academic accounting. Another pointed out that business does not understand reality, which is getting more complicated every day. It stands to reason, therefore, another professor intoned, that *Praktiker* need the professors and their science because of its abstractions, or, as still another professor explained, precisely because most scientists are interested in generalities, not like the *Praktiker*, in particulars.[4]

This cleavage from praxis did not stop academia from changing. In the 1970s German business school curricula developed. Operations research became a popular examination subject, and personnel or human resource management emerged as sought-after electives. Because of the influence of other disciplines (law, sociology, social psychology, statistics and mathematics) the older disciplines, too, changed from what they had been fifteen years before. The transformation became especially marked when electronic data processing finally invaded German business economics. The adoption of new business techniques and perspectives (such as EDP, decision theory and systems analysis) greatly altered the content of traditional studies in accounting and organization. This transformation required considerable effort among students and professors to upgrade their science and mathematical skills.

The limits of post-war reform

Because the educational groups discussed in this chapter lived mostly separated from others and each other, if in different ways and to greater and lesser extents, the limits of reform were set by the inability of groups to cross boundaries.

French and German engineering schools had good horizontal contacts with people in praxis, especially the *Techniker*, but a big

[4] *Die Welt*, 1965; analysis from Locke, 1985, pp. 244–45.

occupational and educational gap existed in both countries between engineers and people in economic studies. Engineers have always tended to discount the usefulness of economics, and economists have resented it. Sometimes the engineers try to be light-hearted in their comments. Locke recalls a luncheon in the faculty club at the University of Manchester Institute of Science and Technology. Ten men sat at table, all engineers or scientists but one, and he was not an economist. One engineer, with an amused air, asked the table: "If you have a problem and twelve economists are in a room, how many solutions will you get? The answer: thirteen, because the Keynesian man will have two." All the people laughed. Sometimes the comments are simply more dismissive. Schöne encountered this attitude in interviews twenty-five years after Locke's, when two professors from a French engineering school described the difference between engineers and merchants: "Engineers hold to their products; merchants sell the wind" (Trémembert and Le Traon, 2002). Engineers, walled off from economists and other non-engineers intellectually, psychologically and – to some extent – physically, lived, as another interviewed French professor said, in "two worlds" (Fonrouge, 2002).

The professional educational systems that grew up in France and Germany before World War II projected this separation into the era of post-war reform. Again, an interview can illustrate the point. Professor Riveline readily discussed how he networked vertically with engineers in firms, ministries and the *grandes écoles* of engineering, but when he was asked about contacts with the *écoles supérieures de commerce* and with FNEGE the question drew a blank. There might have been common participation on committees, but there was no real intensive cooperation in project work.

French and German engineers lived apart from commercial managers and economists, but there were major differences in the way engineers related to each in the two countries. French engineering professionally and educationally separated into the graduates from the *grandes écoles*, who were destined – as Degot phrases it – "to rise higher" to top jobs, and the university engineers, who did the specialist jobs under them. The separation reflected strongly ingrained attitudinal patterns of belief about the necessity for the country to be run by educationally pre-selected elites. Geert Hofstede in *Culture's Consequences* sees this submissive attitudinal pattern in France in the "power distance" that exists between the leaders and the led (Hofstede,

1980). Frenchmen might be democratic but they wanted an elite to take charge.

The same vertical separation existed between non-engineering French groups. The *grandes écoles de commerce* grew up over a hundred years, establishing good contacts with praxis, but they avoided the university, which itself ignored commercial studies until the reforms after World War II. Despite the reform of business and economic studies top to bottom in the post-1968 university, the *grandes écoles de commerce* remained separate and aloof. They retained the stiff competitive entrance examinations (*concours*) based on *culture générale*, which let them cream off the best business students. This deleteriously affected the development of management education in university faculties, which did not recruit students by *concours*. While the *grandes écoles de commerce* had contacts with business leaders, many of whom were their former students, the new university faculties of commercial/business studies, developed in institutions traditionally dedicated to learning, scholarship and research, did not and could not easily establish contacts with business leaders. In the reformed French educational scheme, then, the best students went to the *grandes écoles*, got the best jobs, and had the best careers.

The French clung tenaciously to their schools, fighting attempts to deprive them of their educational prerogatives. The "general attitudinal pattern" that survived in France for two hundred years into the postwar world protected and retained separate and isolated educational components, which tend to degrade the effectiveness of systems. The obvious example is the bifurcation of the French educational system into *grandes écoles* and the university, but it is expressed as well in the separation of the *grandes écoles de commerce* from the *grandes écoles* of engineering, in the separation of the faculties from each other in the university, and in the separation of each school from the other physically and psychologically. And the bifurcated French system persistently separated the place where an academic business research culture existed (the universities) from the place where the future managerial elite studied (the *grandes écoles*).

In Germany engineers and business economists after the war seldom had contacts with each other in universities and different contacts with praxis (the academic engineers plenty, academic *Betriebswirte* few), but the sort of separation that happened between the *grandes écoles* and universities in both engineering and business education in France did not exist in Germany. German engineering education integrated vertically. *Dipl.-Ingenieure* educated in *Technische Hochschulen* taught in the lesser engineering schools (which in the 1970s became *Fachhochschulen*) that produced the *Graduierte Ingenieure* (now *Dipl.-Ingenieure FH*) so sought after in industry. Both the *Graduierte Ingenieure* and the *Dipl.-Ingenieure* found their way to the top in German firms. Professors of business economics in university faculties and *Handelshochschulen* might, in contrast to professors of engineering, be cut off from praxis, but they had good relationships with schools in the non-university sector of commerce education because they educated the teachers (*Dipl.-Handelslehrer*) who now teach there (commercial *Fachhochschulen*).

Isolation is relative. Since no group is an island, contacts take place between the isolated groups that have been identified. Considerable efforts were made even after the war to end these instances of isolation. In France, for example, the *grandes écoles de commerce*, unwilling just to be undergraduate teaching institutions (which is what they had always been), and eager in an era of management science to retain leadership in commercial studies, got involved in research. Because of the universities' exclusive authority to grant graduate research degrees, certain *grandes écoles de commerce* worked out arrangements for their own Ph.Ds. in management to be granted by a university (Paris-Dauphine, for example). The admission of engineers into HEC's newly created programs is another instance of this crossing of borders.

German reformers, too, tried to cross borders in management education. Active BWL professors who did cultivate relations with business brought the management academics and praxis together in more formal ways. One was the *Universitätseminar der Wirtschaft*, which, beginning in the late 1970s, met near Cologne at Schloss Gracht. BWL professors on leave from their faculties take up residence there to teach courses to people from praxis, who, equally, are released from their jobs for a short time. It has been a great success, but, as Tom Lupton, head of the Manchester Business School, said after a short visit, "It is not a business school." It is only a neutral ground where academics and business people meet. Other German reformers created independent management schools. The most obvious example is the school of management established with private funding outside Koblenz (the WHU). New BWL faculties set up in new universities in the 1970s and 1980s started MBA programs for post-experience students with a diversity of degrees (engineering, science, economics, etc.) to spread the reach of BWL academically. Examples of such efforts to connect separated groups can be multiplied in both countries. They were, however, sporadic, non-systematic and highly selective, and on the whole comparatively limited in their impact on inherited educational structures.

This failure to promote institutional interconnections limits more than anything else the extent to which the reforms in post-war European business and management education can be called "Americanization." Two things make post-war American business and management education different from the European. First, American corporations since World War I have not been run by engineers but by moneymen – financial accountants, controllers, etc. Even though the world of engineering is different from that of non-engineers in the United States, as it is in Europe, American engineers have been compelled to take a back seat in corporate governance. The prestigious moneymen, CEOs and their sons frequently studied at American management schools (or wished they had), which they generously funded. And the engineers, watching the moneymen (their bosses), have learned to speak the language and appreciate the talents of these successful managers. American engineering schools have, accordingly, been open for some time to the study of business administration. The Sloan School at MIT, funded by and named after the former head of General Motors, is a manifestation – if a spectacular one – of the early contacts established between business management and engineering.

The second peculiarity of American business and management education is its location primarily on university campuses. Some universities are old: Harvard dates from 1636, Yale from 1701. But most, and especially the state universities, started in the late nineteenth century. Many of them also began as land grant colleges that the American government set up to provide agricultural and engineering education. Instrumentalist in outlook, they had to serve the community. And they reflected the community in their governance. Generally, the regents who run American universities are businessmen and industrialists as well as educators. They are flexible in viewpoint and insistent that universities be integrated into the life of the community. Since business schools grew in this community, it was relatively easy – although at times difficult – for them to cross-reference courses and create combined degrees with other faculties on campus. And, since business schools thrived under the university's educational roof, it was possible for them to provide undergraduate and professional education and also be graduate research institutions.

Because, in their post-war reforms, the French and Germans did not create similarly vertically and horizontally integrated educational communities, their schools could not be a mirror image of American business and management education. The reformed *grandes écoles de commerce* did not, like American business schools, become research institutions. They only made extramural gestures in this direction by coordinating Ph.D. programs with universities. The schools primarily remained teaching institutions, which even in this regard differed from the American business school. French *écoles supérieure de commerce* often translated the name on their letterheads into English as "business school" or "school of management," and they call their degrees "MBA equivalents." But American MBA students are quite different from those in the *grandes écoles*. Whereas the latter are young and inexperienced, the MBAs at the best American business schools are older post-experience students with a variety of first degrees drawn from a broad educational spectrum (history, engineering, economics, law, etc.). They constitute a different student body with closer ties to the business and research community than their French counterparts.

As for the universities, their newly created management study departments did not resemble the American business school either. Since top managers came from the *grandes écoles*, the sort of lucrative connection that exists between the managerial elite and the business schools in American universities, which funnels money into management research and innovation, has not taken place to any great extent in French university management education. Reformers in this French system could only with difficulty coordinate the joint research and degree programs that American business schools worked out regularly with schools and departments of engineering within a university. For the French, Americanization required that they take on a scientific culture where one had not existed, and teach that culture to the most promising students. But even after their reform the *grandes écoles* had not become research institutions like American business schools. Research remained a university province.

The German failure to integrate BWL into the community of praxis also left the discipline, after reform, quite unlike the American. German BWL professors greatly admired the research and publications produced in American business schools, and they prided themselves on their own *Wissenschaft* tradition. But they did not admire the professional postgraduate education of the MBA type, because it required an intense interaction between educators and practitioners. Because German professors had so much control over university reform, they could frustrate efforts to bring about the necessary change that interaction requires. Frustrated management in German firms, therefore, often hired MBAs from foreign business schools (INSEAD, the London Business School, etc.) in their search for the sort of educationally qualified managerial talent that was the mainstay of US business schools.

Thus, serious curriculum reform, reforms in teaching methods, and reforms in the training and recruitment of professors and in commercial and engineering education – much of it along American lines – took place. But, when reform required changing the educational systems in order to foster horizontal relationships between isolated groups, then reform was quite effectively resisted. And if the Americanization of post-war French and German management education meant creating these horizontal relationships, then there Americanization reached its limits. The limits were set primarily by persistent attitudinal patterns, which prevented the integration of inherited educational institutions into the type of community in which American business education thrived.

4 | *Creating German and French entrepreneurship studies*

"**E**VERY historical undertaking," Merleau-Ponty affirmed, "has something of an adventure about it, as it is never guaranteed by any *absolutely* rational structure of things. It always involves a utilization of chance; one must always be cunning with things (and with people), since we must bring forth an order not inherent in them."[1] Despite Merleau-Ponty's warning there are, if not inherent structures in the German and French education systems, at least historical ones that – as just described in chapter 3 – shaped the management education reforms in both countries after the war. Because of their persistence they also affect the insinuation of entrepreneurship studies into the German and French systems of higher education. Before plunging into this subject, however, it is best to begin with some preliminary observations about what constitutes the Americanization of entrepreneurship education, and with a few remarks about how the discussion will be handled.

An Americanization beyond language adjustments and technology transfer

The first chapter briefly considered the language adjustment that encounters with Silicon Valley produced in the French and German worlds of thought and language. This analysis can easily be extended to the language that Europeans used when describing the nature of the entrepreneurial process. A random search through French and German periodicals on start-ups shows as much. The authors' perusal of several publications that were at hand gave the following results: *en High Tech, Das Entrepreneurship Forum, bei Start-Ups, le business plan, Businesspläne, le coaching, Coach und gezieltes Feedback, le venture capital, l'incubateur, der Venture-Track*, and numerous other instances of

[1] Quoted in Sartre, 1948, pp. 163–64.

fractured French, franglais and German English that American contacts have induced. It is remarkable how quickly and completely the French and Germans involved with entrepreneurship and entrepreneurial education have taken to these American expressions. If Americanization means the adoption of American expressions and words into the language of this French and German business community, then the two countries in the high-tech entrepreneurial era have indeed been Americanized.

But these remarks apply only to a relatively small and active group in each society. When the subject becomes people's general predilection toward entrepreneurialism, Americanization is much less clear. We noted in the introduction that the study does not propose to establish a "neutral analytical category" that defines American values as entrepreneurial in contradistinction to those of other countries. There were many eras when entrepreneurs were esteemed outside the United States (e.g. Victorian England, the *Gründerzeit* in Germany, Japan after World War II) and times in US history when entrepreneurs were not particularly praised (e.g. the Robber Barons of the Gilded Age). Our reference is historical, to the enthusiasm for high-tech entrepreneurship that pervaded American society first and made it an example to others at the end of the twentieth century.

The historicity of the subject allows in this period for attitudinal changes toward entrepreneurship, even within Silicon Valley itself. There perceptions have evolved, for example, about what is meant by "spin-off" firms (Beer, 2000). At first the Americans looked at them as civil applications of military and space technology; then, in the late 1960s, they considered them to be new ventures that came out of established firms. The idea that start-ups emerge from university faculties is a third version of the spin-off idea, which gained strength only in the 1980s. Books written in the mid-1980s still did not stress the university's involvement in entrepreneurial activity because the notion, as explained in chapter 1, had not yet become clear in the first phase of Silicon Valley development.

But by the 1990s an enthusiasm for entrepreneurship had come to exist in American politics and society from the top down. The Clinton administration expressed a deep appreciation and admiration for Silicon Valley. The Vice-President even claimed to be a high-tech entrepreneur, through his efforts to develop the Internet. On the enterprise level, the American Business Conference specifically lauded the entrepreneur and set up programs of recognition. The information media voiced entrepreneurial values by highlighting the entrepreneur heroes of the information age and praising their achievements. Entrepreneurship studies grew rapidly in response to student demand in the midst of an entrepreneurial effervescence. First came the entrepreneurship, then came the studies.

Since Americans touted entrepreneurial values in the information era and accepted them throughout their society, for the purposes of this study to be "Americanized" means for non-Americans to do the same. When leadership cadres from foreign countries, besotted by Silicon Valley's achievements, begin to sing the praises of high-tech entrepreneurs, then they are being Americanized. If polling shows that the general public does not share this appreciation of entrepreneurialism, if studies of certain groups (e.g. engineers and business economists) reveal a lack of appreciation of entrepreneurs, then the public or the identified group has non-American values. For the nation or the group to be going through a process of acquiring this appreciation for entrepreneurship means they are being Americanized.

Just as high-tech entrepreneurialism gained adherents among Americans in the 1990s, so did it among Europeans. When the French and Germans first reacted to Silicon Valley, they relied on government programs and big companies to transfer information technologies and develop them back home. Then, when Silicon Valley entered its second phase of development, they discovered the importance of the high-tech start-up culture and education. Joseph Orlinski, of the Université de Technologie, Compiègne, describes this transformation of mentality in France. "In the 1980s the government had the idea to create jobs by stimulating the technology sector, so it created the technopôles ... After the policy failed, the government understood that it was necessary to create proper conditions to favor technology transfer. That implied changing the mentality of civil servants in the national research laboratories and in the universities and schools" (Orlinski, 2002a). The same thing happened in Germany. The regional governments' technology start-up centers (TGZ), beginning more with employment problems and industrial decay in mind than high technology, left high-tech education out of the equation. Popular discussion of Silicon Valley in the mid-1980s ignored the educational dimension. Schmidt's book about the valley, for example, does not discuss start-up entrepreneurship, much less university involvement (Schmidt, 1986). It touches on technology transfer and innovation and mentions venture capital, but business angels and university interaction are not treated. Another Silicon Valley work, by Rogers and Larsen, 1986 (to cite a frequently read German-translated version of an American text), also ignores this university spin-off entrepreneurial culture.

With the intensified awareness about the need for high-tech firms in the 1990s, people in France and Germany discovered that they had a problem. Studies done after years of start-up activity in Germany and France show not only that people in both countries are not entrepreneurial, but that they do not much appreciate entrepreneurs either. In 1998 one study reported to the French Minister of Economics, Finance and Industry that the number of start-ups *ex nihilo* amounted only to 15 percent of new firms (the others were inherited or restarted firms), and that their number had been falling over the decade (Beranger et al., 1998, p. 12). Citing a 1996 APCE report, it stated that, of the start-ups that year, only 5,000 were in industry and only 0.7 percent of all start-ups were in high technology. They were "of little importance in France," primarily because of the entrepreneurial lethargy of French engineers (Beranger et al., 1998, p. 12). Compared to the United States, where the ratio of college to non-college graduates who start firms was 1:1, in France it was 1:2 (p. 12). Educated people were the least entrepreneurial of all. A number of carefully organized comparative national surveys carried out since 1997 by the *Global Entrepreneurship Monitor*, which quickly became the standard reference on comparative entrepreneurial performance, produced similar results. The national teams that surveyed France and Germany concluded that people in both countries are not entrepreneurial and they do not appreciate entrepreneurs very much. The *Global Entrepreneurship Monitor's* 1999 report on Germany, for example, ranked it next to last – and Japan the last of ten surveyed countries – in the public's appreciation of successful entrepreneurs.

Thus, from the point of view of European policy makers, who thought that economic growth, job creation and technological prowess in the information society stem from the development of a high-tech start-up economy similar to the one thriving in the United States, something had to be done.[2] Something had to be done to evoke this entrepreneurial spirit generally within the population, but specifically within certain target groups – engineers, students of business and

---

[2] See the reports cited in chapter 1 commissioned by ministers and parliamentary committees.

management, and college graduates – whose talents and knowledge were especially needed to close the entrepreneurial gap. Those who visited Silicon Valley had come away deeply impressed by the capacity of the valley's environment to facilitate the entrepreneurial process. *The Silicon Valley Edge* discussed elements of this start-up culture: university interaction, venture capital, workforce mobility, community action, quality of life, etc. Chapter 1 identified some more specific instrumentalities: the use of stock options to facilitate building a start-up's leadership, the founding of business angel network or high-tech equity markets to ease capital formation, etc. In Silicon Valley there were plenty of agencies involved in setting up incubators, running business plan competitions and holding private get-togethers (e.g. First Tuesday) that brought venture capitalists, business angels, scientists and public relations people into contact in one room with the hope of entrepreneurial spin-off as an outcome.

Universities did not at first have an obvious role to play in fostering high-tech entrepreneurialism. People perceived them as a source of high-tech science and engineering ideas, which university interaction commercialized for the market. Then universities began to pay attention to the start-up effort essentially as "how to" instructors, to help people with a big idea develop business plans, find capital and build effective organizations. The university got involved in the start-up process. Subsequently it was called upon to promote the level of consciousness about entrepreneurship itself, on the assumption that an aroused entrepreneurial awareness would produce more active entrepreneurs. The issue was complicated. It required the schools to add what the French call *sensibilisation* (stimulating people to be entrepreneurial) to the "how to do a start-up" dimension of education. Even more significantly, some reformers decided that success depended on the creation of a new academic discipline in entrepreneurial studies. Only with the separation of entrepreneurship from economics and management studies, they felt, and its development into a separate field could an education policy of entrepreneurial enhancement fructify.

Educational policy change aroused opposition. Many people in each country were quite content with non-entrepreneurial values. They might subscribe to a service or a community ethic instead. Within the management education establishment, people might belittle efforts to make entrepreneurship a separate discipline on the grounds that start-up enterprises were only a special case within finance, marketing, decision theory, accounting and/or some other management sub-field. Engineering schools might be quite willing, and were, to participate in start-up programs and to "sensibilize" their students to entrepreneurship. In cooperation with various agencies, they set up incubators and start-up units in technology parks to help scientists and engineers commercialize their ideas. But they saw no place in an engineering curriculum for a "soft" subject such as entrepreneurialism. There were barriers to the creation of entrepreneurship studies that had to be overcome, and these barriers differed in each country because – as described in the last chapter – of educational heritage.

Obstacles to reform, moreover, arose from more than conflicts of interest within and between educational groups and institutions. Academics in France speak about entrepreneurship as a *transversale* phenomenon; those in Germany talk about it in terms of *Interdisziplinarität*. "Transversal" means crossing boundaries to places outside the normal province of management in order to pull together the complicated elements necessary for entrepreneurial success. Instrumentalities that foster entrepreneurship facilitate this coming together; those that stop it are obstacles to entrepreneurialism. When French professors use the term *transversale*, they are talking about the configuration of disparate forces that combine in an entrepreneurial act. But the term can also be applied to the elements that must come together to make entrepreneurial studies themselves effective. Research and teaching about the entrepreneurial habitat require an interdisciplinary effort by people knowledgeable in city and regional planning, economic geography, sociology, economics, finance, the environment, marketing and other areas. An effective academic-run start-up program cannot be achieved without crossing non-academic boundaries – without a host of non-academic affiliations with local entrepreneurship clubs, incubators, venture capitalists, entrepreneurs, chambers of commerce, research laboratories, etc., as well as effective cooperative work among people of various academic fields. It is this that American entrepreneurial study programs had demonstrated to the world.

Because of the subject's complexities, therefore, it is necessary to extend the definition of American influence in entrepreneurial education. It is about the adoption of entrepreneurial values in French and German higher education, but to have an American-influenced system of entrepreneurship studies also means to have higher education that has not only learned a lot about entrepreneurial process as an object of academic study but has created instrumentalities, similar to those in America, that permit it to act itself as a catalyst in that process. To have Americanization going on in a country's entrepreneurship studies means to be in the process of transforming a system of higher education from one that separates the elements essential to entrepreneurship, with itself being one of them, into one that promotes through research, teaching and outreach the effective combination of the transversal elements that contribute to entrepreneurial synergy. To oppose or delay Americanization in entrepreneurship studies means not just, or even, to reject these values but to resist the creation of instrumentalities, similar to those the Americans developed, that make an effective educational program possible.

In one respect the European reform challenge exceeded the American. When Europeans looked at the United States, and found entrepreneurialism and a lusty entrepreneurial studies program side by side, they assumed that a connection existed between the two. Perhaps inevitably they got that connection back to front. In the United States entrepreneurialism created entrepreneurial studies; Europeans sought to use entrepreneurial studies and university-involved high-tech start-up programs to create entrepreneurialism. Their reform had a dimension that differed from that of the Americans, who took their entrepreneurialism for granted.

The entrepreneurial educational problematic just described bundles two rather different phenomena together: 1) entrepreneurship study programs and 2) entrepreneurial activities that involve educational institutions. Both are important to the story of entrepreneurship education: both implicate the systems of higher education; and both are subjects of Americanization, to a greater or lesser degree, as it has been defined above. But entrepreneurship study programs have to do with building an academic discipline and action teaching programs (pedagogy), while entrepreneurial activities promote actual start-up firms. They are quite different functions. Again, the difference can be clarified through a comparison of the terms interdisciplinarity and transversality, for if the two illustrate the breadth of entrepreneurship studies they also reveal dissimilarity. Indeed, it is easy to fall into the trap of using the terms interchangeably even though they do not represent the same thing. Simply put, interdisclipinarity has to do with academic disciplines – with, in this case, crossings of academic boundaries. Transversality includes interdisciplinarity but it casts the net wider to include boundary crossing into non-academic groups whose inclusion is essential to carry out an entrepreneurial act – for example, the business angels, venture capitalists, public relations experts, civic entrepreneurs, etc. who figure so prominently in descriptions of Silicon Valley's high-tech start-up habitat. It is, therefore, possible to be engaged in interdisciplinary studies without being transversal. Accordingly, interdisciplinarity without transversality would be classified under the subject "academic entrepreneurship studies" and transversality under the subject "entrepreneurial activities."

Since the two subjects are not the same and manifest themselves differently in each country, they are best discussed separately even though both are part of entrepreneurship education. This chapter, therefore, deals with entrepreneurship study programs in France and Germany; the next deals with the role that institutions of higher education played in the promotion of entrepreneurship activities, with particular emphasis on high-tech start-ups.

Remarks about method

The second chapter described American entrepreneurship studies with regard to the growing complexity of curricula, research and community outreach. These yardsticks served to measure the new subject's maturity. Since research methods should fit research goals, originally we intended, in order to allow comparisons, to measure the maturity of French and German entrepreneurship studies the same way. We collected and scrutinized bulletins, brochures, announcements, catalogues and flyers issued by various schools in France and Germany about their entrepreneurship study programs. But this research model broke down. We discovered that the story of Americanization in Europe cannot be told through an extensive comparison of the development of curricula, research and outreach in American, French and German entrepreneurship studies. Such an argument structure is invalid because of the time factor: Germany and France have not had the time the United States has had to develop curricula, research and outreach in these studies. Detailed comparisons of programs would, under these circumstances, simply register obvious points about the inadequacy of European achievements vis-à-vis American achievements, and not explain them. The argument structure consequently needed to change to one that would clarify why French and German business studies started so late and developed in such a truncated fashion. That is the explanatory design used here.

To that end we have downplayed the discussion of programs to the extent of not including school brochures, catalogues, flyers, etc. in our bibliography. Instead, we stress the educational institutional history that produced the current management educational culture (the last chapter), and focus our attention in this chapter on the actors in each country's system who have been charged with developing entrepreneurship studies, and on the businessmen, politicians and administrators preoccupied with matters of management education reform.

As well as the written reports and studies about entrepreneurship education cited in the bibliography, this longitudinal analysis of current study programs depends on interviews. The people contacted are academics, mostly professors in entrepreneurship studies in German universities and *Fachhochschulen* and their counterparts in French *grandes écoles de commerce*, engineering schools and university faculties. In both countries we approached all institutions that were seriously engaged in entrepreneurship studies at the time of investigation – summer, fall and winter 2002–03. "Seriously" means that they have been offering more than "some" sensibilization actions.

In Germany, forty-two institutions at the time were active in entrepreneurship studies. Nineteen people out of the pool of academics drawn from these institutions agreed to an interview, all from different institutions. They are listed in table 4.1. If cited in the text, they are referred to in the format given in the footnote.[3]

Two of the interviewees are young scholars, and two professors, Mancke and Dowling, are Americans. They were educated in America and had careers there before entering German academia. They bring a knowledgeable comparative perspective to the subject. With the exceptions of Würth and Gering, the others had German degrees. They had obtained doctorates, usually in business economics (*promoviert in BWL*), and a few had done a *Habilitationschrift*. Würth is a non-*Akademiker*, and Gering has a Ph.D. from the University of Wyoming. But some of the German-educated interviewees have also studied in the United States. Schefczyk, for example, has done graduate work at the Georgia Institute of Science and Technology.

---

[3] Achleitner, 2002; Bayer, 2002; Dowling, 2002b; Eickhoff, 2002; Gering, 2002; Hering, 2002; Kieser, 2002b; Klandt, 2002; Mancke, 2002; Masberg, 2003; Moser, 2002; Rumpf, 2002; Schade, 2002; Schefczyk, 2002; Uebelacker, 2002; Wassenberg, 2002; Witt, 2002; Würth, 2002; and Zühlsdorff, 2002.

Table 4.1 *List of interviewees in Germany*

Interviews of entrepreneurship academics in Germany			
Name of interviewee	Institution	Date of interview	Type of interview
Prof. Dr. Ann-Kristin Achleitner	TU Munich	September 10, 2002	Telephone interview
Ingo Bayer	Mannheim University	August 21, 2002	Telephone interview
Prof. Dr. Michael Dowling	Regensburg University	July 16, 2002	Telephone interview
Prof. Dr. Matthias Eickhoff	FH Mainz	September 10, 2002	Telephone interview
Prof. Dr. Thomas Gering	IU Bruchsal	September 10, 2002	Telephone interview
Prof. Dr. Thomas Hering	Fernuniversität Hagen	September 5, 2002	Personal interview
Prof. Dr. Alfred Kieser	Mannheim University	May 25, 2002	Personal interview
Prof. Dr. Heinz Klandt	EBS Oestrich-Winkel	September 20, 2002	Personal interview
Prof. Dr. Richard Mancke	HHL	August 9, 2002	Personal interview
Mathias Masberg	RWTH Aachen	January 8, 2003	Telephone interview
Prof. Dr. Reinhold Moser	FH Trier	August 28, 2002	Telephone interview
Prof. Dr. Maria Rumpf	FH Friedberg	September 4, 2002	Telephone interview
Prof. Dr. Christian Schade	HU Berlin	September 11, 2002	Personal interview
Prof. Dr. Michael Schefczyk	TU Dresden	August 28, 2002	Personal interview
Stefan Uebelacker	Regensburg University	July 14, 2002	Written answer
Prof. Dr. Rolf Wassenberg	FH Gelsenkirchen	August 19, 2002	Telephone interview
Prof. Dr. Peter Witt	WHU Koblenz	September 2, 2002	Telephone interview
Prof. Dr. Reinhold Würth	TU Karlsruhe	September 12, 2002	Written answer
Prof. Dr. Henning Zühlsdorff	Lüneburg University	September 20, 2002	Written answer

In France, thirty-three institutions were seriously engaged in entrepreneurial studies at the time of the investigation. Twenty-seven people from them agreed to interviews. All of them are French and French-educated. They work in every sector of French higher education (nine from engineering schools, ten from *grandes écoles de commerce*, eight from universities and one with no school affiliations). The interviewees are listed in table 4.2. They, too, are cited in the text as given in the footnote.[4]

[4] Albert, 2002; Boistel, 2002; Bouchikhi, 2002; Certhoux, 2002; Cordonnier, 2002; Danjou, 2002; Deblois, 2002; de Metz, 2002; Dubois, 2002; Fayolle, 2002b; Fonrouge, 2002; Frugier, 2002; Gallouin, 2002; Giraud, 2002; Guillot, 2002; Jouandeau, 2002; Lescat, 2002; Marion, 2002; Orlinski, 2002a; Orlinski, 2002b; Papin, 2002; Peccoud, 2002; Rebouil, 2002; Schieb-Bienfait, 2002; Schmitt, 2002; Senicourt, 2002; and Trémembert and Le Traon, 2002.

Table 4.2 *List of interviewees in France*

Interviews of entrepreneurship academics in France			
Name of interviewee	*Institution*	*Date of interview*	*Type of interview*
Philippe Albert	CERAM	November 26, 2002	Telephone interview
Philippe Boistel	IAE Rouen	November 26, 2002	Written answer
Hamid Bouchikhi	ESSEC	November 18, 2002	Telephone interview
Gilles Certhoux	EM Nantes	November 26, 2002	Telephone interview
Michel Cordonnier	UTC	December 16, 2002	Personal interview
Isabelle Danjou	ESC Lille	September 16, 2002	Personal interview
Christian Deblois	UTC	December 17, 2002	Personal interview
Alain de Metz	Ecoles des Mînes de Douai	November 18, 2002	Telephone interview
Béatrice Dubois	ESC Lille	September 17, 2002	Personal interview
Alain Fayolle	ESISAR-INPG	July 29 and November 11, 2002	Telephone interview
Cécile Fonrouge	University of Evry	November 20, 2002	Telephone interview
Dominique Frugier	EC Lille	September 16, 2002	Personal interview
Jean-François Gallouin	EC Paris	November 18, 2002	Telephone interview
Patrice Giraud	ESISAR-INPG	September 18, 2002	Personal interview
Bernard Guillot	ESC Clermont-Ferrand	September 18, 2002	Personal interview
Alain Jouandeau	INSA Lyon	November 25, 2002	Telephone interview
Gilles Lescat	ESC Le Havre	November 14, 2002	Telephone interview
Stéphane Marion	University Lyon III	November 25, 2002	Telephone interview
Joseph Orlinski	UTC	September 18 and December 16–18, 2002	Personal interviews
Robert Papin	HEC	December 17, 2002	Telephone interview
François Peccoud	UTC	December 16, 2002	Personal interview
Martine Rebouil	Research Ministry	September 18, 2002	Personal interview
Nathalie Schieb-Bienfait	IAE Nantes	November 19, 2002	Telephone interview
Christophe Schmitt	INPL	November 19, 2002	Telephone interview
Patrick Senicourt	ESCP-EAP	November 28, 2002	Telephone interview
Pierre Trémembert and Jean Le Traon	ENST Bretagne	November 20, 2002	Telephone interview
Lydia Wilmin	ECD Besançon	November 15, 2002	Telephone interview

Of the French interviewees, those in universities have doctorates or are Ph.D. candidates, since universities, as research institutions, insist on academically qualified appointees. But there are exceptions. Philippe Boistel, IAE Rouen, for example, was a marketing consultant, a *praticien* with start-up experience, before taking up his position. Since no field of entrepreneurship studies exists, those with doctorates have acquired them in management. There exist in French management studies prejudices against establishing an independent field in entrepreneurship studies. Cécile Fonrouge testifies that the management faculty at Bordeaux was so concerned about the field's integrity that it would not permit the word *entrepreneuriat* to appear in her dissertation title, even though that was the research subject. This at the time when, on a visit to Babson College, she heard people discussing the field of entrepreneurship in great complexity. Doctorates seemed to be less important to faculties in *grandes écoles de commerce*, and contact with the professional world more. This suggests that the French interviewees in the *grandes écoles* were less academically oriented than the German, in the scientific sense. But they have confidence in themselves, as graduates of these elite schools, and they know the system. Three of them, Philippe Albert, Robert Papin and Patrick Senicourt, led the entrepreneurship education movement. The French interviewees had not studied formally in the United States as often as the Germans, but they were well informed about US entrepreneurship study programs. Both groups of interviewees fairly represented the educational systems from which they came.

Each interviewee received a standard questionnaire in his/her national language. The English version of it is given in table 4.3. This questionnaire permitted interviews to be conducted in a way that elucidated not only the content of the entrepreneurship study programs in which the interviewees were engaged but the obstacles they encountered in their creation. The interviews were carried out either on the telephone or in person. Both interview techniques were pre-tested and appeared equally valid. We left it up to the interviewees to choose whether to be interviewed in person or by phone. E-mail responses were accepted only when the interviewee clearly insisted on giving the answer in this form. The interviews, supplemented by parliamentary reports, books and articles, are valuable sources for a comparative analysis of entrepreneurship study programs in each country. The presentation of the results of the analysis starts with the Germans.

Table 4.3 *Interview questionnaire for Germany and France*

Interview questionnaire	
Main questions	*Specifying questions*
1. How has entrepreneurship education developed at your institution?	a) Who started it when and why? b) How did events in Silicon Valley stimulate the introduction of entrepreneurship studies? c) Which education has been offered in the course of time (programs, chairs, specifics)?
2. Which schools/programs served as a reference point and in which way?	a) Which schools/programs inspired the development of entrepreneurship studies at your institution? b) Which schools have been visited by the teaching staff? c) What are your teaching materials based on?
3. How have relations with business, especially with start-ups and venture capitalists, been organized?	a) Has your institution been involved in the organization of conferences and/or business plan competitions or in the creation of technology parks and/or incubators? How and since when? b) If not, why? And who, then, has been involved in it?
4. What obstacles have stood in the way to the development of entrepreneurship studies (attitudes, structures, finances, qualified personnel, demand, publication possibilities, etc.)?	a) At your institution? b) In Germany/France in general? c) What are the challenges to the further development of entrepreneurship as a field study and as a field of research?
5. How do German/French entrepreneurship studies compare to the American?	a) What are the strengths and weaknesses of the American higher education system in terms of entrepreneurship studies? b) What are the strengths and weaknesses of the German/French system?

The introduction of entrepreneurship studies in Germany: a reluctant BWL

Several investigations can be used to orient oneself inside the world of German entrepreneurship studies. Two look at the recently created professorships in the subject. In their analysis of the organization and establishment of the chairs, Jürgen Schmude and Stefan Uebelacker counted twenty-three: thirteen *Lehrstühle* in universities and ten *Professuren* in *Fachhochschulen* (Schmude and Uebelacker, 2002, p. 3). In the other slightly more recent study (September 2002) Klandt and Knaup identified forty-nine "planned and established chairs in the management of start-ups in Germany" (Klandt and Knaup, 2002, p. 12). Twenty-one of them were chairs in universities and the remainder professorships in *Fachhochschulen*.

The first professorship was established in 1998, at the European Business School in Oestrich-Winkel; the rest followed in a flurry of creations over the next four years. The first thing that can be said about entrepreneurship studies in Germany, then, is that their formal establishment through these professorships is of very recent origin indeed. Of the forty-nine professors that Klandt and Knaup identified in their report, thirty-eight were educated in the economic sciences (mostly in BWL), five in science and engineering, and six in other disciplines or in praxis (p. 12). These are the principals involved in this story about entrepreneurship studies in German universities, which revolves around the creation of the professorships and the chairs.

If the interviewees and their colleagues in BWL mostly got the chairs, the economic faculties whence they came had not particularly sought them. Professor Alfred Kieser explains: "It was not BWL faculties that took the initiatives to introduce entrepreneurial programs or business plan competitions; it was banks that asked BWL faculties to establish the chairs for start-up management, and it was the consulting companies that organized the business plan competitions." The initiative came from government and from praxis. The Deutsche Ausgleichsbank, which specifically promotes start-ups, funded four chairs (Leipzig, Magdeburg, Munich and Oesterich-Winkel); the software giant SAP funded three (Berlin, Dresden and Karlsruhe). A variety of banks, firms, chambers of commerce and trade associations financed the rest. Sometimes two, three or more sponsors combined to fund one chair, and there were small sponsors who joined the major ones in

supporting a professorship. American academics would find this sort
of funding perfectly acceptable. But German academics felt somewhat
uneasy about the sponsorships, since in some cases funding lasted five
years instead of the usual ten and there was no assurance that public
funds would be forthcoming to sustain a chair once the private support
ended. For German business economists there was something wrong
with a science based on such financial insecurity. They preferred the
permanency of science guaranteed by state-funded chairs.

They were even more concerned about scientific deficiencies than
money. Their stance can be clarified by revisiting the last chapter, where
it was noted that BWL faculties, in contrast to those in *Ingenieurwe-
sen*, treasured *Wissenschaft* more than relations with praxis. It was
not BWL's business to service praxis but, as Kieser puts it, "to teach
a basic understanding of business problems to students and how to
confront them systematically."[5] This knowledge did not come straight
from praxis but was built into the discipline of business economics
through research and publication by scientifically prepared academics.
Traditionally, too, BWL concerned itself mainly with the administrative tasks that appointed managers faced in big firms. As a body of
knowledge it tried, and tries, to control and optimize already existing
functions, organizations and processes within companies. Its world is
that of Nietzsche's Apollonian man.

Entrepreneurial studies have to be different because the entrepreneur,
in contrast to the company manager, concentrates much more on
creating new structures and managing in a world of discontinuities.
Entrepreneurial education has to escape Apollonian managerial func-
tionalism to reach interdisciplinarity and transversality; it has to teach
people how to exploit a business opportunity, how to start growth-
oriented enterprises of their own. Advocates of entrepreneurial studies
claim that, by their transversality and interdisciplinarity alone, they
have had to go their own way.

Because BWL apologists asserted that entrepreneurship could be
handled within the discipline of business economics as a special case,
in their work they need not – and did not – completely shun the start-
up problematic. Modern research on start-ups probably began in the
1970s with the work of David Birch on *The Job Generation Process*
(Birch, 1979), but German professors of business economics showed

[5] Kieser, 2002b; for his view, see Kieser, 2002a.

an interest in them about the same time. In the 1970s Norbert Szyperski focused on start-ups in his *Seminar für Allgemeine Betriebswirtschaftslehre* in Cologne; the *Institut für Mittelstandsforschung* in Bonn and the *Betriebswirtschaftliches Institut* in Stuttgart worked on the subject as well. In the mid-1980s, sociologists and psychologists who turned their attention to start-up research, thereby giving those in the economic sciences a taste of interdisciplinarity, joined BWL scholars. Dieter Bogenhold and the group working with Rolf Ziegler in the *Institut für Soziologie* at the University of Munich worked, among other things, on the start-up boom of the 1980s. This diversity of interest led people in various fields, including those in geography, to the Heidelberg Interdisciplinary Symposium on start-up research in 1994 and to the establishment of the start-up *G-Forum* to push this interdisciplinary work.

Despite these efforts, interdisciplinarity in German entrepreneurship remained quite limited. Professors and researchers interested in it had few contacts with natural scientists and engineers. The list of participants in DFG's 1994 Interdisciplinary Symposium on start-up research, for example, included people from economics, business economics, law, economic geography and sociology but nobody from natural science or engineering fields.[6] The interdisciplinary research that non-scientists and non-engineers did, therefore, almost ignored the concerns of the scientists and engineers who were preoccupied with high-tech enterprise. Of the 100+ books and articles listed under *Literatur* in the DFG's interdisciplinary start-up research program, works on high-tech ventures are literally conspicuous by their absence.[7] Moreover, even among the social scientists interdisciplinarity faltered. After the DFG established interdisciplinary research as a *Schwerpunkt* (major emphasis) program, the *G-Forum* met yearly to promote it. The group produced valuable work, especially the geographers, whose studies have been so helpful to our own. One of them, Jürgen Schmude, discloses the limited state of interdisciplinary research in start-up studies through the tally of participants (table 4.4) at the *G-Forum* meetings held in Cologne in 1999 and 2000 (Schmude, 2001, p. 94).

[6] Deutsche Forschungsgemeinschaft. List of participants given on www. DFG-Schwerpunktprogram–Interdisziplinaere Gruendungsforschung.uni-regensburg.de._FAKIII/Geographie/wirtgewo/ forschung.

[7] Schmude and von Rosenstiel, 1997. Most of the works were published in the 1980s and, in increasing numbers, in the late 1990s.

Table 4.4 *Interdisciplinarity in German*
entrepreneurship academia

Provenance of G-Forum *participants*		
Field	1999	2000
Business economics/economics	79	104
Geography	8	3
Social sciences	5	4
Engineering	5	7
Sociology	4	4
Other	21	33

Source: Schmude, 2001.

The presence of so many business economists at interdisciplinary meetings indicates that entrepreneurship studies were, essentially, in their hands. And people with a more negative attitude toward the subject could scarcely be found, for opposition in BWL faculties to the establishment of entrepreneurship professorships almost exceeded the academic will to create them. Entrepreneurship studies long retained an "exotic status" within BWL, their practitioners remained a small academic community working outside the mainstream, and their work never blossomed – as similar work did in the United States – into a new academic discipline (Schmude and von Rosenstiel, 1997, p. 92). People in BWL particularly objected to the appointment of non-qualified people to chairs. And academically qualified people were in short supply in entrepreneurship studies within the German system since, as it had not been accepted as a scientific subject, they had not been incorporated into the corpus of BWL. People had not been able to write the doctoral dissertations and *Habilitationsschriften* that provide candidates for positions in Germany with the requisite qualifications.

The conflict between science and praxis about academic appointments has a long history in BWL. It reaches back to the controversy over Richard Ehrenberg before World War I (Ehrenberg, 1910). The academics successfully thwarted his appointment – and the minister's will – because, although an experienced business operator, he lacked academic qualifications. It also appeared in conflicts between businessmen and academics trying to reform management education in Germany after World War II, and it appeared now in the struggle to create this new field.

Since academically qualified people were not available, when the chairs were offered some BWL faculties refused to establish them. This happened in very famous places, such as Cologne and Mannheim, but in less prominent places as well, such as Trier. The Technische Universität in Karlsruhe did hire a non-academically qualified businessman (Professor Würth), but the university housed the chair in the Department of Electrical Engineering. Elsewhere they found people with academic credentials. Most had doctorates in business economics; only one (Klandt) had actually written a dissertation about start-up enterprises. Not one of the appointees educated in German faculties of economic science had started up a firm (in the sense of being a "full-blooded" entrepreneur without having had an academic "career").[8] Although most had worked, mainly in consultancy, they were longer on academic qualifications than on entrepreneurial experience.

The appointees to entrepreneurship professorships in interview seemed to share the general opinion of their BWL colleagues about these studies. When asked what obstacles existed to the development of their chairs, they invariably mentioned its lack of scientific respectability. One professor of entrepreneurship studies replied that he doubted the viability of the subject as an independent discipline; he thought it should be incorporated into BWL. To questions about who founded their professorships and why, they sometimes replied that "the motivation was not a rational one" (Schefczyk); it was a "fashionable subject at the time" (Hering); or that it was done out of "hysteria" (Bayer). Hysteria? Yes, because the flourishing American start-up culture in the late 1990s made people in government and industry think that *something* had to be done. So they started founding chairs. It was as if this had little to do with the desires of the chair holders or the seriousness of the subject. The interviewees (especially with the stock market decline) also expressed the fear – and for some, perhaps, the hope – that this start-up economy had ended and student interest faded. Perhaps,

---

[8] Schmude and Uebelacker, 2002, p. 13. By contrast, as noted, a study of best entrepreneurship programs in twenty-five top American business schools revealed that 90 percent of the professors in entrepreneurship studies in them had created or owned a firm; in ten of the schools the percentage was 100 percent. See Debourse et al., 1999, p. 9.

with it, entrepreneurship studies would go away too, and BWL could return to normal. This was not said but it was implied in some of their remarks.

If Americanization means the adoption of entrepreneurial values and the spirit that went with them, the professors holding these chairs – with talk of irrationality about the founding of their own chairs and worries about the scientific acceptability of their subject – hardly seem to be exemplary specimens of Nietzsche's Dionysian man. Perhaps their hesitancy is natural for people involved in an early stage of the start-up process. It is easy for American centers for entrepreneurship studies, with up to twenty full-time professors and well-equipped conference rooms, lecture halls and offices, to exude the start-up spirit. But the German professors' responses to interview questions were hardly entrepreneurial.

The professors did not cut themselves off from the United States. These interviewees and other chair holders could scarcely avoid the "Mutterland des Entrepreneurship, den USA" when setting up programs since Americans already had a developed discipline (Schmude and Uebelacker, 2002). Some professors (mainly in *Fachhochschulen,* where teaching is emphasized) did, however, show a surprising ignorance of American entrepreneurship studies in their interviews. But most had read American research literature and knew something about the most famous programs (Babson College, MIT, UCLA, Stanford and Harvard). They could compare US entrepreneurship study programs with their own, and they expected their students to read the English-language research literature. To prepare their report on the new German entrepreneurship professorships for the Deutsche Ausgleichsbank, which sponsored four of the new chairs, Schmude and Uebelacker not only examined the German situation but, for comparative purposes, made a special trip to interview people and visit institutions in the United States. For holders of these chairs in German universities the American yardstick was always at hand.

When they used it, they did not do so to copy the Americans. German professors in their interviews denied having engaged in any wholesale borrowing of manuals and teaching programs from them, explaining that they needed manuals, curricula and outreach programs that fitted German conditions, in the German language, which they had to create themselves. But surely the issue ran much deeper than the rejection of a few externalities. "German science," Professor

Hering noted, "is theory and thus is developed according to the Humboldtian ideal of unity of research and teaching. The US follows a casuistic approach in research and teaching" (Hering, 2002). The BWL professors rightly worried about the scientific acceptability of entrepreneurship studies, and therefore BWL's future, because, if entrepreneurship studies had no scientific credibility and remained part of BWL, BWL's reputation would suffer within the German university. BWL in Mannheim, Professor Bayer explained, would lose status if a non-academically qualified person were appointed to a chair in entrepreneurship studies. The academic system, as theory-led science, would break down if it conferred "*Habilitations- und Promotionsrecht an Nicht-Promovierte/Habilitierte*" (Bayer, 2002). This consequence, understood within the German academic context, added significance to Professor Würth's observation that "the University of Karlsruhe had taken a courageous step when it nominated a non-academic [himself] to the chair" (Würth, 2002).

The problem, however, is that the justification of this theory-led BWL rests on an old epistemology that had exploded in the twentieth century.[9] Hence, the theory these professors talk about is not scientific but a professorially derived – if not contrived – discipline that grew from internal scholarly debates carried on in books, periodicals and meetings among academics with little reference to praxis. This procedure accounts for the derisory comments of scientists and engineers about BWL as science, and for the very serious doubts of people in praxis about its usefulness. The BWL faculties behaved much like cloistered clerics, who cling, as many people do, to the traditions and illusions that define their existence. By insisting that entrepreneurial studies needed to establish themselves academically on BWL's terms, the professors automatically hamstrung the efforts to adopt these studies – and American influence with them.

Entrepreneurship study programs in France: diffusion within a system of different cultures

French education as characterized in chapter 3 is, to borrow A. Broder's precise formulation, "a heterogeneous system, vertical, cloistered, put together along the way under the pressure of needs and without any

---

[9] See, in particular, Capra, 1982.

internal logic."[10] This bifurcated program separating *grandes écoles* from universities survived the war undeterred, but, because within one of its branches (the *grandes écoles*) a distinction held between those in engineering and those in commerce, the system can be understood best as one of two cultures and two worlds. The schools of commerce and the university social science faculties formed the two cultures. In Cecile Fonrouge's words, the *écoles supérieures de commerce* had "a culture of excellence to draw students, the university a scholarly culture, a culture of rigorous research, of quality" (Fonrouge, 2002). Both cultures were separated from the schools of engineering, which constituted another world. The two worlds also existed in Germany, for academic business economists and engineers scarcely worked with each other. Among French "general attitudinal patterns," it is this belief in a tripartite system (universities, *grandes écoles de commerce* and schools of engineering) that has most resisted change. Hence, the "two cultures and two [scarcely bridgeable] worlds." The structure shaped the development of management education during the post-war reforms, posing the greatest obstacle – because of its lack of interconnections – to American influence. And it governs the introduction of entrepreneurial studies into French higher education.

The engineer's world can be left aside for the moment. Among the interviewees involved in entrepreneurship studies, those from engineering schools especially pooh-poohed the pretensions to disciplinarity. The subject was not, one professor remarked, "a real field – just a *pratique*" (Jouandeau, 2002). But they said the same thing about management. They might be interested in entrepreneurship as an activity; they were not concerned about it as a discipline. Alain Fayolle's survey of engineering schools supports this claim: only 1.6 percent of the responding schools offered a diploma in entrepreneurship studies (Fayolle, 2000, p. 88). The engineer's part in the story of entrepreneurship studies, like that of the German *Techniker*, belongs in the next chapter.

In the two cultures, entrepreneurship studies located inside universities potentially draw on many of the resources necessary for their development. The advantage that American entrepreneurship studies enjoy, Jean-François Gallouin claimed, results from "the collaboration of all the actors aiding in the creation of a firm on one campus: the project

[10] Broder, 1990; quoted in Fayolle, 2000, p. 82.

carriers, the researchers, the teachers, the financiers, the consultants, etc. This proximity is a great advantage" (Gallouin, 2002). But being in a university is not always a "great advantage" to an academic discipline in its start-up phase. In Germany, opposition to entrepreneurship studies in the economic science faculties delayed their progress. In France, almost all the complaints that BWL academics in Germany voiced against entrepreneurship studies could be found in universities too; and entrepreneurship studies made little headway there. Consequently, in 1996, Denis Mortier could characterize their status in French universities as "le grand vide" (the great emptiness). "Each year the French university educates hundreds to work and manage small firms, and produces 40,000 diplomas in management and economics . . . but only a few dozen in entrepreneurship" (Mortier, 1996, p. D3). Had the university dominated higher education in France as it did in Germany, the progress would have been just as slow, but because the French educational system was *éclaté* (scattered) and a second education culture existed within it – that of the *grandes écoles de commerce* – it proved to be more receptive to entrepreneurship studies. Mortier, in the same report that spoke of *le grande vide* in the university's entrepreneurship studies, added that "the *écoles de commerce et de gestion* play a most important role in the education of entrepreneurs in French higher education" (p. D6).

The first movers: grandes écoles de commerce *and "la pédagogie active"*

Grandes écoles de commerce are not by tradition academic research institutions. But they are elitist teaching institutions with active alumni associations, which signifies, since the alumni are successful businessmen, that they are schools close to praxis. Before the post-war reforms this had not been of much significance to pedagogy, but, after the *cours magistraux* were dropped and student participative education techniques borrowed from the Americans, the pedagogy underwent transformation. Whether the subjects were marketing, strategy, finance or human relations the students no longer learned about them passively but actively, using the tools they learned about in classrooms in project work. Although this did not necessarily imply working closely with praxis, in entrepreneurial studies it was easier, within the educational context of the *grandes écoles de commerce*, to make them transversal by incorporating people in praxis into the academic process. Pedagogy in French schools of commerce needed more projects than American business schools because of the nature of the student body. French students were not raised in an entrepreneurial culture. They were less capable of finding their way entrepreneurially than Americans. Young, inexperienced, they had to be led by the hand in carefully structured project work in order to bring them closer to the entrepreneurial process. They could not, like the Americans, be left to find their entrepreneurial way on their own.

Since the schools primarily concentrated on educating managers for big firms, the introduction of entrepreneurship studies in them required the presence of prescient individuals – educational pioneers. Robert Papin at HEC was prominent among them. Under his guidance, HEC started a special program on enterprise creation in 1978, which ten years later became a master's option with the designation "HEC Entrepreneurs." Out of an incoming class of about 400 at HEC, 140 become candidates for "HEC Entrepreneurs" in the third of their three years of study, and twenty are selected. To this twenty add ten recruited from engineering schools, and another dozen (half from foreign universities and half from French), and that makes up the "promotion." Between 1978 and 2002 some 2,200 people went through "HEC Entrepreneurs." Five hundred of them have become CEOs or general directors of firms; a quarter of them work overseas.

Papin refers to the education of "HEC Entrepreneurs" as "la pédagogie active," because it combines course work with projects ("missions" – Papin, 2002). Students are organized into "Trinômes," groups of three, each of whom are drawn from a different educational background (mostly engineering, management and economics). Project members go through seven operations together under the tutelage of an experienced professional. In a recent manifestation the seven operations were: (1) four weeks learning about starting up a firm; (2) four weeks dealing with companies in receivership; (3) four weeks studying takeovers and transmissions; (4) twelve weeks working as assistants ("the right arm") to a senior manager; (5) five weeks working in a consultancy; (6) one week working in retail sales; and (7) four weeks working on communications. HEC professors kept in touch as resource persons with each project through the steps; otherwise, specialists in praxis handled the theoretical and practical problems that the project encountered at each stage. And, at HEC itself, visitors from praxis taught alongside the regular academic teaching staff.[11] Thus, the "HEC Entrepreneurs" course offers a transversal educational experience in its student recruitment and its teaching program. And the success of its graduates permits networking to extend back to incoming students. Graduates could, with this network at their disposal, get jobs.

The second pioneer, in terms of seniority of programs, is Philippe Albert at EM Lyon. After setting up marketing and MBA programs and a business research institute, he was, as he testifies, looking for a new challenge, which he found in the *création d'entreprise* (Albert, 2002). Before introducing external six-month programs in 1986, which combined courses with coaching, he went on a journey to the United States – the "country and mirror of entrepreneurship," as he phrases it in a report about the trip (Albert, 1986, p. 15). He visited American business schools with established programs (Kansas State University, Wichita; Baylor, Texas; University of Texas (Austin); UCLA; University of Southern California; Santa Clara University; University of Washington, Seattle; and Pace University, New York). But he also visited at least one university, Stanford, where the business school in 1985, skeptical about the academic merits of entrepreneurship studies, refused to accept an endowed chair that was proffered. He also met with people and visited institutions, especially in Silicon Valley, that were important in the high-tech start-up environment: Rubicon Group, a high-tech incubator in Austin; Onset in Palo Alto; Sofinova Ventures, venture capitalists in San Francisco; and the Stanford Research Institute, in Menlo Park. No doubt Albert learned a lot from this tour of institutions, but the real inspiration to go into entrepreneurship studies came, he later affirmed, from a conversation he had during the trip with Carl Vespers, one of the American pioneers in entrepreneurship studies (Albert, 2002).

After creating the external program, Albert introduced one for third-year students at the Ecole Supérieure de Commerce and the Ecole Centrale de Lyon. This program's success brought funds from

[11] Chief executives or top executives in rather famous companies – e.g. SOEXHO Alliance, Groupe Bollore Delmas, Dassault Aviation, Dupont de Nemours, Publicis, Microsoft Europe, BNP Paribas, Pernod and Saint Gobain. Information taken from www.hec-entrepreneurs.com/fr/index.php.

the regional council of Rhône-Alpes and from the general council of Rhône. The Credit Lyonnais financed a professor's chair in
entrepreneurship studies, which became the Centre d'Entrepreneurs in
1990. This chair permitted the centre to engage many professors from
different disciplines. After 1990 EM Lyon developed the course structure to meet increasing student demand. In 1993, in order to give all
students a complete view of management, the school made the "virtual"
creation of a firm an obligatory part of every student's first-year studies.
Then it made entrepreneurship a study option in all diploma programs
(MBA, master's, etc.) and introduced an entrepreneurship stimulation
program for science students and an intrapreneurship course.

Patrick Senicourt, at ESC Paris, also counted among the pioneers. He
tried as early as 1977 to introduce a course on the *création d'entreprise*.
He could not use the word "entrepreneur" then because, he said, it still
had in France the connotation of a firm that constructs or reconstructs
buildings. In any event, this attempt failed because of the big firm
placement prejudice of the school's students. But in the early 1980s
he succeeded in making entrepreneurship a second-year study option.
There was no model at the outset; he and his French colleagues mutu-
ally inspired each other. But in 1980 he analyzed start-up promotions in
France, Germany, the United Kingdom, the United States and Quebec.
And he made a tour of the United States and the United Kingdom, with
Marc Benoun from Paris IX Dauphine, in order to learn about their
entrepreneurship study programs. Senicourt was involved in the first
competition for business start-ups in 1985, organized by ANCE (the
Agence Nationale pour la Création d'Entreprises), which was founded
in 1979. Senicourt in interview confirms that people in the mid-1980s
did not talk about Silicon Valley in terms of start-ups. It was known
then for its hardware. And in the first start-up competitions people
prepared *dossiers de faisabilité*, not business plans. He participated in
the first incubators in France and attended the opening of ELAN, the
French association of business incubators, in 1990. And his work at
ESC Paris led to the establishment of a special master's, "innover et
entreprendre."

Another pioneer, Jean-Pierre Debourse, fostered the development of
entrepreneurship studies in ESC Lille. The first program for the education of students in the *création d'entreprise* started in 1975 (Debourse
et al., 1999, p. 14). Between 1982 and 1988 ESC Lille, with a regional
development agency, organized a "strategy" for the creation of firms

in the Nord, Pas-de-Calais region, with financial aid for start-ups. The number of annual projects varied between about 100 and 150 – a total of 700 to 800 during this period. In 1991 ESC Lille organized a master's in "project management," which later became the program for "the education of the educators" in project management. ESC Lille's program also included an elective major option on entrepreneurship for third-year students, which was, after 1999, offered conjointly to the engineering students in the Ecole Centrale (Lille) and ENSAIT. These project-oriented programs expressed ESC Lille's commitment to an active pedagogy.

A final example of pioneering work in entrepreneurship education in *grandes écoles de commerce* comes from ESC Nice (Albert et al., 1999). Founded in 1963, the school moved to the Technopôle Sophia-Antipolis in 1978. ESC Nice became CERAM. In the late 1980s a group of professors in the school increasingly concentrated on start-ups in their teaching.[12] They regularly invited entrepreneurs into the classroom. Michel Bernasconi presided for two years over an association in Sophia-Antipolis of small firms in information technology before going to Silicon Valley on a sabbatical year (1992/93) to "observe the conditions for the development of start-ups and, in particular, the modalities of finance." On his return, he, with François-Xavier Boucand, accepted a commission from the *département* of Alpes-Maritimes to investigate the start-up situation in the region. Their study concluded that the start-up models in vogue were invalid guides to prospective entrepreneurs. In the meantime (1992) CERAM introduced a model for *création d'entreprise* inspired by other schools, in particular by PIMENT, in the ESC Clermont-Ferrand. The program favored group project work – about forty to fifty projects each year. CERAM intensified its preoccupation with start-up education after 1993. This included the coaching of start-up entrepreneurs by students enrolled in a third-year course, *création d'entreprise*. The students, dividing into groups of two or three, helped scientist-entrepreneurs, especially, on the strategic, financial and marketing aspects of their undertakings. The school's efforts culminated in the diploma option "entreprises innovantes," first offered in 1997. Proposed by Bernasconi and Boucand, this elective includes 150 hours of work on the creation and the development of

[12] Michel Bernasconi, François-Xavier Boucand, Cathérine Gasiglia, Hervé Gasiglia and Eric Viardot.

enterprises, principally in technology. The program leans heavily for course materials on the testimony of entrepreneurs. Student engineers, of whom about twenty are admitted each "promotion," work closely with CERAM's business students in some designated courses.

Senicourt says that the pioneers amounted to perhaps a dozen people. Cécile Fonrouge claims that they "turned the most towards the United States. In the second generation [of which she is a part], we stay rather among ourselves" (Fonrouge, 2002). This comment underscores the importance of the work of the pioneer institutions to other *grandes écoles de commerce*. Interviewees from ESCs invariably, when asked about their reference points, cite more frequently EM Lyon and "HEC entrepreneurs" than American programs. Because of the French pioneers, entrepreneurship courses could quickly multiply within *grandes écoles de commerce*. After polling these institutions in 1998, Fayolle reports that 71 percent of them had at least one course and 15 percent of the others planned to introduce a course in the near future (Fayolle, 2000, p. 87).

This complicates discussions about American influence. *Grandes écoles de commerce* were closer to American business schools than any other French institutions of higher education. That is one reason why they developed an early awareness about entrepreneurship studies. But the study programs created in the 1980s made it easier for the post-pioneer generation to look inside France and less to the United States when the start-up boom of the late 1990s prompted the rapid expansion of entrepreneurship studies. The French believed, moreover, that the active pedagogy in the *grandes écoles de commerce* made it likely that the programs in ESCs would be even more tranversal than entrepreneurship studies in run-of-the-mill American business schools.

The latecomers: universities and their search for a discipline

French university faculties could never rival the *grandes écoles de commerce* as teaching institutions. The passive nature of their learning and their poor connections with business prevented them from engaging in the outreach essential to an active pedagogy. Moreover, perhaps because of their relative isolation, they had never developed a compelling desire to do so. That is why in 1996 entrepreneurship studies in them were *le grand vide*. Fayolle's poll in 1998 in the midst of the start-up mania shows that entrepreneurship studies had made some progress in universities in two years (1996–98). Thirty-seven percent of them had at least one course in entrepreneurial studies and 19 percent planned to introduce one soon. However, 44 percent of the universities still had none (the corresponding figure for the ESCs was 14 percent). The development of a field of study is not one-dimensional. It requires both teaching and a scholarly culture – a culture of research. Critics claim that this scholarly pursuit of a discipline "serves nothing," in UTC's Orlinski's words (Orlinski, 2002b). But it does; it serves scholarship, and it is the university's task to create and develop scholarly disciplines. The fact that no discipline in the university recognizes entrepreneurship studies as a field of knowledge is less a refutation of its scholarly possibilities than an affirmation that it does not yet fit into its current structures. For academics interested in entrepreneurship developing into a discipline, this constituted a challenge, for initially neither had business economics nor management studies "fitted" until they actually established themselves in the university community. Since the old German idea of an integrated discipline that Kurt Schmaltz wrote about in 1930 could no longer pass muster, it was becoming somewhat easier for new subjects to carve out a niche in academia.

Inasmuch as entrepreneurship was not a recognized field, and those interested could not do a doctoral dissertation in it, they had to work in other, established, disciplines. In Germany this meant business economics, in France management (*gestion*). And French research scholars in management, like Germans in BWL, had not totally neglected the subject. In 1985 Henri Le Marois in the Faculty of Management Sciences (Lille) and in 1986 Lucien Kombou in the Faculty of Management Sciences (Bordeaux) did theses on entrepreneurial subjects.[13] They stood alone in this decade, but in the 1990s they were joined by eleven dissertations. As in the *grandes écoles de commerce* there were several pioneers at universities. In Bordeaux IV Bertrand Saporta counted among them. He started the Bordeaux DESS (major) in *création d'entreprises et gestion des projets innovants*, "after a trip to Quebec's Université Trois Rivières" (Fonrouge, 2002). The director of CREGE, he guided students towards research on entrepreneurship. Cecile Fonrouge mentions two other university pioneers (Emile Marchesnay in Montpellier and Emile-Michel Hernandez in Reims). They and their students started DESS programs in entrepreneurial studies.

[13] Le Marois, 1985, and Kombou, 1986.

One of Saporta's students, Fonrouge, on her appointment was given the task of introducing a DESS on *création d'entreprises et ingénieurie entrepreneuriale* at the University of Evry.

Scholars interested in research did not necessarily restrict themselves to universities. The boundaries between them and the *grandes écoles of commerce* could be blurred in this respect. Stéphane Marion states that there was an absence of researchers and not much research at his university, Lyon III; Natalie Schieb-Bienfait, IAE Nantes, asserts that research in Nantes was not "well established." Cécile Fonrouge observes that, for research, "one looked, of course, at the Americans." The research lab at her university was filled with sociologists and management people; she was the only one researching entrepreneurship. On the other hand, Philippe Albert at the Centre d'Entrepreneurs of ESC Lyon and Robert Papin at HEC had developed complete academic research and teaching programs. "These two centers," Mortier writes, "had, simultaneously, permanent staff, a critical mass (in number of students enrolled), a research activity in these disciplines that produced new pedagogical tools, a network into the economy, and an identity as a school in entrepreneurship studies. In brief, they would bear comparison with the best foreign universities" (Mortier, 1996, p. D9). Mortier overlooked research efforts in other *grandes écoles de commerce*. Jean-Paul Debourse at ESC Lille pushed research programs that culminated in a new research "Centre de Développement des Entreprises et de l'Entrepreneuriat," but Mortier's omission is understandable, since the centre had been established after his report. CERAM, the graduate school of management and technology, had also created a center for research on high-tech start-ups, dubbed "Dynamis," which commenced operations in 1994. Six professors interested in a multidisciplinary approach to the subject worked in the center, which, when Philippe Albert resettled there from EM Lyon in 1998, was continuing to enhance its reputation in entrepreneurship process research (Albert, 2002).

But the point needs to be emphasized that, when researchers sought *knowledge* rather than *creation,* they had to forsake the domain of the *grandes écoles de commerce* for the scholarly milieu of university research. Patrick Senicourt, at ESC Paris, completed a dissertation at Paris IX and Alain Fayolle, while at EM Lyon, at the University of Lyon III.[14] Most *grandes écoles de commerce* with serious research

[14] Fayolle, 1996, and Senicourt, 1997.

interests had contacts with universities (at Lille, ESC with the IAE in the University of Science and Technology; in Paris, ESC with Dauphine). On leaving the precincts of the ESC for the university, the preoccupation changed from *création d'entreprise* to questions of disciplinarity. For this reason, perhaps, the discipline of entrepreneurship studies in France found its most detailed critics in universities. Whereas people in *grandes écoles* of engineering and commerce simply dismissed them, the university researchers, since disciplinarity is the university's province, had to explain what elements necessary to disciplinarity were absent in entrepreneurship studies.

In order to promote a discipline, advocates of entrepreneurship studies had to provide a scholarly arena in which debate about the content and shape of entrepreneurship studies could take place. Since people in universities focus on disciplinarity, they were the major force behind the organization of the Académie de l'Entrepreneuriat. At its first congress in 1999 Bertrand Saporta and Thierry Verstraete headed the program committee, and all twenty-three of the committee members were drawn from university faculties. The same thing was true of the *Revue de l'Entrepreneuriat*, which the academy founded. Its director of publication, Thierry Verstraete, lectures in the IAE, University of Lille; its two chief editors, Robert Paturel and Bertrand Saporta, are university professors. Five of the *Revue*'s scientific committee are professors in French universities, and two in Quebec. The *Revue*'s scholarly intent is clear from its subtitle: "Revue Scientifique dediée à la Publication des Travaux de Recherche sur l'Entrepreneuriat." It was also expressed in its first publication, a list of "Thèses et Revues Francophones sur l'Entrepreneuriat." University-affiliated scholars also dominated French academic discussions about the nature of entrepreneurial education. Alain Fayolle, Bertrand Saporta, Thierry Verstraete, Nathalie Schieb-Bienfait and two Quebec scholars wrote the articles on "L'enseignement de l'entrepreneuriat," published in the Belgium journal *Gestion 2000* (for the article concerning France, see Fayolle, 2000). The professors, moreover, wrote reports about the state of entrepreneurship teaching and research in France. They attended and hosted regional, national and international congresses, workshops and colloquia on entrepreneurial education, which increased in frequency as the 1990s ended.

At every point, the scholars confronted the fact that the subject of entrepreneurship covered a vast arena. The researcher in quest of a discipline in entrepreneurship had to embrace interdisciplinarity, but their economic science backgrounds limited their range, just as BWL did that of the Germans. The French work on entrepreneurship particularly left out what one group of scholars, in a report, called the *devenir social* – that aspect of entrepreneurial action that encompasses the general environment and its multiple elements (economic, institutional, social, political, cultural and religious). "Rather curiously," this report emphasized, "one must state that in the multiple definitions of entrepreneurship proposed by French researchers this dimension is always absent" (CIDEGEF, 2001, p. 3).

The national culture factor, however, did take on a great importance. In their debates the French, like the Germans, stressing the lack of entrepreneurship in their societies, assumed that something could be done to promote it. The venture capitalist Jean-Bernard Schmidt, who participated in the Assises de l'Innovation in Paris, was optimistic in this respect. "It is striking," he observed, "with what facility the French adapt to Silicon Valley and contract the ambulant virus of risk and the spirit of conquest" (Assises de l'Innovation, 1998). Everybody could not go to Silicon Valley, so institutions of higher education in both countries underlined the importance of stimulation programs.

French concerns about national culture went much deeper than the German. If they wanted to stimulate their compatriots to be entrepreneurial, they did not want French entrepreneurialism or entrepreneurial studies to mirror the American. Sometimes their anti-Americanism was xenophobic and funny. François Peccoud, president of UTC, for instance, called Americanization "a collective intoxication for a model of errors which is not even a model" (Peccoud, 2002). Despite the hyperbole, they were serious educators in search of a discipline that would reflect French culture in order to serve better the French entrepreneur. Still, their inquiries and investigations into entrepreneurship usually began with the Americans. The communication of Debourse, Danjou and Dubois to the first congress of the Académie de l'Entrepreneuriat in Lille is mostly about entrepreneurship education in the best American business schools (Debourse et al., 1999). Danjou's analysis of research in entrepreneurship, moreover, focuses primarily on the Americans (Danjou, 2000). The report by Beranger, Chabral and Dambrine to the Ministère de l'Economie, des Finances et de l'Industrie on the entrepreneurial education of engineers and Fayolle's report to the Ministère de l'Education Nationale, de la Recherche et de la Technologie on entrepreneurship education in French universities also discuss American entrepreneurial education extensively.[15] But the purpose in so doing is clear. As Debourse, Danjou and Dubois explain it, "Our object here is to analyze how the university can be an effective partner in the creation of firms and how it can define and implement a global strategy to this end, in order to apply it to the Group ESC Lille. To do this, we shall proceed to analyze the 'best practices' of American university programs" (Debourse et al., 1999, p. 7).

Because their real concern was French entrepreneurial studies they wanted to distinguish them from the American, and they scrutinized both to achieve this effect. But it was not an easy task. People in the *grandes écoles de commerce* claimed their *pédagogie active* made them different from the Americans. But others said that it made them the same. Alain Fayolle, one who has much studied the subject, concludes that "French entrepreneurship education is a partial declination of the American . . . principally on the level of pedagogical modalities, which are built on the principles of diversity of sequence and alternation of modes. Professors, entrepreneurs, and professionals intervene together to start up an enterprise . . . but we do not find [in France] all the varieties of modalities and apprenticeship methods utilized in American universities" (Fayolle, 2000, p. 93). Apparently, Americans also had an active pedagogy, which was more developed than, and influenced, the French. Fayolle states this view in another study when he writes: "The osmosis between universities and entrepreneurs is typical in America, and is no doubt a trump card of the American system" (Fayolle, 1999b, p. 32).

In research the university scholars also sought to identify certain especially French themes. In the preface to the first issue of the *Revue de l'Entrepreneuriat* (published in 2001) the editors went out of their way to compare French research to American "by their (the French) qualitative, sometimes constructivist approach, [which contrasts] with the more mechanistic, often quantitative methods of the Anglo-Saxon researchers in their specialized reviews, notably the *Journal of Business Venturing*." This was true. Patrick Senicourt's thesis used constructivist methods and Thierry Verstraete's was "inspired by a constructivist model that utilized a cognitive dimension with three elements in it: strategic thought, reflexivity (the capacity to interpret and understand

[15] Beranger et al., 1998, and Fayolle, 1999b.

an action and thus learn through action) and an apprenticeship which resulted in lived knowledge."[16] At the conference "Entrepreneurship Research in Europe," Alain Fayolle and Christian Bruyat reported on the research at their universities, the Institut National Polytechnique de Grenoble and the Université Pierre Mendès-France de Grenoble:

> The research framework is grounded in a constructivist approach and is based on a new type of action research, involving three categories of individuals: researchers, nascent entrepreneurs, and those that we call accompanists. In our research framework, these different individuals interact mainly through a set of tools, based on computer systems technologies, which are playing a double role. On the one hand, the tools are conceived to strongly help the nascent entrepreneurs and the accompanists . . . On the other hand, the tools give to the research team the opportunity to track a lot of cases of innovative business activities . . . [and] also to collect data which concern the entrepreneurial process from the beginning to the final point (Fayolle and Bruyat, 2002).

Whether or not qualitative and constructivist research approaches can be found under the big tent of American research is debatable. But it will not be debated here.

What the French university researchers thought and did is the issue. Fayolle and Bruyat knew that, in entrepreneurship studies, "our knowledge is unstable. When we look at the scientific literature the first impression is more related to the reading of a fragmented and heterogeneous catalogue and less to the reading of a well-structured knowledge handbook" (Fayolle and Bruyat, 2002). They realized and said that their constructivist approach was only one of many promising research methods that might contribute to the creation one day of that entrepreneurship knowledge handbook. In their research choice they seemed to rule out habitat analysis in order to concentrate on entrepreneurial process. That had always been the stated focus of people in the *grandes écoles de commerce*.

Conclusion

Entrepreneurship studies in Germany and France have a very short time trail. Although that trail extends further into the past in French academia than in the German, in scope and intensity the French history

[16] Senicourt, 1997, and Verstraete, 1997; quoted in Danjou, 2000.

is restricted, too. In the first chapter the establishment of a high-tech entrepreneurial consciousness in Silicon Valley was the theme. Phenomenal Silicon Valley directly affected France and Germany by awakening their leaders to the importance of start-up entrepreneurship. The outpouring of comments about the entrepreneurial challenge coming from the United States provoked a series of visits to the country, including one from top policy makers in the French government: Dominique Strauss-Kahn, Claude Allègre and Christian Pierret. Their visit did not "cause" subsequent events in France, but it was the catalyst to the rapid succession of ministerial action that led to the Law on Innovation and Research of 1999. This law, which everybody cites as a defining moment in French entrepreneurial studies, did not directly promote them in institutions of higher education. The law eliminated obstacles to and established aids for entrepreneurial action in France. And it did help schools by providing for thirty-one public incubators to be established by institutions of higher education in order to stimulate outreach. In this heady atmosphere, entrepreneurship studies thrived. The chambers of commerce and industry, traditional supporters of the *écoles supérieures de commerce*, found funds for entrepreneurship studies. Private industry, general councils and regional councils gave money for these studies in universities. French universities never created endowed chairs on the German scale. There is no national source of funding for academic entrepreneurship studies in France as there is in Germany and the United States. Money has always been tight. But interinstitutional patterns of cooperation begin to emerge: the Académie de l'Entrepreneuriat was founded, the *Revue d l'Entrepreneuriat* started, and conferences, symposia and workshops met; all this happened to entrepreneurship studies in France, after two decades of gestation, in just a very short period of time – i.e. after 1996.

In Germany entrepreneurship studies grew rapidly in higher education after 1997, primarily because of government support. This support and encouragement led to the professorships that finally set entrepreneurship studies in German *Hochschulen* on the search for disciplinarity. Not that the private sector was inactive. It provided money for chairs and helped pay for the business plan competitions that McKinsey and other consultancies managed. But the discipline, even compared to financially starved French entrepreneurship studies, has not moved very far. The German academics did not provision themselves with the research instruments needed for serious national research programs. There are no academic journals specializing in entrepreneurship studies in Germany. No academic publisher focuses on the subject. German professors attempted to float a monograph series on entrepreneurship, but there were no takers since the market and the money were unsure. Academics publish on entrepreneurship in management journals in their own countries, but they probably publish as much in American journals – in the *Journal of Business Venturing* or in Babson College's *Frontiers of Entrepreneurship Research* – when they publish at all.

Moreover, the French advantage increases over the German if the comparison is labeled "pedagogy of start-up process" rather than "maturity of academic discipline." Since German BWL neglects its relations with praxis and the new professors of entrepreneurship are more academically qualified than experienced in business, the sort of *pédagogie active* that developed in *grande écoles de commerce* did not occur in German entrepreneurship studies. No strong voices speak out in German academic business studies, as in France, against the preoccupation with questions of disciplinarity. In France, when asked what obstacles hindered the effectiveness of entrepreneurship education in France, Patrick Senicourt, ESC Paris, replied: "Efforts to make entrepreneurship education academic"; Robert Papin, HEC, answered: "Too academic criteria for evaluation [publications], distrust of professionals"; and Gilles Certhoux, EM Nantes, pointed an accusatory finger at "French cartesianism, the desire to structure and demonstrate."[17] These remarks were not from engineers, who often say the same thing, but *commerçants* in the *grandes écoles de commerce*, whom engineers criticize for a lack of practicality.

Still, the *grandes écoles de commerce*'s achievement in *pédagogie active* should not itself be exaggerated. Fayolle claims that French entrepreneurship education follows approaches that are too often "functional and not sufficiently processual" (Fayolle, 2000, p. 93). In other words, it is still mired too much in management education in both the *grandes écoles de commerce* and the universities. He also complains that entrepreneurship teaching is "little anchored in tradition and French culture" (p. 93). Perhaps he and Bruyat believe that the constructivist method in research that they pursue could eventually

[17] Senicourt, 2002, Papin, 2002, and Certhoux, 2002.

make the new field in research and teaching an essential part of the French entrepreneurial process.

Neither Germans nor French interested in the development of a new academic discipline worked in a reform environment that completely resembled the American. Entrepreneurship studies based on the US model required research to be fused with an active teaching pedagogy. The same institutional obstacles that hindered the growth of management education along American lines after World War II hampered reforms in the 1990s. The *Wissenschaft* tradition in BWL stymied the independent development of entrepreneurship studies and the transversal activity necessary to make them flourish. French research like the American, was more casuistic than theory-led, but the institutional gulf between *grandes écoles de commerce* and university entrepreneurship studies prevented the French from integrating research with outreach on a scale commensurate with that taking place on the American university campus. Because natural scientists and engineers did not think entrepreneurship a discipline, in all three countries they ignored or resisted the creation of entrepreneurship as a field of study. But the institutional isolation of scientists and engineers from people in business studies in France and Germany meant that efforts to promote entrepreneurship studies went on in a low-tech milieu. The isolation stopped them from taking the first, tentative steps – as elite business schools and engineering and natural science faculties had in American universities – toward creating a discipline in high-tech entrepreneurship.

If they could not work with each other in formulating a discipline and a pedagogy in entrepreneurship studies, could the social science academics work with engineers and natural science academics in actually achieving start-ups? "Everything comes from structure and from event at the same time," Sartre says. Structure dictates that the educational heritage will keep the social scientists and scientist-engineers apart. But event, Merleau-Ponty says, is capricious, ruled by chance, and is an agent of change. The issue to be confronted in the next chapter is whether the unpredictable event of Silicon Valley's emergence drove people into transforming structures enough in each country to bring natural scientists, engineers, business economists and management scientists together to further the high-tech start-up process.

5 | Networking for high-tech start-ups in Germany and France

wo factors must be considered when dealing with the networking necessary for high-tech start-ups. One is the networking that natural scientists and engineers use when starting firms, especially reaching out from the university community. German and French natural scientists and engineers may not be interested in cooperating with social scientists in building an academic discipline in entrepreneurship studies, but if they want to start a firm they readily admit that they need a lot of help in the non-technical aspect of entrepreneurship. The historical example of Silicon Valley, where plenty of expertise (consultants, venture capitalists, public relations firms, etc.) is available to scientists and engineers looking for assistance, instructed them.

The other factor is the specific networking that could occur, if it is really useful, between people in entrepreneurship studies, the social scientists in institutions of higher education, and the scientists and engineers whose high-tech ideas foster firms. People in entrepreneurship studies believe they can assist the scientists and engineers in this regard, specifically in the non-technical aspects of start-up activity, but those with high-tech ideas generally have not seen how they would benefit from networking with their colleagues in business schools or faculties of business.

The divorce between the two is longstanding and understandable. In Germany, BWL focuses on building an academic discipline that scientists and engineers mistrust, and BWL professors' contacts with praxis are so tenuous that they have not acquired much sapiential knowledge about start-ups from which natural scientists and engineers could profit. This has not always been the case. German professors of accounting, led by Eugen Schmalenbach, had worked closely during the efficiency drive of the 1920s with engineers in the *Reichskuratorium für Wirtschaftlichkeit* when devising charts of accounts and cost accounting systems, but the post-war decision to make BWL a theory-led *Wissenschaft* opened the gap between working engineers and *Betriebswirte*. Professors in the new field of entrepreneurship studies have not been around for sufficient time to close it. Interviewees in BWL faculties in engineering schools even share the engineers' doubts about BWL's usefulness. Mathias Masberg, of Gründerkolleg, RWTH Aachen, expresses himself succinctly: "Too much weight is given to the BWL aspect in entrepreneurship education" (Masberg, 2003).

In France, engineers and natural scientists dislike the academic emphasis in university entrepreneurship studies, and the *écoles supérieures de commerce*, despite their *pédagogie active*, also drew criticism. Pierre Trémembert and Jean Le Traon, ENST Bretagne, observed that it was "easy to collaborate with business schools in the area of *intervention* [lecturing] but not in the sphere of projects." Some provided cultural explanations for this lack of concordance. Jean-François Gallouin, Ecole Centrale de Paris, said, "Entrepreneurship is not accepted in the French culture because of its social values and organizational traditions. Diplomas and technocracy are important; money and business are rejected." Other engineering school interviewees spoke more precisely about the source of this lack of cooperation, and sometimes they were pejoratively frank. Alain Jouandeau, INSA Lyon, explained: "The collaboration with the *écoles de commerce* is done by teacher exchange; it is not done in teamwork. The marriage does not work because of constraints on the use of time. The student-engineers work and learn what is necessary quickly. They do not need business professors for that." Engineers felt that the student-engineers could easily learn on their own the content of business studies required in the start-up process. For the rest of the business studies curriculum they had neither time nor inclination.

The subject of this chapter, then, is how and to what extent natural science researchers, academic engineers and social scientists in entrepreneurship studies have managed – and are managing – to transform their education system from one that separates the elements of higher education from each other and from praxis into one that promotes the effective combination of the elements that contribute to start-up synergy. This collaboration had to come, if it came, out of common experience. Whether and how people in entrepreneurship studies could network with scientists and engineers in building high-tech start-up networks, and thereby emulate the Americans, also depended less on the general strength of the entrepreneurship study programs that social scientists had devised (described in the last chapter) than on industry-university networking between praxis and the greater university community that existed before the creation of the entrepreneurship studies programs in each country. The presence of developed university-industry relationships allowed entrepreneurship studies, when they came, to be co-opted into an operating networking system, provided one existed. In this regard the industry-university networking heritages differed greatly, for the French had much less robust traditions than the Germans. The German story will be related first, the French second. Then a general assessment of the participation of both countries' systems of higher education in high-tech start-up networks will be made.

Networking in Germany: the eager universities

Entrepreneurship education beyond chairs and study programs

German entrepreneurship study programs could be traced rather easily because they were fashioned by the people holding professorships in German *Hochschulen*. And a lot has been written about them and their new field. It is much more difficult to detect and describe systematically university interaction with praxis in the start-up process. Fortunately, a comparative picture of university involvement with praxis can be gleaned from other studies. One especially revealing work was written by Schmude and Uebelacker a year before their investigation into professorships in entrepreneurial studies (Schmude and Uebelacker, 2001). In this earlier work the authors concentrated on universities, not chairs. They conceived of the university interaction as community involvement in entrepreneurialism, and this conception enhances the usefulness of their analysis because it permits the role of various groups implicated in the building of entrepreneurship studies to be taken into consideration – even that of scientists and engineers. The authors ignored the *Fachhochschulen*, but they covered seventy-eight universities, leaving out only special ones such as the Army University.

In order to determine a university's effectiveness in fostering entrepreneurism, they selected eight factors for measurement, some weighted differently from others. The first two factors were a university's entrepreneurship programs (30 percent) and a university's marketing of its programs (20 percent). These two factors added up to 50 percent of the possible points in their evaluation schema. Factors

3 to 8 together accounted for the other 50 percent. They covered the intensity of: (3) stimulation programs (learning by doing, business plan preparations, etc.); (4) spin-off relevant events; (5) technology transfer center activities; (6) motivation of students; (7) networking inside and outside the university; and (8) communication and exchange within the university's greater academic community. Professorships and academic programs were weighted heavily in their evaluations but factors 3 to 8, with 50 percent of the possible points, were very significant indeed. And they dealt with start-up processes and outreach within and outside the university's community, crossing boundaries, which made entrepreneurship interdisciplinary and transversal. Schmude and Uebelacker's study, then, provides a good basis for analyzing start-up networking and entrepreneurship studies in German universities.

The striking things about the study's results are the incongruities that exist between the ranking of universities under factors 1 and 2, and under factors 3 to 8. An analysis of two factors – (1) university entrepreneurship programs and (7) networking – is used to make this point (table 5.1). The table lists only the top third (twenty-nine universities) of the seventy-eight universities included on their lists because they represent the best universities in terms of program excellence. The table shows on the left side the ranking for entrepreneurship programs, and on the right side the ranking for networking. Networking is about the extent to which entrepreneurial activity connects various academic disciplines inside the university with a variety of groups outside. The top third of the seventy-eight universities ranked in both categories is given in the table in descending order of excellence.

Ten schools that rated in the top third in terms of entrepreneurship programs did not make it into the top third with regard to networking, and half of these ten had established chairs of entrepreneurship studies (identified in the Klandt-Knaup report). They were Oestrich-Winkel, Münster, WHU Koblenz, Magdeburg and TU Darmstadt. The other five had not established a chair. Nine schools that ranked in the top third in terms of networking were not in the top third with respect to entrepreneurship programs. Only one of the nine (TU Munich) had established a chair in entrepreneurship studies. The others without chairs were Paderborn, Cottbus, Duisburg, Oldenburg, Bochum, Saarbrücken, Braunschweig and Halle-Wittenberg. Since Klandt and Knaup identified twenty-one chairs of entrepreneurship

Table 5.1 *Ranking of German universities in terms of entrepreneurship programs and networking activities*

Entrepreneurship programs	Place	Networking
UGH Wuppertal	1	TU Karlsruhe
EBS Oestrich-Winkel	2	UGH Wuppertal
TU Dresden	3	TH Aachen
University of Witten-Herdecke	4	UGH Paderborn
TU Karlsruhe	5	Augsburg University
Hockenheim University	6	TU Clausthal
Fernuniversität Hagen	7	TU Cottbus
Münster University	8	TU Dresden
University of Cologne	9	UGH Duisburg
HU Berlin	10	Hanover University
TU Chemnitz	11	Oldenburg University
WHU Koblenz	12	HU Berlin
Magdeburg University	13	TU Berlin
Regensburg University	14	Bielefeld University
Trier University	15	Bochum University
Bremen University	16	TU Chemnitz
Hamburg University	17	Hockenheim University
TU Illmenau	18	TU Illmenau
Bonn University	19	TU Munich
Munich University	20	Stuttgart University
UGH Siegen	21	Bremen University
TU Darmstadt	22	TU Hamburg-Harburg
TU Hamburg-Harburg	23	University of Cologne
Hanover University	24	Regensburg University
Bielefeld University	25	Saarbrücken University
Jena University	26	UGH Siegen
Kaiserslautern University	27	Trier University
Rostock University	28	Braunschweig University
University of Stuttgart	29	University of Halle-Wittenberg

Source: Schmude and Uebelacker (2001).

studies in German universities (the others were in *Fachhochschulen*), and only five of them were in universities rated in the top third with respect to networking, a lack of connection appears to exist between the intensity of networking and the excellence of entrepreneurship programs.

The placement of technical universities and technical *Hochschulen* on the two lists warrants special attention. Most (all but two: Darmstadt and the Bergakademie Freiberg) of these thirteen schools ranked in the top third in networking. Six of them also rated in the top third under entrepreneurship programs. Of these, five had established chairs for entrepreneurship studies and one (TU Hamburg-Harburg) had not. The five were Dresden, Karlsruhe, Chemnitz, Illmenau and Darmstadt. This indicates a slight disconnection between entrepreneurship study programs and start-up networking activities in engineering schools.

The creation of every new university discipline, especially one with economic and social ramifications, is a complex process that involves university politics, government policy and private interests. The contrasting university rankings under study programs and networking suggest that a bifurcated story – or, rather, two stories – about entrepreneurship education has occurred in German higher education, and the two amount to different tales about American influence as well. Story one was examined in the last chapter. It was about the reluctant professors of BWL. The second story is not about reluctance. On the contrary, it can be called the eager universities.

University rankings in the Schmude and Uebelacker study point to the second story. A disconnection emerges between entrepreneurialism as study programs and entrepreneurialism as networking activities. The disconnection could have something to do with lateness. Universities with entrepreneurship chairs did not have much time in the few years after their establishment to engage in outreach. But what about the universities – and that was most of them – without entrepreneurship chairs that ranked high under the networking factor? It appears that they have been engaged in the networking necessary in a high-tech start-up culture before the creation of entrepreneurship professorships. Hence Schmude and Uebelacker's comment about transfer centers. These centers, they state, are "the classical conduits between university research and science on one side and the private economy on the other. Most of the universities [before the establishment of entrepreneurship study programs] already had extensive activities going on in transfer centers with regard to start-ups . . . This leads to the conclusion that the universities' involvement with start-ups had begun very early under the roofs of numerous transfer centers, which accounts for the intensity of their activity today."

Governmental networking incentives

This second story extends, then, beyond professorships and chairs of entrepreneurship studies into the broader university community, German society, and overseas to the United States and Silicon Valley. The first chapter catalogued some of the German individual responses in the 1990s to phenomenal Silicon Valley. Government involvement began earlier in a limited way with regional authorities' support for technology start-up centers. Although these TGZ started outside the universities, with employment problems and industrial decay on the minds of their sponsors, the German federal government changed this emphasis when it sponsored a series of programs to induce a start-up culture in the universities. The Federal Ministry for Education and Research (BMBF) ran a program between 1983 and 1988 that supported technology-oriented start-ups (Förderung technologieorientierter Unternehmensgründungen). It provided financial aid for three phases of start-up activity: (1) early business and market planning; (2) research and development; and (3) production build-up and market entry. A seed capital program for start-ups (1989–94) followed (BJTU – Beteiligungskapital für Junge Technologieunternehmen), which furnished much-needed early-phase capital, and a BMBF-initiated special program following on after that was used to support start-ups, after unification, in the new federal states.

Government programs multiplied in the 1990s, culminating in the BMBF EXIST initiative. It spun off various instruments (such as EXIST-High TEPP – High-Technology Entrepreneurship Postgraduate Program – and EXIST-Seed) designed to promote regional cultures of entrepreneurship. And the Federal Ministry for Economics and Innovation (BMWI) fostered the establishment of the professorships in entrepreneurship when it asked its affiliate, the Deutsche Ausgleichsbank, to promote their foundation.

The government programs sought to establish high-tech cultures of entrepreneurship in which government, business, industry and *Hochschulen* networked. To these federal programs can be added regional programs and initiatives. In Baden-Württemberg a "young innovator" program guarantees the income of start-up entrepreneurs during the early phase, and an initiative called "start-up bonds on campus" gives access to *Hochschul* research laboratories and other resources during the start-up phase. In Bavaria the program FLUEGGE

(Bavarian program to ease start-up transition) allows entrepreneurs to work half-time in the university during the first stage of a start-up, and "high jump" – a program for start-up entrepreneurs in fourteen Bavarian *Hochschulen* – offers counseling, assistance in finding partners, and material support. In Berlin the project "support for start-up entrepreneurs," set up by a consortium of *Hochschulen* for their graduates, arranges contacts between them and science laboratories. The program "start-up jobs", in Hamburg, offers graduates as well as former researchers in *Hochschul* laboratories six months' secure income during the conception phase of their start-ups. The program "GO" (start-up offensive) in Nord-Rhein-Westfalen offers networking possibilities throughout the state to start-up entrepreneurs from various *Hochschulen*, and the program PFAU (Programm zur Finanziellen Absicherung von Unternehmensgründern aus Hochschulen – program to secure finance for firms started from universities) supports graduates in Nord-Rhein-Westfalen for up to two years in start-up preparations. In Mecklenburg-Vorpommern, Saarland and Sachsen-Anhalt there are special state programs to help young graduate start-up entrepreneurs found technologically oriented firms.

Building on the engineering schools' tradition

University participation in high-tech networking was especially important to the process since, if scientists and engineers needed capital and commercial know-how to start a firm, nothing much could be done in high tech without the "big ideas" coming out of universities. And German engineering and science faculties responded. Professor Wassenberg notes: "Silicon Valley [was] rather a reference point for German universities pioneering in entrepreneurship studies in the 1980s, which were RWTH Aachen, TH Berlin, and TH Karlsruhe. The engineering schools were the first because they had always been in contact with the business world" (Wassenberg, 2002). This was true. Professors and their students in *Technische Hochschulen* at Charlottenburg, Karlsruhe and Aachen in particular, but elsewhere as well, not only worked with firms of the *Gründerzeit* and Wilhelmenian era (Siemens, AEG, M.A.N, etc.) but researched industry-funded projects in industry-supported *Hochschul* laboratories, too. Masberg says of RWTH Aachen, which claims to have spawned more high-tech start-ups after World War II than any German university, "The co-operation with industry and the economy and the technology transfer idea that springs from it have been a special feature of the [*Technische Hochschule*] since its foundation in 1870" (Masberg, 2003). And that again is true. Professors of metallurgy and their students in Aachen played a key role in transforming the German steel industry at the end of the nineteenth century from a process industry to a science-based one.

The cooperation between industry and *Hochschulen* restarted with the recovery of German higher education in the 1950s. Government policy distinguished between pure and applied research. It funded the Max Planck Institutes to carry out value-free, disinterested research on a number of themes. But it left the universities and *Technische Hochschulen* to exploit technological ideas commercially. The Fraunhofer Institutes, where firms and professors met in the post-war decades on project work, acted as agencies of transfer. In 1972 the Fraunhofer Gesellschaft expanded its province beyond science and technology. It created the Fraunhofer Institut für Systemtechnik und Innovationsforschung (ISI) in Karlsruhe. The Fraunhofer ISI investigates the border between technology, the economy and society. Numbers of and funds for these institutes increased steadily after the war. Generally, cooperative work went on between professors and established firms, so the system had to be adapted to a start-up culture. Consequently, at Aachen the existence of the networks and a tradition of cooperation between engineers and industry made the creation of a high-tech start-up process in the information era more one of network adaptation than network invention.

German universities did not have venture capital to invest, nor did the professors. But they cultivated contacts with recently developed venture capital sources. Moreover, university-affiliated transfer centers and incubators facilitated the work. Two networks of incubators existed in the 1990s, and one emphasized technologically oriented start-ups. Most of the successful spin-offs came from this network's incubators, in which universities participated.

Throughout the 1980s and 1990s, moreover, Germans, carefully examined and sometimes copied what they believed contributed to US high-tech start-up networking prowess. Governments took notice of the effects of the Bayh-Dole Act, which, beginning in the early 1980s, permitted American universities and professors to patent government-funded discoveries and exploit them commercially. This led to a dramatic increase in the number of patents in just a few years. Following suit, the state government in Baden-Württemberg established a technology licensing bureau (Lizenz-Büro), and BMBF created INSTI (INnovations STImulierung – stimulation of innovations) for the same purpose and with the same inspiration. The universities took an interest in patents. TH Dresden adopted measures that emulated Bayh-Dole. Schools set up patent service centers, which helped researchers through the difficult patenting process. The private sector borrowed U. S. programs, too. The business plan competitions, as Kieser remarks, came from consultancies, the most important of which were American (Kieser, 2002b). McKinsey in 1996 managed the first business plan competitions in Munich and Berlin. It used the successful "Silicon Valley business plan competition model," after adjusting it to the German market. In 1998 McKinsey supervised the business plan competition in northern Bavaria, which became the most successful regional competition in Germany.

The unfolding of German entrepreneurship networking along American lines

Programs promoting university start-ups reeked with American nomenclature. BMBF's EXIST, with its five regional programs (GET UP, KEIM, Dresden EXISTS, BIZEPS and PUSH), burden the German language with energetic-sounding but empty American formulations. If the words do not really represent anything in the United States, the programs do. At the start of the last chapter, the definition of American influence was extended to an acceptance not only of the entrepreneurial ethic but also of the implantation of "instrumentalities that transform the system of higher education from one that separates the elements essential to entrepreneurship into one that effectively promotes the combination of the transversal elements that contribute to entrepreneurial synergy." The success of the Americans depended on the building of transversality and interdisciplinarity into their entrepreneurship studies, and to the extent that the German programs did the same thing their educational systems were being Americanized.

Transversality and interdisciplinarity in high-tech management refer to concepts about the entrepreneurial process that had been incorporated into American research and teaching. One such process in America is called MOT – management of technology. It was developed by leading researchers in business schools in the United States – e.g. at Harvard and the Sloan School at MIT – "as a new interdisciplinary sub-field of strategic management, separate but complementary to organizational theory." It was, Professor Dowling in Regensburg University explains, "more than just the management of the research and development function" (Dowling, 2002b). Dowling, who introduced MOT in Regensburg when he assumed Regensburg's professorship in innovation and technology management, continues:

To define this field, one first has to define technology. Technology is partly the knowledge and the science of engineering. But technology is not only knowledge; it is also the ability to create new products or services. In other words, technology is the knowledge embodied in products and processes, and also the knowledge to produce, and to replicate these products and processes. Innovation and Technology Management . . . includes creative thinking about innovation processes, and above all about how organizations can improve their performance through organizational change (Dowling, 2002a).

Accordingly, successful MOT, as an educational process, could not come from the engineers and natural scientists alone but required interdisciplinary input from organization scientists and – because knowledge in it is inseparable from practical realization – from the active participation in MOT of people in praxis. Dowling writes specifically about MOT's usefulness to established firms that "seek new technologies to strengthen their performance and competitiveness through new products and services (intrapreneurship)" (Dowling, 2002a). But MOT procedures require crossing traditional borders between academic disciplines and between academia and praxis in order to create educational environments necessary to flourishing high-tech start-up habitats. And this is what the new field had done in the United States.

   If this left most German business economists out of the MOT story, it did not exclude all the new professors of entrepreneurship and innovation studies. It did not leave out Dowling, of course, who was an outsider in German business economics. When asked in the interview why he did not have a "chair" in entrepreneurship studies created for him at Regensburg, he replied: "I decided against it because of the German university structure. A chair is held by one academic who 'does everything,' like Klandt at the EBS. Since entrepreneurship is an interdisciplinary subject, I wanted to create a program in which academics from many chairs [fields] are involved" (Dowling, 2002b).

It also did not leave out the other American, Professor Mancke, of the Handelshochschule Leipzig, who stated that his professorship "has been entrepreneurially oriented since the school's re-foundation in 1996 because supporters wanted to create what has been traditionally missing in German BWL – the link between academics and praxis" (Mancke, 2002). And it did not leave out the Ph.D. from Wyoming, Professor Gering of IU Bruchsal, who, in any event, did not fear a confrontation with BWL in his institution since it "had been conceived in an American way: all teaching is in English, there are only American degrees, and the overall orientation is interdisciplinary" (Gering, 2002).

Moreover, it did not shut out German business economists who had chairs in universities, where natural science and engineering faculties had consistently taken a great interest in high-tech start-ups and are, thus, part of this second story. In some big universities, such as Cologne, the opposition of the BWL faculty to a chair had not dampened the enthusiasm throughout the university for start-ups. But this happened above all in THs and TUs, which have scored so high in the "networking" ranking. They were attracted to MOT and the interdisciplinarity it entailed. They were prepared to help dissolve barriers to interdisciplinarity while building, at the same time, university entrepreneurial studies into start-ups networks.

This was the thrust of BMBF's EXIST program. In 1997 the ministry asked for three partners to step forward; one had to be a university (*Hochschule*). Some 200 *Hochschulen* responded, with 109 ideas for regional networks. Out of them the ministry selected five EXIST regions: Wuppertal-Hagen (BIZEPS), Dresden (Dresden EXISTS), Illmenau-Jena-Schmalenkalden (GET UP), Karlsruhe-Pforzheim (KEIM) and Stuttgart (PUSH). The purpose of EXIST was to cultivate entrepreneurial self-reliance as educational and business goals in order to further innovation and start-ups. Although the specifics differed by region, the *Hochschulen* in each had to work within regional networks that included research centers, firms, capital providers, technology and start-up centers, consultants, chambers of commerce and local government authorities. Follow-up evaluators assessing the program noted that, to succeed, its research centers had to be placed outside the university in order to facilitate extramural networking, and people from praxis had to be involved in teaching, although that presented problems in how to anchor the teaching in curricula and examinations. The Fraunhofer ISI took on the job in EXIST of neutral scientific coach, appraiser and advisor. It was specifically charged with scientifically analyzing selected projects in the program, with monitoring the goals and the extent to which they had been attained, and with a general strategic evaluation of the program's "best practices." EXIST actively publicized its work, through publications on "entrepreneurial self-reliance" and *EXIST News*, a quarterly that propagandized their efforts. The project has its own data bank on the Internet and a network map.

Other programs also accompanied the main project. One, EXIST-Seed, concentrated on the discovery and development of business ideas in the universities located in the EXIST regions. EXIST-Seed provided students, graduates and university scientists with financial support (up to DM15,000) for one year of coaching and start-up preparations. A second, EXIST-High TEPP, assisted graduate students at the Universities of Jena, Bamberg and Regensburg. Twenty-one of its grantees, in business economics, science and information technology, currently manage start-up projects in IT and the life sciences. The interdisciplinary approach seeks to expose business economists to science and scientists to business administration, and both to the rigors of praxis, by providing grantees with work partners – consultants, venture capitalists, entrepreneurs from start-up firms and from technologically oriented firms – who accompany them on their way to the doctorate. The plan also includes international networking, especially with American business schools, and research trips outside Germany to work on dissertations. The goal, then, is an education that combines knowledge in the form of a Ph.D. degree with practicality in the form of participation with people in praxis in the founding of a future high-tech start-up firm.

Among the active professorships in Germany, two – those of Professor Lambert Koch, with a start-up chair, and Professor Ulrich Braukmann, with a chair in start-up pedagogy – worked in one university, the Bergische Universität Wuppertal. They have striven in the short time since assuming their chairs (Koch in 1999 and Braukmann in 2001), as participants in EXIST's regional BIZEPS program, to make Wuppertal an entrepreneur career development center. Braukmann worked out a firm start-up pedagogy especially for students in non-economic fields. And the Open University at Hagen offered its students a distant learning start-up entrepreneurship program. Besides this entrepreneurship education, BIZEPS brought the Technical Academy of Wuppertal into a network of fifteen educational units dedicated to creating a regional start-up culture. With Braukmann and Koch's award-winning "Wuppertal model of entrepreneurship education" and active start-up efforts, Wuppertal University scored first in "entrepreneur programs" and second in "networking" in Schmude and Uebelacker's study.

At Regensburg Dowling not only developed and co-coordinated an interdisciplinary course on entrepreneurship and growth management, he was project co-leader of EXIST-High TEPP, while also acting as co-director of GoH-Net (Gründernetz der ostbayerischen Hochschulen-Net), an initiative of the Hans Linder Foundation to network the entrepreneurs of five eastern Bavarian universities. No doubt Dowling's activities contributed to Regensburg's strong rating in the Schmude and Uebelacker study under both "networking" and "entrepreneurship programs." As for scholarship, under the EXIST High-TEPP program he directs five dissertations.[1]

At TU Dresden networking had begun long before Professor Schefczyk filled his chair and applied in 1999 to join BMBF's EXIST program. In the 1990s a professorship in innovation management and technology evaluation, held by Helmut Sabisch, had preceded his. Sabisch, who had worked in the Fraunhofer ISI in Karlsruhe, returned to take this chair, where he ran business plan seminars with a professor of electrical engineering. In these seminars roughly 50 percent of the students came from engineering and 50 percent from economic and social science faculties. Schefczyk, profiting from the efforts of forerunners, worked under Dresden EXISTS with other chairs (computer science, finance, organizations, law and psychology), so his chair in innovation – in his own words – "has got a broad base within the TU.

---

[1] They are (in English) Holger Kollmer's "licensing strategies of young technology firms – an empirical study based on the biotechnology industry"; Julia Lampe's "delegative leadership and new venture growth – a theoretical and empirical study"; Christian Lendner's "critical success factors of university incubators"; Tobias Schmidt's "initial public offerings and investment strategies of young, growing e-commerce firms – a theoretical and empirical study based on new international e-commerce companies after their IPO"; and Isabell Welpe's "cooperation between VC firms and start-ups – an empirical study." They are all works on start-up process, not academic themes.

Dresden EXISTS," he reflects, "surrounds and broadens the academic core: motivation events (lectures by entrepreneurs in the *Studium Generale*), information events (start-up-oriented introduction to BWL), lectures and coaching for non-business students, and a start-up space (*Raum*) for the development of ideas." Schefczyk also observes that "the chairs at other TUs (Aachen, Munich, Darmstadt, Karlsruhe) have an interdisciplinary integration posture similar to TU Dresden" (Schefczyk, 2002).

It is not necessary to follow the activity of the professors of entrepreneurship in all five EXIST regions. EXIST is itself only symptomatic of a greater awareness within German higher education of high-tech start-up phenomena. The response of the schools to the government's call for EXIST proposals proves that, as does the ability of the schools in the regions selected to participate in the programs. Three years into EXIST, an advisory board of experts, evaluating the program, declared itself – with some reservations – "very satisfied with the overall performance of the *Hochschulen* and regions" (EXIST, 2002). A poll of student populations in ten universities in EXIST regions, carried out by the Fraunhofer ISI, supports this conclusion.[2] Some 40 percent of the 5,324 responding students expressed an interest in starting up a firm. Of these respondents, 9 percent, selected on the basis of age and experience, were characterized in a special group as the most promising "potential *Gründer*." Of the 40 percent only 14 percent had had contact with the start-ups program in their university, but around a half of the 9 percent designated as potential *Gründer* had. "Here," the study concludes, "is a big development potential for start-up initiatives in *Hochschulen*" (Görisch et al., 2002).

In the former West Germany, many universities in developed regions had advanced so far in start-up networking that they did not need – or, for that reason perhaps, did not get into – EXIST. This was true in Berlin, Munich and Aachen. All of them, but especially Munich, had been highly recognized regions of entrepreneurship for some time, and newly created professorships in entrepreneurship studies in their regional universities could easily be drawn into and contribute to their start-ups habitat.

---

[2] The ten universities were: Bergische Universität Gesamthochschule Wuppertal, TU Dresden, Friedrich-Schiller-Universität Jena, FH Jena, TU Illmenau, FH Schmalkalden, Stuttgart University, Hockenheim University, FHT Esslingen and FH Nürtingen. Görisch et al., 2002.

At Berlin's Humboldt University, which rates high in both of Schmude and Uebelacker's rankings, Professor Christian Schade in the economic science faculty cultivated his American contacts. Frequently in the United States, he invited prominent professors from there as regular guest speakers on entrepreneurship and innovation in a funded speakers' forum that he has at his disposal. Schade notes that 95 percent of the readings used in his entrepreneurship and innovation courses are American, and that this would increase to 100 percent because the MBA would soon be taught in English (Schade, 2002). He organizes a series of lectures and discussions about start-ups in a club that meets the last Thursday every month, and he sponsors bistro evenings (*Kneipenabende*) where entrepreneurs, venture capitalists, public funders, etc. mingle with interested guests. Start-up enthusiasts access HU's incubator, which dates from 1994, HU's Technology Transfer Center, a patent counseling service, and HU's Career Center. Schade observes that in the United States the biggest research field is technology venture, which in Germany is represented by himself and by Professor Schefczyk (Schade, 2002).

Professor Ann-Kristin Achleitner's chair at Munich TU reflects its location inside a high-tech start-up *Hochschule* in Germany's most active high-tech region. Before she assumed the chair in 2000, students in the university had initiated their own start-up club called "Tomorrow," and Professors Bode, Reichweil and Heinzl had taught a course there on entrepreneurship. She characterizes the chair's entrepreneurship approach as integrative and its special features as the tie-up with a *technical* university and instruction in English (Achleitner, 2002). Professor Achleitner's sub-field, entrepreneurship finance, is particularly useful to scientists and engineers interested in starting a firm. She offers a course to non-business majors on the subject. In her courses she draws heavily from the work of Americans, at Harvard (Gompers, Lerner and Kuemmerle) and at Stanford (Saalman), and utilizes American teaching materials (e.g. case studies that deal specifically with venture evaluation). Her chair exists, she notes, "in a very contact-oriented environment with invited guest lecturers from praxis" (Achleitner, 2002). The TU network passes through a biotech start-up center, an entrepreneurship center (Unternehmer TUMunich GmbH) and the Munich Business Plan Competition, held annually at Schloss Elmau. The creation of the entrepreneurship chair at TU Munich, then, simply added to the constellation of start-ups activities that make Munich so important a part of the second story.

RWTH Aachen's early work with industry continued after World War II, particularly in the machine tool laboratory (Werkzeugmaschinenlabor). Its research gained notice steadily, which persuaded the Fraunhofer Gesellschaft in 1980, with support from the state government of North Rhine-Westphalia, to found the Fraunhofer-Institut für Produktionstechnologien (IPT) in Aachen. Four of WZL's professors joined the board of directors of the IPT. The cooperation between research and industry in WZL fostered "the quick and effective transfer of scientific knowledge into business practice," and earned the laboratory a number of awards, from the Society of Manufacturing Engineers (United States), the Verband Deutscher Maschinen-und Anlagenbau, and others. Although networking between the *Hochschule* and industry was intense, none of it included the management sciences, which the engineers excluded from their province. Originally, too, the networking went on with established firms. But the department of technology transfer and innovation in RWTH's bureau of technology transfer and scientific post-experience education found start-up counseling to be an increasingly demanded part of its work. The economic science faculty of RWTH decided in the late 1990s to establish a lecture series on start-ups, a *Gründerkolleg*, which Mathias Masberg took over in 2000, and to create a chair – funded by the regional savings bank (*Sparkasse*), on "business economics for natural scientists and engineers," to be filled in 2003. In 1999 they thought of adopting MIT's program, but it was too expensive. So they devised their own, which was smaller than but similar to MIT's. The chair in Aachen focuses on start-up coaching, start-up training and start-up mobilization. Start-up training is carried out in cooperation with firms in praxis. The program includes BWL and law for start-ups, the examination of various start-up themes, and work on a business plan, plus a "network dinner" with eight to ten venture capitalists. The mobilization effort has included the establishment of a First Tuesday Club, working with Düsseldorf's First Tuesday Club, and lectures by professors in other fields (Masberg, 2003).

The chair and the *Gründerkolleg* aroused opposition from engineers. Masberg says that the professors in WZL saw "no necessity for BWL (within a *Gründerkolleg*) in high-tech start-up management." But he goes on to remark that this "old prejudice of the engineering professors is slowly changing and, with the new chair, the students' thinking will inevitably change, too" (Masberg, 2003). BWL people in Aachen are careful to tailor their program to the needs of engineers and scientists and to downplay the usual BWL theoretical emphasis in favor of an action-oriented pedagogy. The Aachen experience is new, like all attempts in *Technische Hochschulen* to provide student engineers and natural scientists with knowledge of a non-technical nature about the start-up process. But it promises to lower the barrier between engineering and business studies that an education suited to the transversal and interdisciplinary nature of entrepreneurship seems to require.

The activities of other professors in entrepreneurship studies could also be traced. Those in the *Fachhochschulen* have been neglected because they are not included in the Schmude and Uebelacker rankings. But one, who was interviewed, can be included. Most of the *Fachhochschul* professors are teachers. Professor Richard Mancke at the HHL is a teacher, too, but he brought an American approach to the job. HHL was the first *Handelshochschule* in Germany (1898), but after World War II the Communists closed it. On its reopening in 1996 it organized along American lines, to close the gap between business economics and business, with instruction in English, US entry requirements (GMAT, TOEFL) and an American in the professorship. Some of Mancke's teaching materials are drawn from Timmons, his former classmate at MIT, and Mancke has had another former classmate, Kenneth Harrington (who runs an entrepreneurship program at the University of Washington) guest lecture at HHL. He organizes conferences and *Stammtische* (regular meeting places), to bring Leipzig people together, and a business plan competition. He has started up enterprises himself. He is also involved as chairman of the board in two incubators: Biotech World and the Business Innovation Center. But he complains about the ineffectiveness of this start-up networking because of the general lack of money (Mancke, 2002). Other professors in schools that do not rank high in networking have tried to enter the high-tech start-up culture. Gering at IU Bruchsal is an example. He has suffered, despite his penchant for interdisciplinarity, from the absence at his school of engineering and natural science faculties. He compensates by working with Heidelberg's incubator in biotech and in Karlsruhe's KEIM (Gering, 2002).

This *tour d'horizon* suffices to show that an active culture of networking exists between Germany's *Technische Hochschulen* and praxis, and that the scientists and engineers involved in it have slowly started to include occupants of the newly appointed professorships in entrepreneurship and innovation into their networks, as they adapt them to support start-ups. The more high-tech the venue, the more susceptible it is to Americanization. German business, science and government are not shy about learning from the United States inasmuch as the high-tech future of the country seems to be at stake. Academic engineers, moreover, had always been interested in process and product. They seldom let *Wissenschaft* separate them from praxis, and their faculties eagerly sought to learn ideas about MOT coming out of the United States. Where science and technology dominated, in technical universities and institutes, so did high-tech start-up interest and activity. Their interest, however, invariably stopped at the point where entrepreneurship turned into an academic discipline.

They left that to the non-natural-science people. In Germany this meant people primarily in economic science, and, within it, principally those in *Betriebswirtschaftslehre*. People who have entered entrepreneurship studies from BWL learn the difference between the new knowledge field and the traditional business economics they studied; as of necessity they reach out to the scientists and engineers. Out of practicality alone, they have had to move away from BWL. Consequently, according to Hering, "in German entrepreneurial studies there is a stronger adoption of American research and teaching traditions (case study method, descriptive, empirical research) than in traditional BWL" (Hering, 2002).

Networking in France: overcoming disintegration

In France, as in Germany, the ranking of schools in high-tech networking would have, had a French study comparable to Schmude and Uebelacker's been done, differed from those ranked in entrepreneurship studies. This is true because engineering schools had little interest in entrepreneurial studies and because only slight contact existed between the *grandes écoles de commerce* and industry. The intensity of the networking between industry and the French schools of engineering and faculties of natural science did not, moreover, match the German. Two aspects of the French heritage in higher education hindered them from doing the networking that took place in Germany between industry and academia. One is the system of French engineering education outlined in chapter 3; the other, the French system of research discussed briefly in chapter 1. The French had to figure out ways to overcome these systemic weaknesses before high-tech entrepreneurial networking could thrive.

Elitist engineering education

Within engineering education the elite from the *grandes écoles* of engineering, with a generalist (polyvalent) education, were separated from the graduates of the "lesser" schools, with a specialist education. The separation has produced a bizarre result for start-ups. It removes the most brilliant youth, those from the *grandes écoles*, from the pool of potential high-tech entrepreneurs and streams them into the civil service and management hierarchies of *la grande industrie*. Alain Fayolle, in *L'Ingénieur-Entrepreneur Français*, writes:

One constant to underline is the determinant role of the school of origin. It appears that there is a clear opposition between the *grandes écoles d'ingénieurs* that educate the future directors of large public and private firms and the other schools of engineering. The *grandes écoles* of engineering form, in fact, constituent bodies that permanently feed the system. For the engineers who are not able to integrate themselves into this system, the access to a top position is considerably reduced (Fayolle, 1999a, p. 94).

A member of the staff at the Ecole Polytechnique, the grandest of the *grandes écoles*, is on record as saying: "The vocation of the school is to educate people for entry into the *grands corps d'état* (mines, bridges, telecommunications and armaments) or to gain access into the engineering schools of application, but not to educate entrepreneurs" (Fayolle, 1999a, pp. 83–84). G. Ribeill, in an article published fifteen years before Fayolle's book, describes the situation aphoristically: "The entrepreneurial propensity of engineers is inversely related to the fame of the schools from which they come" (Ribeill, 1984, p. 89).

This posed no disadvantage for start-up activity in ordinary industrial enterprises. Most of them required the specialized knowledge that the "lesser" engineering schools provided. Moreover, the specialist engineers had more hands-on experience and human relations skills compared to the aloof, self-conscious generalists from elite schools, which gives advantages to the specialists in a start-up environment. But high-tech start-ups need the most scientific and intellectually accomplished. A 1996 study, for example, showed that 63 percent of the high-tech start-up entrepreneurs in France had a bac+5 (master's) level of education.[3] The United States could draw on the milieu of the most gifted in Silicon Valley, at Stanford and Berkeley, and along Route 128 outside Boston, at MIT. The German start-up enterprise could tap talent from *Technische Hochschulen* at Aachen, Munich, Karlsruhe, Dresden and Berlin. Because graduates of the elite French engineering schools were not entrepreneurial, the pool of potentially exploitable engineering talent available for high-tech start-ups diminished in France.

A scattered, mainly exclusive research system

The scientific research system is the second aspect of the French heritage that hindered entrepreneurship. Since the engineers from the *grandes écoles* ran the *grands corps d'etat*, they assumed that the state could best manage the resources of the country. Inasmuch as the universities recruited less accomplished people, they could not be relied upon, in the judgment of the *grandes-écoles*-educated elites that ran the country, to fill elite functions. No function seemed more important to them than scientific research. And so the French leaders from *grandes écoles* organized a research system that ignored the universities. Philippe Mustar and Philippe Laredo, from the Ecole des Mines (Paris), put it this way: "[The creation of the CNRS in 1939 was] justified by the weak state of university research at the time" (Laredo and Mustar, 2002, p. 60). This might have been true, but policy makers had a choice. They could have set up a "a project-funded agency, in the style of the Anglo-Saxon 'research councils,'" that left research largely in the hands of universities (the triple helix) and then pump a lot of money into the French university research labs, or they could have set up "public research institutions, employing professional researchers," which would thrust the universities aside. They made the second choice with the creation of the CNRS and "developed the model of the full-time professional researcher," setting aside the "university model, which entails the dual activities of teaching and research" (Laredo and Mustar, 2002, p. 60). Moreover, the various government agencies (forestry, fisheries, food and health safety, etc.) developed their own research structures, which gained "degrees of autonomy in the form of government laboratories. These public research institutions adopted the CNRS model of

[3] SOFARIS, 1996, quoted in Fayolle, 1999a, p. 70.

recruitment of researchers at a young age (following postgraduate study) by discipline-specific committees, based on academic career criteria" (p. 62).

Thus, in France public research after the war mainly went on in institutions outside the universities. To the extent that research still occurred in schools it was scattered about like the educational institutions themselves. The *grandes écoles* of engineering developed their own scientific research laboratories, by far the most important of which was the Ecole Supérieure des Mines, Paris. The *écoles supérieures de commerce*, institutionally isolated, had limited contact with scientific research laboratories. University laboratories still did important research but under the tutelage of the CNRS. It, ostensibly in order to reinforce university research, organized a partnership scheme in the late 1960s between "CNRS personnel and university groups on the basis of periodic evaluations by committees" (Laredo and Mustar 2002, p. 62). The "associated CNRS-university research teams" that the partnership created became an increasingly important aspect of university research, which gained steadily in significance. When CNRS researcher partners moved in partnership into university laboratories, however, the arrangement led to the separation of "teaching departments" in universities from "research structures" – the very reverse of what happened in the German *Wissenschaft* tradition.

This is a distinction worth stressing, and French critics of their system emphasize it. Jean-Michel Yolin points out how the German universities combined teaching with industrial research in the Fraunhofer and Steinbeis Institutes.

They are directed by professors teaching in schools that are the equivalent of our *grandes écoles*; they work in close cooperation on their projects with firms, particularly the *Mittelstand* (small and medium-sized firms); and they have a 'light' structure of senior researchers, which embraces numerous teams of quality, composed of Ph.D. students and postdocs who will continue their careers afterwards as a natural course in industry (Yolin, 1997, p. 14).

The educational structure of the French engineering schools limited student access to their research laboratories. The research emphasis on fundamental science at the CNRS produced structures that were incompatible with industry-related projects. Yolin complains that Robert Chabbal's attempt in the late 1970s to create a department of engineering science in the CNRS never really succeeded. Placing it in laboratories preoccupied with basic research rather than economic innovation neutralized it. The CNRS and the Atomic Energy Agency had aging permanent research staffs, a low turnover rate in researchers, and poor connections with small and medium-sized firms.

The career researcher thus predominated throughout both the state and the university laboratory structure. This system worked well during the *trentes glorieuses*, the era of big projects (telecommunications, atomic energy, aerospace, etc.). Inasmuch as the system neglected the needs of small and medium-sized firms and start-up entrepreneurs, it became increasingly an object of criticism after 1980. The French interviewees mostly count among the critics. They call the people in the research laboratories *fonctionnaires*, by which they mean that they are career laboratory workers who cook up research projects without any concern for their applicability in industry; people without spirit or desire to exploit research commercially. And this says nothing about the effect that the separation of research from teaching had on entrepreneurialism amongst students in French higher education. The Beranger, Chabbal and Dambrine report, with reference to Fraunhofer Institutes, specifically notes the need in France to bring students in the engineering schools regularly into scientific laboratories (Beranger et al., 1998, p. 37).

From an entrepreneurial networking point of view, then, reformers faced three problems. First, something needed to be done about the detrimental effects that the division between research and teaching had on entrepreneurialism. Second, something needed to be done to entice the more brilliant students from the elite *grandes écoles* of engineering into high-tech start-up entrepreneurship. Third, something had to be done to overcome the detrimental effects that the separation of schools (the absence of horizontal contacts) had on networking. Little help in overcoming these problems could come, at least initially, from within the institutions themselves. People in research laboratories were not about to leave them abruptly to risk everything on entrepreneurial ventures. Graduates from the *grandes écoles* of engineering were not going to leave their prestige jobs in big firms to join the graduates from the lesser schools in start-up ventures. France is a country of entrenched self-interests and knows how to protect them. That is, no doubt, the source of the proverb *plus ça change* . . . The system had survived ruder shocks before. So, anybody concerned about reforming it had to leverage engineering education and research in some way from outside.

The agents of change: government and local initiatives

The French state government was the chief agent of change, but not the only player. As in Germany, reform had to come out of the life of the wider community. There exists an historical community in France that the state elite tends to denigrate. It exerts itself industrially and educationally, by creating useful institutions, when the agencies of the traditional state elite fail France. This happened in the aftermath of the Franco-Prussian War (1870–71), in the high-tech era of the second industrial revolution. Germany's electrical and chemical industries led this revolution. But certain areas in France developed the new technologies as well. This happened in the Alpine region, for instance, which became an aluminum/hydroelectric center. It also happened in Lorraine, where steel and electrical product industries grew. Since the education in the *grandes écoles* of engineering scarcely touched on the new technologies, the engineers in the *grands corps d'état* were not much help in their development. In order to get them – the needed specialist engineers – local businessmen, industrialists and educational officials together founded faculties of engineering studies in regional universities – for instance, at Grenoble and at Nancy. Thus, over a hundred years ago, local need and networking – not some state fiat from Paris – led to the creation of the first special schools of engineering in French universities (Laredo and Mustar, 2002, p. 69).

After 1980, in a nation beset with unemployment and industrial decay, facing the challenge of a new high-tech information revolution, the French state turned in partnership to regional authorities. The cooperation started with the Decentralization Act of 1982, which created regional councils. It continued with a law in 1984 that granted autonomy to universities. Regional research and innovation policies got a boost from the "unprecedented success of the [state's] experimental Community programs aimed at supporting the regions in the formulation of their own policies" (Laredo and Mustar, 2002, p. 69). The regional authorities needed no central government prodding. The experimental community programs, originally limited to twenty regions, "had to be extended because of pressure from regional executives." Meanwhile, the government created the Agence Nationale de Valorisation de la Recherche in 1974, which took over the resources (money, technical centers and the management) left over from the productivity missions financed under the Marshall Plan. By the mid-1980s ANVAR's chief activities focused on small and medium-sized businesses and regional development.

At the same time the state undertook fewer large programs. Some disappeared completely. France Télécom, with privatization, is an example. Reforms after 1980 reduced the state's financial control and dominance over science, education and industry. New partnerships developed not only between the regions and the central French state but also between the regions and the EEC, which gave the regions greater leverage in the formulation of educational and industrial policy and an ability to create effective networks among interested parties. With these developments, well could Mustar and Laredo talk about the progressive dismantling of the Colbertist state. "With regard to technology," their study concludes, "the state's capacity in the future will stem less from direct financial interventions (the central mode of intervention within the Colbertist model) than from its role of strategic impetus and anticipation, of evaluation of past action and of the promotion of public debate to promote common visions between innovation actors" (Laredo and Mustar, 2002, p. 69).

The reforming national and local governments, assemblies and civil servants confronted the high-tech entrepreneurial challenge. First, they had had, as in Germany, to realize that one existed. Mustar and Laredo note that the public research laboratories finally went to work for industry. Between 1983 and 1996 the number of contracts between the CNRS and industry multiplied tenfold, from a few hundred to around three thousand per year. But Joseph Orlinski of UTC observes that the *ingénieurs-doctorants* – the future researchers – remained too academic and wanted to work for big firms (Orlinski, 2002b). Putting them in large firms to do industrial research might make them slightly less academic, although that is doubtful, but it could not in itself turn them into entrepreneurs. Nor had the "firm nurseries" started in the Ecoles des Mines (e.g. at Douai, Alès and Saint-Etienne) during the 1980s come into existence to prompt high-tech start-ups. The national and local governments and the schools themselves sponsored them in order to fight a recession in the coal-mining regions, like the Germans at the time, by increasing the number of firms and decreasing unemployment. Only in 1992 did the public powers really start to emphasize the creation of high-tech innovative enterprises, after phenomenal Silicon Valley had drawn world attention to them. Then came a national campaign that brought the *assises d'innovation*, the gathering of prominent industrialists, educators, scientists, engineers, venture capitalists and civil servants at regional meetings and in Paris to consider what was to be done. The press and broadcast media took up the theme; there were round-table discussions on innovation. The government orchestrated the campaign, which it spiced with a series of policy declarations and laws designed to develop an entrepreneurial culture in the country. The French equivalent of the campaign that occurred simultaneously in the German Federal Republic, it culminated in the law on innovation at the century's end, which provided for national high-tech start-up competitions and for the establishment of thirty-one university-affiliated high-tech incubators (the so-called "Allègre incubators," named after the Minister of Education who led the campaign). Thus, government and notables used their powers to leverage change in the research establishment and in engineering education during this decade; but with what effect?

A transforming research system

At the national level, the ministries responsible for research, industry and defense opened up their programs through research grant contracts to high-tech start-ups. Mustar reports that one in three of the firms he surveyed that had been started by public laboratory researchers got contracts from these ministries, which helped them survive in the tough start-up years. The CNRS also changed. It expanded the CNRS-university mixed-research tie-ups to the point that, by 2000, ten new appointments occurred in university laboratories for each one in the CNRS laboratories. The number of researchers in university laboratories grew to some 45,000, as opposed to 14,000 CNRS researchers and engineer researchers – a proportion of four to one. The university laboratories ended with double the research potential of the CNRS. ANVAR progressively extended the range of its operations. On top of loans granted for innovative projects, it supported the contracts let by SMEs to ANVAR-approved research societies, and "the recruitment by SMEs of Ph.Ds. and qualified research engineers" (Laredo and Mustar, 2002, p. 65). Over 2,000 SMEs received ANVAR support yearly in the 1990s, and a quarter of them were new firms (in existence for less than three years). The government also used research tax credits to encourage the development of high-tech firms. In 1987 around 3,500 firms applied for the research tax credit; ten years later the number exceeded 7,000 every year, with reimbursements that amounted to F3 billion. That constituted twice as much money for SMEs as provided by ANVAR. The government employed non-financial procedures to help SMEs as well. These included aid from the Ministry of Industry (the "Atout" project) for the diffusion of techniques to SMEs. Local authorities, primarily the newly created regional councils, devoted an increasing proportion of their budgets to research and innovation. They, for example, provided assistance through job-creation grants to start-ups. CIFRE (the Conventions Industrielles de Formation par la Recherche) provided subsidies to firms in order to encourage them to hire young students for a period of three years to carry out research, with, according to Mustar, the correct expectation that these researchers would start firms. European Union policies, such as ESPRIT (in information technology) and RACE (Research and development in Advanced Communications for Europe), directly assisted French researchers to start up firms. One-fifth of Mustar's sample of successful firms had taken part in ESPRIT. It amounted to a major policy instrument, which brought firms into heterogeneous networks composed of participants from scientific research laboratories, technical research centers and industries. During the last decade of the twentieth century innovative state policy formulators created "a new kind of partnership" that brought "together universities, industries and local authorities to cooperate on the same [start-up] projects" (Mustar, 1997, p. 40). Other government policies had indirect high-tech start-up effects. Pierre Trémembert and Jean Le Traon, at the ENST, in Brittany, point out that it and its four sister institutions had done contract research for some time, but that up to 1997 the results of research at these schools of telecommunications remained the property of France Télécom. "After the separation of the ENSTs from the newly privatized telecommunications company, and the law on innovation that encouraged researchers to commercialize scientific results, relations with firms have become much more important" (Trémembert and Le Traon, 2002).

No doubt a reforming French research system fosters high-tech commercialization. But is it enough? In 1997 Mustar stated, "For the past ten years or so the creation of enterprises by researchers seems . . . to have reached . . . forty new firms born every year"

(Mustar, 1997, p. 39). Public researchers, principally from the CNRS, the Atomic Energy Agency, the National Computer and Automation Research Institute and university laboratories, started 28 percent of the new firms in biotechnology, 15 percent in computer science and software engineering, and 10 percent in opto-electronics. They worked in every region of France but mostly in greater Paris (Île-de-France) and in Provence-Alpes-Côte d'Azur. The firms would not have succeeded without constant financial support from the state and the European Union, but because of that Mustar does not conclude that public laboratory researchers are "mediocre entrepreneurs." On the contrary, he describes modern high-tech entrepreneurship as a complex team effort that succeeds when the entrepreneur knows how to exploit the network of research, government supports, markets and partnerships that the environment offers. After surveying 250 high-tech firms started by academic researchers, Mustar concludes that capable public research laboratory entrepreneurs skillfully set up and manage networks internal and external to their companies. "Typically, they have surrounded themselves with professionals in the field of management, finance and marketing for high-tech products, exploiting national and international networks efficiently" (Mustar, 1998, p. 217). Mustar asserts, too, that the reformed research system no longer necessarily separates teaching from research. He and Laredo point out that one Ph.D. thesis in every five is completed in engineering school research laboratories – an excellent result considering that these schools have only 6 percent of all teacher-researchers in France (Laredo and Mustar, 2002, p. 61). Beranger, Chabbal and Dambrine add that in the late 1990s the *écoles des mines* at Paris, Alès and Saint-Etienne began to offer instruction to their doctoral students on an option basis (a week's instruction in each of three years in Paris, a hundred hours over three years in Saint-Etienne, five days in an enterprise at Alès) to stimulate and instruct the Ph.D. students to learn how to achieve a start-up (Beranger et al., 1998, pp. 62–63).

Mustar's assertions invite response. The fusion of research with teaching, despite the progress, is still not typical of the French system. Normally students are not brought into contact with the entrepreneurial process in French research institutions. Although recently the public researcher's entrepreneurial performance has compared impressively with past achievements, it must be evaluated within an international context. Mustar states that none of the firms he tracked are real "success stories." Five years after their creation the surviving firms had, on average, three or four employees. The success criterion applied to firms in *The Silicon Valley Edge* is rapid growth from small-ness. Nor does the number of "successes" make a case for the commercial efficacy of public research laboratories. France's huge investment in them should have achieved a better return in start-up firms.

Entrepreneurship education at engineering schools

To be Americanized, French engineering schools would need to introduce entrepreneurship education. And they did – but primarily in the form of project work. It differs from that of the ESCs, which do project work too, for the project work in engineering schools is technical in nature. When high-tech project work results in start-ups, student coaching is needed, which normally requires the presence of a high-tech incubator where non-technical services can be secured. French engineering schools could have been doing projects for industry for a long time without having developed networking start-up skills. During the first phase of their existence (the 1970s and 1980s) incubators were managed by chambers of commerce (e.g. Novacité in Lyon), which had a limited interest in fomenting high-tech start-ups. Rarely did these incubators, as Beranger, Chabbal and Dambrine observe, "transform the local industrial fabric to the point where it became a center for the accelerated development of innovative enterprises" (Beranger et al., 1998, p. 58). Success for entrepreneurial education in engineering schools demanded the establishment of close networking between project teams of engineering schools and the newly created high-tech incubators.

Among French engineering schools there were pioneers in entrepreneurship networking. People usually mention the *écoles des mines* at Douai, Alès and Saint-Etienne in this regard. Philippe Albert names them all as the first in France to have had incubators. But, because they were small schools, they were not the important innovators. A better example of an innovator is Promotech, an incubator created in the 1980s by the universities and schools of engineering at Nancy.[4] Promotech created more firms by far than the mining schools.[5] It continued the creative educational tradition of the entire region.

[4] Discussed in Beranger et al., 1998.
[5] At Douai, for example, there were thirteen firms in ten years; at Promotech 180 in the same timeframe.

Too much should not be read into beginnings. The numbers involved in entrepreneurship education were few everywhere in the early years. At the Ecole Centrale de Paris, for example, the school had a coaching program in entrepreneurship for fifteen years, but during the first ten of them only four or five students participated yearly. The number jumped to twenty per year in the late 1990s. "Pressure from the government, students, and the media," Gallouin explains, "and consciousness of retardation vis-à-vis the USA" were the causes (Gallouin, 2002). The same rapid expansions occurred in other schools. At Nîmes an incubator opened in 1998 (EERIE – Ecole pour les Etudes et la Recherche en Informatique et Electronique), presenting far greater opportunities than before for nearby Alès engineering students on start-up projects. Promotech at Nancy expanded when the new high-tech incubator opened at the technical park Nancy-Brabois in the late 1990s. Entrepreneurship education did not expand steadily over fifteen years; it came suddenly in the last five years of the 1990s.

Government reformers often took the United States as a point of reference. Schools of engineering did, too. American engineering schools eagerly hawked their entrepreneurship programs. Alain Fayolle remarks that US institutions such as MIT at the round-table discussion of "le monde des *écoles des ingénieurs*" showed "how they do it" (Fayolle, 2002a). French engineering schools also consulted American high-tech programs when making up their own. Joseph Orlinski, who came to UTC in 1998 specifically to "dynamize the entrepreneurial education of engineers," examined the programs at MIT and Carnegie-Mellon (Orlinski, 2002b). Christian Schmitt at INPL consulted the program at MIT. Beranger, Chabbal and Dambrine extolled the American pedagogy. They observed that MIT, Stanford and Wisconsin, in their entrepreneurship study programs, brought engineering students to visit famous start-up firms located in neighboring high-tech habitats. Dominique Frugier at the Ecole Centrale de Lille comments that the new diploma "ingénieur-entrepreneur," recently approved by the ministry, was based on MIT's (Frugier, 2002). The engineering school teaches it jointly with the business school (ESC Lille).

American influence need not be exaggerated. The engineers knew perfectly well about the entrepreneurship programs in France, frequently citing "HEC entrepreneurs" and EM Lyon. And they occasionally mentioned the Dutch program at Twente, and the work in Fraunhofer institutes. But French engineering schools probably learned more from US engineering school programs than from project work in the French commercial schools, because engineers had to find out how an engineering school handled projects, and French schools of engineering had no projects comparable to those in American schools of engineering. Reformers in the *écoles de commerce*, by contrast, could draw on entrepreneurship study programs in their pioneering sister institutions.

Since entrepreneurship education in engineering schools amounts to project work, its progress depends on networking in the greater environment. This requires high-tech incubators. Good study programs also depend on effective networking. Even an apparently simple subject such as *sensibilisation* demanded it. These entrepreneurship stimulation "actions" lasted mostly for half a day, sometimes less. By 1998 80 percent of the engineering schools responding to Fayolle's poll said that they had stimulation programs, but 70 percent of them had had them only for two years. Their effectiveness depended on the quality of the stimulators. That Beranger, Chabbal and Dambrine understood when commenting about the usefulness of the American visits to local start-up firms in high-tech centers. If the area lacked high-tech firms or the school had poor contacts with them, then the stimulation program would not work. Thus, even though 80 percent of the schools had programs, effective ones only really occurred in high-tech areas.

The same is true of engineering school programs that offer *specialization* in entrepreneurship. In Fayolle's poll 18.7 percent of the engineering schools had them. This meant that over 80 percent of the schools had no entrepreneurship project programs for their students. They can be left out of the analysis. The effectiveness of the 18.7 percent varied according to the size and nature of their networking environments.

There are schools that identify with the concept of the engineer-entrepreneur. The best known is the *école des mines* at Alès, which has committed itself to being the first "engineer-entrepreneur" school in France. It structures education accordingly. All students on entering are put into contact immediately with the CEO of a firm. They are obliged to participate over a six-month period in a start-up simulation exercise. Much of their study time is devoted to electives. Students can also choose to work on a start-up project. They are permitted to take sabbaticals in order to work on projects or to pursue their studies elsewhere (an MBA in the United States, for example). The school entered into partnership with "HEC entrepreneurs" to structure a pedagogy that gives the student *le goût d'entreprendre*. More entrepreneurially oriented studies in an engineering school could scarcely be found. If French schools of engineering were ranked in terms of entrepreneurship process study programs, Mines-Alès would rank number one.

By contrast, the Ecoles des Mines (Paris) has a modest program in entrepreneurship. Although in 1997 it started "l'acte de l'entreprendre," the program is not obligatory. Each student who elects to join works on a project of his/her choice under the guidance of a tutor. There is no grade for the project at the end, no sanctions for failure or awards for success, and the student's regular program is not reduced. If "l'acte de l'entreprendre" were to be rated as an entrepreneurship study program, it would certainly rank far below that of Mines-Alès.

But, in terms of entrepreneurship effectiveness, the two schools' ranking would be inverted. It is a question of networking versus entrepreneurship studies again. The Ecole des Mines d'Alès's entrepreneurial hinterland is restricted. Its program, even with the new incubator in Nîmes, has only created thirteen start-up firms in recent years. The Ecole Supérieure des Mines in Paris is the premier school of engineering in France, with access to the best incubators in the country and a vast network to tap. Eighteen percent of the high-tech start-ups came from the laboratories of the *grandes écoles* of engineering, most of them from Mines-Paris (Laredo and Mustar, 2001).

It is not necessary, therefore, in a chapter on networking to describe the programs that the schools of engineering have recently developed in France. Most are variations on the same theme: project work on start-ups carried out with a tutor in liaison with an incubator. The scope of the programs has grown everywhere in the past few years because of the new incubators the government helps fund and the annual business start-up competitions it supports. The issue here is not programs but the patterns of networking in which the programs are enmeshed. The engineering schools' involvement in this networking has grown strikingly in some regions in the past few years. Here are some representative examples of this development.

In Picardy, at Compiègne, president François Peccoud of the university of technology is the principal agent of change. Created in 1973, following an "American model," this university operates on the semester system with diplomas granted on the basis of credit units accumulated by course. The school provides a general cultural education for engineers at the first-degree level and undergraduate and graduate training, including research doctorates. From its origins, moreover, it has sought to integrate the school into the business and industrial community (Orlinski, 2002a). It has done this through networking. According to Michel Cordonnier, director of the school's enterprise relations, the school has two off-campus agencies that work to this effect. One, Gradient, is an association of UTC researchers. It signs hundreds of research contracts with firms and is active in patenting. The second, Divergent, which UTC researchers started in 1987, is an industrial training and consultant agency. It has a staff of thirty and a network of 150 consultants (Cordonnier, 2002).

In the mid-1990s, Peccoud intensified support for activities that add value to knowledge through its commercialization. He was a principal behind the organization of a regional venture capital firm (SECANT). ANVAR, the regional council, a number of local banks and branches of national ones, and the University of Picardy Jules Verne all support this firm. Orlinski, who organized "dynamique entreprendre" at UTC, did not establish it as a degree program but concentrated on start-up project work and coaching. The program plugged into Gradient, Divergent, and SECANT. The project carriers work in UTC and in regional incubators. In the national competitions to aid in the creation of technologically innovative enterprises, UTC deposited thirty-four of the 150 dossiers presented for Picardy and garnered nineteen of the province's twenty-five prizes. Since 1997 UTC has created twenty-two new firms; since 1990 one hundred (Orlinski, 2002b). This is a splendid record for a university that was overlooked in the 1997 Beranger, Chabbal and Dambrine report about the state of entrepreneurship education in French schools of engineering.

In Lorraine the schools of engineering coordinated their start-up networking primarily through Promotech. By the late 1990s it had become a Centre Européen d'Entreprise et d'Innovation (CEEI) with a multifaceted program. It had an incubator, a high-tech *pépinière* (incubator) situated in the technology park at Nancy-Brabois, and a system of education for future entrepreneurs in which all institutions of higher education in Nancy could participate, including the engineering schools of the INPL. Promotech's educational modules covered the entire start-up process: stimulation, training on how to begin a firm, the development of a business plan, and its implementation and follow-up. The incubator specialized in the preparation of business plans, and students benefited from the counsel of Promotech's permanent staff, with a network of over 200 specialists. The students also had access to laboratories and other facilities. About thirty business plans were prepared yearly, with fifteen to twenty-five turning into start-up firms. The incubator was also open to projects from local small and medium-sized businesses that wished to launch an innovative project based on their own ideas. About half of the start-up entrepreneurs came from the universities, the others from praxis. About half of the start-ups moved to the high-tech *pépinière*, where they received further coaching. Promotech organized its own start-up competition "Entreprendre" with the support of Nancy's urban community and other nearby communities. Eighty-eight projects entered the competition of 1998, seventy of them from the INPL. The schools also participated in other competitions – i.e. "sinergie," the "boutique de gestion" and the "1-2-3 go" business initiative of McKinsey. Local agencies supported the efforts. The regional council of Lorraine provided a scholarship of FF17,000 for each firm during its incubation period, and capital was available from SARL (up to FF200,000) for the later phases.

In the north, long-term efforts to rehabilitate an old industrial region culminated in a concerted community effort to create high-tech incubators. The first was founded in 1990, and by 1997 the region had a dense network of incubators and a group of business angels and venture capitalists that regularly visit the engineering school and university laboratories (Frugier, 2002). But the business incubators did not focus sufficiently on high technology, so in 1997 a group led by Jean-Pierre Debourse, ESC Lille, created the Centre Frederick Kuhlmann (CFK), a high-tech incubator. Although situated at the ESC, the CFK works in partnership with regional engineering schools, university laboratories, the CNRS, the Pasteur Institute and organs devoted to the creation of firms, i.e. Nord Entreprendre, ANVAR and the regional council of Nord and Pas-de-Calais. The CFK is a reception center, a secretariat, an Internet contact point and a source of help in the preparation of market studies and engineering and commercial projects. In less than a year's operation it launched six new high-tech firms. Since a business school is behind this high-tech movement, the most interesting aspect of the story, from our perspective, is the collaboration between the engineering and business schools. During the start-up boom of 1998, ESC Lille, EC Lille and ENSAIT put together a common program for the teaching of entrepreneurship and the creation of enterprises.

The regions described so far are in the northern and eastern parts of the country. Regions elsewhere could be included; indeed, some even better known for their entrepreneurism have not been covered. Greater Lyon and greater Grenoble are good examples. EM Lyon's work with EC Lyon and other regional engineering schools, including Ecole des Mines-St-Etienne, breached the barrier between the two types of schools in the same way as the cooperation between ESC and EC Lille did. The project work that Alain Fayolle and his colleagues are doing at the INPG is of the same order. The INPG, in partnership with UCLA's Anderson School of Management, started the Hall de l'Entrepreneuriat Technologique, which supports the creation of firms with a global reach. The list could be extended – to the strong project coaching at the Ecole Nationale de Télécommunication, Bretagne, for example. But, as in the German case, there is no need to analyze networking in every region of the country. Each story is unique and, therefore, different, but the patterns of networking are familiar because they are similar to those already presented.

Two regions, however, should not be overlooked, because they produce the most high-tech start-ups in France. One is the Île-de-France. Greater Paris concentrates the most prestigious schools, consultants, venture capitalists, civil servants, politicians and scientific talents in France. The *grandes écoles* of engineering, and the science faculties in universities, with proper networking, should create a powerful high-tech start-up culture. The example of the Ecole des Mines (Paris) has been cited, and it is an important one. But the *grandes écoles* of engineering, including Mines-Paris, were not particularly innovative in entrepreneurship programs. Perhaps the charge against them is correct: that their graduates desire and are destined for the boardrooms of big corporations and top civil service posts. The excitement of starting up a great high-tech firm could stir the imaginations of the few but not of the many. There is one exception: the Ecole Centrale. It is a private school that has produced many of France's great civil engineers. The school's interest in entrepreneurship, Gallouin states, "centered on creation, not management" (Gallouin, 2002). It did not start entrepreneurship courses but expanded its project-coaching program at the end of the 1990s. The innovative aspect of the EC's program stemmed from its interdisciplinarity and interinstitutionality. The EC invested in an incubator, Paris Biotech, along with ESSEC, INSERM and the University of Paris V. It agreed in 2001 with ESSEC to develop common coaching arrangements for their students and also for the establishment of an adult teaching program on entrepreneurship called "catalisateur". And its project carriers entered into the national high-tech start-up competition, ESSEC's competition and those of several associations too ("réseau entrepreneurs," "entretien européen de la technologie," etc.).

The second high-tech region is centered on the technology park Sophia Antipolis. At its origins it was technological but not entrepreneurial. This changed after 1993/94, when Bernasconi spent the year in Silicon Valley. Sophia Antipolis entered a period of high-tech involvement, concentrating on telecommunications, electronics and software engineering. Sophia Antipolis reoriented its strategy to high-tech start-up finance (venture capital) and information technologies. New scientific and technical groups moved into the park: ESSI (Ecole Supérieure en Sciences Informatiques), ESINSA (l'Ecole Supérieure d'Ingénieurs de Nice Sophia Antipolis) and the Eurecom Institute. A new business incubator, CICI, and a group underwritten by the chamber of commerce and industry, Pôles de Compétence Technologique, supported them. The number of high-tech start-ups multiplied in the last two years of the decade to the point where Sophia Antipolis created about a hundred new firms a year, almost one every three days, many of them fast-growing. The business incubator and Pôles de Compétence Technologique furnished the professional coaching, and well-developed business angel and venture capital networks provided the money. CERAM in Sophia Antipolis surfed this wave and contributed to its force. It created entrepreneurship courses for scientists and engineers, and it brought in Philippe Albert – from EM Lyon – and Carole Cohen, who specialized in the management of innovation. Its ambition was not just to be another school of entrepreneurship on the margin of the technical world, but to be part of it. Being "part of it" meant belonging to a group involved in the advanced education of management and technology. This required not only mutual tolerance between engineering schools and schools of commerce but the absorption of both into networks of high-tech entrepreneurship. Sophia Antipolis, because of its success, has probably come closer to this fusion than any other place in France.

Means to ends

Some aspects of German and French entrepreneurship networking are similar. In both countries governments responded to phenomenal Silicon Valley by intensifying their support for high-tech start-ups, with

quite similar programs. Moreover, they started these efforts at about
the same time. But the evidence that is accumulating indicates that the
results are not the same. The BMBF cites, because it is favorable to it,
the results of the *Global Entrepreneurship Monitor* surveys for 1999
and 2000. In 1999 Germany ranked sixth among ten industrial countries on the *Global Entrepreneurship Monitor* entrepreneurship index
and France ranked number eight. The next year Germany's ranking
jumped to number three on the list, far behind number one (the United
States) and number two (Canada), but still number three. France fell
to number nine, just ahead of Japan. Although Germany's position
improved, the results were not a good omen for France's efforts to stimulate entrepreneurial activity. Another study provides more pointed evidence since it deals with student populations. In 2000 IFO Gallup-JE
HEC conducted a poll of students in several countries. To the question
"Have you received or are you receiving training in the creation of
enterprises?" 14 percent of the French responded "Yes," but 41 percent of the Germans responded to the same question in the affirmative.
That is a sizable difference.

There is a third study, cited above, carried out by the Fraunhofer
ISI as a follow-up on BMBF's EXIST programs, the results of which
can be explored (Görisch et al., 2002). EXIST wanted to know the
effectiveness of their programs. The Fraunhofer ISI people asked students in eleven *Hochschulen* located in EXIST regions about their feel-
ings toward entrepreneurship. The responses divided into three groups:
(1) not interested; (2) interested; and (3) potential entrepreneur. The
distinction between (2) and (3) depended on a number of criteria –
e.g. age, experience and the stage of the respondent's education. Then
the students were asked if they had taken part in a university "action"
or start-up course and how many times. The answers are presented in
table 5.2.

Thus, of the potential entrepreneurs, over half had participated in
an action or start-up course.

Although there is nothing comparable in France to this EXIST survey,
a recent ministerial proposal for new laws on innovation indicates that
governmental entrepreneurial actions may not have been very effective. The introductory remarks (December 2002), announcing a government poll, made the following points. Efforts to raise the number of
patents had failed. Despite laws and decrees issued between 1996 and
2001, giving researchers property rights in their research results, the

Table 5.2 *Results of EXIST*

EXIST results (in percentages of interviewed students)			
Subjects studied	Potential entrepreneurs	Interested	Not interested
Economic and social science	12.5	23.0	64.2
Engineering	9.4	29.0	61.6
Participation in *Hochschul* "action" or start-up course			
Economic and social science			
No	47.3	78.2	81.2
Once	22.6	17.0	12.9
More than once	30.1	4.8	5.9
Engineering			
No	52.0	84.8	90.4
Once	22.0	10.7	6.7
More than once	26.0	4.5	2.9

Source: Görisch et al., 2002.

researchers were not applying for patents. There had actually been a decline in the French share of patents issued, as a percentage of world patents, from 8.4 percent in 1990 to 7.2 percent in 1999. The survey's introduction also complained about the failure of the SAICs, which had been authorized in the 1999 law on innovations. SAICs in public research institutes were supposed to group all industry research activities so as to manage them better. After a year only six had been created. The document also lamented that not enough start-ups had come out of the national start-up competitions and that technology transfer was not being executed well. But it suggested waiting on the latter point, before deciding on remedies, until an audit had been made of best practices in the United States and the rest of Europe. The document is not very happy reading for those who have striven educationally to promote a start-up culture in France.

These surveys are different, and they have not been conducted with the problematic of this study in mind. But their results suggest that the German programs generally have had greater success in stimulating entrepreneurial interest than have the French. But does this mean that the Germans policies and programs were better than French? Every policy must be measured in terms of its ability to meet objectives. If the obstacles to it are so great, however, that almost any policy would fail, then policy or programs cannot be blamed for lack of success. Blame for failure must be sought elsewhere. In their attempts to induce a start-up culture in the two countries, the Germans and French confronted populations similar in their outlooks on entrepreneurship. But the French educational heritage had more obstacles to change built into it than the German. This might better explain the slower going for French reforms than the policies and programs themselves.

6 | The Czech Republic: an arrested development

A mixed heritage

THE Czech Republic is a young country but in an old historical region. In modern European history Bohemia formed part of the Austro-Hungarian Empire, which collapsed in defeat in 1918. It broke into several ethnically diverse countries. One of them, Czechoslovakia, had no historical roots as a nation, its two main peoples having less than love for each other. The country lasted twenty years until it was effectively disarmed in the Munich Agreement between four powers (Germany, Italy, France and the United Kingdom) and then partitioned, after Hitler broke the pact and invaded the Czech lands in March 1939. Bohemia was absorbed into the Third Reich and Slovakia became a Nazi protectorate. Restored in 1945, Czechoslovakia fell behind the Iron Curtain after the *coup d'état* of 1948, where it remained until the revolutions of 1989 ended Communism in Eastern Europe. Then, in 1993, the Czechs and Slovaks split apart to form two separate nations.

Because it stayed behind the Iron Curtain for over forty years, the Americanization of higher management education in the Czech Republic is, compared with France and Germany, a very recent development. After 1989 the same forces that had been transforming Western Europe for the last half-century exerted themselves in Eastern Europe. But everything arrived on the doorstep of the Czech Republic at once: democracy, privatization, capitalism, the market system, educational reform, banking reform, management education and entrepreneurship studies. They arrived because the old system had failed and because the Czechs were seeking to join the EU and to gain admittance to the world economic order. This meant that they had choices in their transformation – but restricted choices, since they had to meet the demands of others to gain acceptance. Within the swirl of claims and choices, the Czechs had to figure out the importance of phenomenal Silicon Valley and to recognize the challenge of high-tech entrepreneurship education. This chapter describes how well they have managed this daunting task in ten short years.

Again, some preliminary comment needs to be made about sources. Articles, books and others printed materials have been utilized to carry out the investigation. As for the French and German chapters, moreover, various interested parties have been interviewed. These experts have been drawn from contiguous fields, ranging from those concerned with the promotion of new venture creation and innovation to those in small business and management education. The nineteen people who agreed to an interview are listed in table 6.1. All the interviews were personal. If cited, the interviewees are referred to as in the footnote.[1]

Since, with one or two exceptions, people were not directly concerned with entrepreneurship studies because they have not yet been established in the Czech Republic, they could not be asked about entrepreneurship programs and how they started. Therefore, they were asked – depending on their field of knowledge – about reactions to Silicon Valley in the Czech Republic; about the support for entrepreneurship, especially high-tech entrepreneurship, in their country since the "Velvet Revolution"; about reforms in business education; about the possibilities of high-tech entrepreneurship studies being introduced into their institutions and in the Czech Republic in general; and about academic involvement in entrepreneurial networking. Table 6.2 reproduces the questionnaire presented to interviewees.

Educational background

Although the Communist hiatus is significant to this history of the Czech transformation, so is the pre-Communist historical background. Bohemia has been economically prosperous and industrially important in Central Europe for centuries. Part of that success can be attributed to educational prowess. The oldest university in Central Europe was founded in Prague in 1348; another was added at Olmouc in 1566. When neighboring Prussia and Saxony started creating *Technische*

---

[1] Boráková, 2002; Chaloupka, 2002; Chaloupka and Kameníková, 2002; Jedlicková et al. 2002; Komárek, 2002b; Komárek, 2003; Korab, 2002; Kreim, 2002; Malý, 2002; Mandiková, 2002; Mikoláš and Ludvík, 2003; Němcová, 2003; Rotgeri, 2002; and Vávra, 2002.

Table 6.1 *List of interviewees in the Czech Republic*

Interviews of new business experts and management academics in the Czech Republic		
Name of interviewee	Institution	Date of interview
Tatána Boráková	Czech Management Institute, Prague	December 4, 2002
Jaroslav Chaloupka	Science and Technology Park Association of the Czech Republic and Business and Innovation Center, Brno	December 5 and 6, 2002
Petra Jedlicková	On-line magazine IKAROS	December 12, 2002
Lucie Kameníková	Business and Innovation Center, Brno	December 6, 2002
Pavel Komárek	Business and Innovation Center at the Czech Technical University, Prague	December 5, 2002 and January 17, 2003
Prof. Dr. Vojtech Korab	Management faculty at the Technical University, Brno	December 6, 2002
Roman Kreim	Masaryk Institute of Advanced Studies, Czech Technical University, Prague	December 3, 2002
Peter R. Loewenguth	President of CMC Graduate School of Business	January 15, 2003
Doc. Ing. Ladislav Ludvík	Economic faculty, Technical University, Ostrava	January 16, 2003
Prof. Dr. Milan Malý	Prague International Business School	April 25, 2002
Miroslava Mandiková	National Training Fund	December 2 and 5, 2002
Doc. Ing. Zdenek Mikoláš	Economic faculty, Technical University, Ostrava	January 16, 2003
Kristýna Montfortová	CMC Graduate School of Management	January 15, 2003
Doc. Ing. Lidmila Němcová	University of Economics, Prague	January 14, 2003
Filip Rotgeri	ARP	December 12, 2002
Ivana Sládková	National Training Fund	December 5, 2002
Luboš Vávra	ARP	December 2, 2002

Hochschulen, so did the Bohemians and Moravians. The founding of two technical universities (at Prague in 1806 and at Brno in 1849), a school of mines in Ostrava (in 1849), and a school of chemical engineering in Prague (in 1920) permitted the kingdom to participate in the more scientifically demanding phases of industrialization in the late nineteenth and early twentieth centuries. Inter-war Czechoslovakia also, following events in Germany, established the Advanced Institute

Table 6.2 *Interview questionnaire for the Czech Republic*

	Interview questionnaire
Group of interviewees	*Questions*
Agencies promoting new venture creation and innovation	1. When did entrepreneurship (together with the information revolution and Silicon Valley) become a "hot topic" in the Czech Republic? 2. When was your organization founded, and what does it do exactly? 3. Which organizations started when to promote new firm creation, and how? 4. When were the first technology parks and incubators introduced in the Czech Republic, and by whom? 5. Who is organizing business plan competitions, and since when? 6. Who is involved in entrepreneurship education in the Czech Republic?
University SME and entrepreneurship chairs	1. How has entrepreneurship education developed at your institution? (Who introduced it, when and why? Which education has been offered in the course of time?) 2. Which schools/programs served as a reference point and in which way (exemplary programs, visits abroad, teaching material)? 3. How have relations with business, especially with start-ups and venture capitalists, been organized (conferences, business plan competitions, technology parks, incubators)? 4. What obstacles have stood in the way of the development of entrepreneurship studies (at your institution, in the Czech Republic in general, future challenges to entrepreneurship as a field of study and as a field of research)? 5. How do Czech entrepreneurship studies compare to American studies?
Providers of management education	1. How has management education developed at your institution? 2. What have been the main innovations during this development? 3. Which role has the international dimension played? 4. Has entrepreneurship education been integrated into the program? If yes, when and why? 5. Have you been taking part in business plan competitions? 6. Are you related to an incubator or technology park? 7. What are the most important concerns/problems/challenges at the moment and the near future?

of Commerce in Prague in 1919, where students could learn the new commercial sciences that mirrored the German BWL model. The republic also established an extensive in-company training program (Bata), which trained some 20,000 people between 1930 and 1950. The Czech system of higher education identified with that of the German-language area, which could be expected since German trade and cultural influences dominated at the time throughout Central and Eastern Europe and Scandinavia, and nineteenth-century Germans were great educational innovators. Hitler closed the Czechoslovak universities in November 1939; they were restored briefly in 1945, then Sovietized after 1948. But the point is that the Czechs, by the outbreak of World War II, possessed a rich educational heritage in commerce and engineering.

When the educational system fell under the control of a Communist dictatorship, how it changed depended on what it was allowed to deliver and what demands were made on it. According to Marxist-Leninist principles, "small-scale production brings capitalism closer, each day, each hour" (Matusiak, 2003). Therefore, the Communists based the economy on large scale industrial enterprise, run by a bureaucracy that was by its nature not entrepreneurial but loyal to higher authorities. They left the service sector underdeveloped, and there was a scarcity of small industrial firms. In 1949 all faculties and schools of economics were closed, to be replaced by the new Institute for Political and Economic Sciences. In 1950 the Higher Education Act ended academic freedom as well as the autonomy of educational institutions. Schools were controlled through dogmatism and the educational minions of the local bureaucracy. In 1953 the Institute for Political and Economic Sciences created the University of Economics out of its economic division. Its textbooks and curricula came from Moscow, and its aspiring professors were sent there for training. Inasmuch as the University of Economics replaced the old Advanced Institute of Commerce that had been founded in 1919, it was clear that there was no longer a place in any of this for business economics à la BWL and management studies à l'Américaine, which served capitalist enterprises and the market system.

In 1961 the University of Economics brought forth a new creation, the Institute of Economic Planning in Prague (later renamed the Leadership Faculty), to train the managers needed in the "big state firm" economy. It offered a three-year leadership and economic planning curriculum to students. The program covered political economy, Marxist philosophy, scientific Communism, the history of the Communist Party and the international workers' movement, the history of economics, the world economy, economic planning, the theory of leadership, finance, accounting, mathematics, the theory of statistics, optimal programming, fundamentals of data processing, law, economic psychology and sociology, and Russian (Dvorák, 1994, p. 149). The first part of the curriculum reflected what the political system wanted: political conformity and obedience to established doctrine. That would be useless knowledge after 1990. But there were elements of learning in the education that had a ring of modernity. Accounting, mathematics, the theory of statistics, optimal programming, and the fundamentals of data processing could all serve economic planners in government offices and large capitalist firms after 1989 as well as they had the Communist managers in state ministries.

Ostensibly, technical education should have been handled less ideologically. Technical universities were all retained and a new one founded at Liberec in 1953. Nonetheless, Communism shaped science and engineering education in three ways. First, it affected student selection. The children of workers received special points when applying for entry. This removed bright "bourgeois" students from the entry classes, especially during the earlier years of the regime. Later the policy was abandoned. Second, the state monies for scientific research went to the Academy of Sciences, not to the universities; they were supposed to prepare enthusiastic young socialists – not researchers. Third, the Communist trade bloc Comecon (the Council for Mutual Economic Assistance) failed to keep pace with world economic developments. The high-tech industries suffered both from this lack of demand for new products and services and the absence of industrially oriented research facilities in the technical universities and university science faculties. Backwardness intensified, too, because of the West's embargo on high-tech exports. Innovation in key fields and industries suffered – electronics, robotics and computer sciences – in terms of world standards. This relative retardation had repercussions after 1989, because the Czech industries that provided high-tech products to the Soviet defense industry found themselves hard-pressed to operate in the – for them – new, highly competitive world markets.

But these negative comments must be modulated. If Czech high-tech enterprise had trouble competing internationally after 1990, precocious Czech scientists who had worked for Tesla Roznov (the firm that supplied semiconductors to the Soviet Union's distribution system for forty years) or had done research in the Institute of Mathematical Machines were highly trained programmers and computer engineers. And highly prized: witness Motorola's dispatch to recruit them into the firm shortly after the "Velvet Revolution." Czech engineers and scientists under Communism may not have fully appreciated the entrepreneurial dimension of Silicon Valley's accomplishment, but the science and technology had not escaped their notice. In the 1980s the engineering schools had begun to emphasize them. The fact that there was an "enormous amount of computing and information-technology talent" in the Czech Republic in the 1990s is to some extent the inherited consequence (Korff, 2000). Moreover, some progress – if unsteady – had also been made in management education. In the 1950s students took management in the faculties of economics in the technical universities. The subject was eliminated in the early 1960s, then restored during the Prague Spring, with the establishment of the Institute of Management. It provided post-experience management education for managers in state enterprises.

With this legacy, Czechoslovakia in 1989 faced a new economic and industrial dawn. The challenge encompassed much more than ridding the country of a foreign-imposed Communist despotism; it also involved building a new industrial future in a competitive world context. In confronting this task, the Czechs had a lot of solicited, unsolicited and sometimes conflicting Western advice. But two things seemed certain: (1) the totalitarian central command economy, which had robbed them of their freedom and prosperity, had to go; and (2) US democracy coupled with managerial capitalism set the historical example of success. The exuberant, proselytizing, freedom-loving, self-confident Americans loudly proclaimed it. Aside from opening society to liberalism and democracy, two particular aspects of the American success story seemed especially compelling: modern management methods, and a private property regime. Indeed, American ideologues coupled them together when counting the virtues of their system. And well they might. But the specific ways both had manifested themselves in the United States, as this book has demonstrated, did not automatically produce phenomenal Silicon Valley. The Czechs have spent most of the past ten years learning this historical truth. The learning process contains within it the story of the arrested development of entrepreneurship studies in the rebuilt system of Czech higher education. The tale will be told, as with the Germans and French, with the focus both on entrepreneurship studies as an academic discipline and on the high-tech networking in which educational institutions participated in the start-up process.

Early business education reform: old wine in new bottles

The 1990 law on higher education gave universities academic freedom and a great deal of autonomy. Within the state system it introduced self-administration, limited the state's power and opened universities to future development. The law also created a three-tier system of higher education – bachelor, master and Ph.D. – that conformed to the American- and now European-recommended pattern. It suggested that a course credit system and end-of-semester examinations be introduced, allowing for the easy transfer of credits between universities – another standard practice in American higher education that Western Europe until quite recently ignored. Whereas in 1953 the newly founded University of Economics sent its teachers to Moscow for training, now it and the other fifteen university faculties that taught economic sciences turned to the West. "Through the employment of foreign 'guest' professors and the promotion of their own students, the teaching staffs were brought up to Western levels" (Linden, 2000, p. 73). All but one of the sixteen institutions that offered instruction in economic and social science had programs in business economics, one (Charles University) had a program only in economics, and four offered programs in both. The restored economic studies resembled Central European academic traditions in that they were theoretical in nature and not much informed by interaction with praxis. The few places that restored studies of SMEs returned to the German BWL tradition.[2] The extensive work of Professor Muegler in Vienna drew their attention. Muegler in his work did not make sharp distinctions between entrepreneurship and small business administration, or between entrepreneurship in general and high-tech entrepreneurialism, which was the big subject in the United States.

[2] The institutions that restored SME studies were: the University of Economics, Prague; the Economics Faculty at the Technical University, Ostrava; and the Economics Faculty at the Technical University, Brno.

Management, specifically MBA education, developed outside the university system. Indeed, since private universities could not legally be established until 2001 and the laissez-faire-inspired government had closed the state-run Institute of Management, all business schools in the post-Communist Czech Republic started as subsidiaries of foreign schools. The Czechs relied, with the support of proselytizing American and EU management education agencies (the USAID and TEMPUS programs), directly on foreign educational expertise to raise their managerial know-how quickly to a world-class standard. The programs were not targeted at a pre-experience student population, for, "as opposed to the US," Klara Smolova explains, "where it is the second level of a college education (a master's degree), in the Czech Republic [the MBA] is seen as a type of requalification education" (Smolova, 2002, p. 18). It was meant to help people whose "socialist" education no longer met current management needs. Sometimes former officials in the old Communist managerial hierarchy could be found sitting alongside each other in MBA classes. Professor Milan Malý, of the Prague International Business School, noted that he had three former deputy finance ministers together in one class. Consequently, MBA students in the Czech Republic are older; in 2002 they averaged 35 to 40 years in age, compared to 30 to 35 in the rest of Europe and an even lower age span in the United States. Like all generalizations, this one should be handled with care. In the best American business schools post-experience people also make up the bulk of MBA classes. But Czech MBA education clearly sought to rehabilitate current management more than to educate first-degree school leavers.

Two of these business schools have affiliations with business schools in the Netherlands, one with the Ecole Supérieure de Commerce de Paris and FNEGE, and one with the business school in Barcelona. The Prague International Business School also offers a German-language study course, which is organized by the Europäische Wirtschafts-Hochschule in Berlin. Most of the affiliates, however, are in the United Kingdom and the United States, and the study programs in English. Seven that offered MBAs in the late 1990s had partners in the United Kingdom and four in the United States. They are shown in table 6.3.

Affiliation simply meant, therefore, that the Czech schools imported management programs and teachers from the West. Hence, it was primarily British and American business schools that ran Czech

Table 6.3 *Business schools in the Czech Republic and their affiliations*

Business school	Affiliates
Brno business school faculty, Technical University	Nottingham Trent University
Brno International Business School	Nottingham Trent University
CMC Graduate School of Business	University of Pittsburgh, DePaul University, Calgary University
Masaryk Institute of Advanced Studies	Sheffield Business School
Newport University, Ostrava	Newport University
Prague International Business School	Manchester Metropolitan University Business School
Business school faculty, Technical University, Ostrava	Liverpool University
The Open University	The Open University, UK
The University of New York/Prague	NYU Sterns Business School
U.S. Business School, Prague	Rochester Institute of Technology, USA
College of Economics & Management, Labem	Knightsbridge University, UK

Source: Smolova, 2002, p. 22.

academic MBA education. Moreover, indirectly, the American impact – through the British – extended its presence.

Thirty years before the "Velvet Revolution" no business schools existed in the United Kingdom. They started in the mid-1960s at London and Manchester, very much under American influence, then multiplied in the next twenty years throughout the country. Although British business schools were not American copies, the concepts of the business school, the MBA and post-experience executive programs were, strictly, imported into the United Kingdom from the United States. British partnerships with Czech institutions, therefore, projected the Americanization of post-war British business education a generation later into this part of Europe. The EU's TEMPUS program expressed the same trend. It sought to foster European-standard MBAs, imbied from the United States some twenty years before, into former Iron Curtain countries. From it emerged in 1991 the

Prague International Business School, with a Manchester Metropolitan University Business School connection. European business school accreditation agencies express American behavioral patterns as well. The British Association of MBAs (AMBA), like the more recently established (1998) Czech Association of MBA Schools (CAMBAS), reflects in inspiration and purpose older American associations – e.g. the American Assembly of Collegiate Schools of Business (AACSB). The predominance of British business schools in the Czech partnerships, and the presence of the Dutch, French and Spanish business school affiliations, testify to the continued successful penetration of American business education into West European business education, which started in the post-war years.

By the 1990s American and European business schools delivered a standardized product. Management in Czech firms that had been effectively privatized and restructured learned about the importance of accounting, human resource management, financial analysis, controlling, marketing and other topics from them. Some of the British and American partnerships were somewhat dubious. Although quite good schools affiliated with the Czechs – e.g. business schools in Sheffield, the Open University, New York University and the Rochester Institute of Technology – others (such as Knightsbridge and Newport) were not even accredited institutions. The Higher Education Funding Council for England does not list Knightsbridge among the 131 institutions, including 77 universities, that it funds. Newport University is not in the alphabetic list of regionally accredited American colleges and universities.[3] The TeleCampus Online Course Database warns students to be "very cautious about taking courses" in these distance learning, unaccredited institutions. There seems, in fact, to have been a rush of Western charlatans to take advantage of the MBA education market that opened in Eastern Europe with the fall of Communism.

Charlatans or not, none of the foreign business school affiliates brought entrepreneurship studies into the Czech Republic. Neither in their programs nor in the interviews with people involved in them is there a whisper of a preoccupation with the question of entrepreneurship studies until the turn of the twenty-first century. Interviewees from the European business school affiliates ignore the subject, too. Tatána Boráková, from the Czech Management Institute, Prague (an affiliate

[3] Available at www.utexas.edu/world/unive/alpha/.

of the Barcelona business school ESMA), describes their program as "classical BBA and MBA since 1995 and DBA since 1999" (Boráková, 2002). Vojtech Korab, head of the Management Faculty at the Technical University, Brno, says that entrepreneurship was not a "hot topic" in his institution (Korab, 2002). Professor Milan Malý, head of the Prague International Business School and president of CAM-BAS, states that the "most recent curricula changes in business schools and management faculties [affected] globalization issues: international management, international marketing, etc. No trend [exists] towards entrepreneurship, venture capital and innovation management" (Malý, 2002).

The failure of business schools to include entrepreneurship studies as an academic discipline among their offerings to Czech clients should not be too surprising. The strategic management guru Igor Ansoff, a former dean of American business schools, once said: "Business schools are generally twenty years behind business praxis" (Ansoff, 1983). The Silicon Valley story affirms as much. Business schools at Stanford University and the University of California eventually got involved in high-tech start-up networking, but they were not, Annalee Saxenian has reminded us, part of the start-up networking culture of the valley until it reached a mature stage. University interaction in the Silicon Valley habitat came out of engineering and science faculties, not business schools. Nor did the business schools emphasize entrepreneurship studies. Stanford Business School's refusal of an endowed chair in the subject in 1985 has been mentioned. Even in American business schools where entrepreneurship study centers exist, except for a few places they are sideshows compared to the schools' mainstream MBA education. People involved in MBA programs at Sheffield University, Nottingham Trent University, Manchester Metropolitan University, the Ecole Supérieure de Commerce de Paris and Barcelona's ESMA, where entrepreneurship studies have had a shorter history and smaller presence than in American business schools, are incapable of delivering, and less inclined to pay attention to, entrepreneurship education.

The Americanization the Czechs got through these business schools, then, reflected early post-war management education. This focus appears in books about the educational challenge that Western MBA programs faced in Eastern Europe. In *Management Education in the New Europe*, for example, published in 1996, the contributors range freely over fifty years of management education, quoting the works of Gordon and Howell (1959) and F. C. Pierson (1959) as if the management education in the United States that they were advocating had remained unchanged.[4] It is an old-fashioned book. Since the Czechs commenced at zero in 1989, they could not know that their reliance on foreign business schools would in this regard be misplaced, for it left them ill-prepared educationally to enter the Dionysian start-up world of the 1990s.

Networking after 1990

In his study of Czech innovation policies, carried out for the European Commission's Directorate General for Enterprise, Charles University's Karel Mueller notes that

the institutional development in the Czech lands had followed in principle the German type of science and technology institutionalization: (i) location of academic science at universities; (ii) engagement of industry in the support of industrial science via establishment of in-house laboratories in firms; responsibility of branch-based industrial associations for support of R&D and technology development in respective manufacturing branches (a type of organization similar to the Fraunhofer organizations in Germany); and (iii) involvement of the state in support of academic and industrial science. Such an institutional setting was based on both the informal networks among research community, industrialists, and state administration and the accepted authority of leading persons with high professional reputations in the respective communities. Informal networks and the reputation of leading personalities were helping overcome different valuations and motivation patterns of research and manufacturing (Mueller 2002, p. 40).

The Czech system grew alongside the German in the late nineteenth century, with similar education/research/industrial roots. Not even the Communist attempt to suppress it entirely succeeded; after moments of political crisis, in the 1960s and the 1980s, the informal networks revived.

What Communist ideologues failed to achieve, however, free market enthusiasts nearly accomplished after 1989. The conservative governments, in their justified hatred of the Marxist state, decided to limit

---

[4] Lee et al., 1996. Of the authors, Lee and Crawshaw were from Lancaster University, Letiche from Keele University, and Thomas from Strathclyde University. Where were authors familiar with Eastern European networks?

the new state's support of scientific research in public institutions to universities and government laboratories run by the Academy of Science. The heretofore state-supported industrial research laboratories were no longer funded. Their survival henceforth depended on an ability to secure contract work with industry. This pure expression of nineteenth-century laissez-faire dogma had unintended consequences. It turned the industrial research laboratories away from research, into service centers for firms, for at best they were interested only in new products developed in the laboratories. The industrial laboratories ceased to be research institutions. The economic reforms in the 1990s, Karel Mueller concludes, "deconstructed informal networks between industrial and academic science" because scientists from both had to engage in "severe competition" for limited funds rather than follow "cooperative approaches" (Mueller, 2002, p. 40).

Some other unintended consequences of laissez-faire economic reform exacerbated the decline in industry/research networking. To end socialism irretrievably, the authorities implemented a mass privatization scheme, which relocated an enormous amount of property in a short period of time. In 1990 the private sector produced about 2 percent of GDP; in 1995 it produced 70 percent; in 1997, 80 percent! The process had definite class origins, in that it was carried out in so-called "small' and "large" privatization schemes. The "small" privatization consisted primarily of the auctioning off of shops and small businesses, and it became the prime target of insiders – those who at the end of the Communist system had accumulated capital by operating in a "capitalist" economy under socialism. Vladimir Bénacek calls this group "operators" – i.e. restaurant and hotel staff, cab or any automobile drivers, foreign exchange touts, greengrocers, used-car dealers, repair workers, shop managers, gas station operators, etc.; people with money, well informed and strategically placed to snap up the small businesses being privatized (Bénacek, 1994, p. 11). "Large," big firm privatization, on the other hand, favored the former Communist "nomenclature" directors of companies, their deputies, heads of divisions or financially independent units, party members, high-ranking bureaucrats at ministries, district and municipal councils, etc. The non-competitive direct sales (e.g. management buyouts) or the competing projects (e.g. leveraged buyouts through bank loans) were their most "attractive targets." Investment privatization funds (IPFs) were another invented vehicle through which the representatives of the old state corporations and high bureaucracy got hold of the portfolios of companies being privatized under a voucher system. "Since practically 100 percent of the top and middle-ranking managers prior to 1990 were members of the Communist Party and a high proportion of the low-ranking managers [were too]," Bénacek calculates, "approximately half of the Czech emerging capitalist class were people chosen by the C[ommunist] P[arty]."

The consequences of this privatization operation were as follows: the leveraged firm buyouts left firms with no capital and large debts. The voucher system created a long period of ownership vacuum, lasting three to four years in state-owned enterprises. The Czech state ceased to control these firms during this hiatus, leaving their managers a free hand. This led to a "tunneling" of assets from state-owned enterprises, which could not be prevented by the voucher holders, who were not yet stockholders in the firms. From the "tunneling," this stripping off of assets from firms, the managers profited personally, but the firms they managed lost valuable properties. In many cases they decreased output, and without an adequate concomitant reduction in employment their indebtedness soared (Chytil and Sojka, 2001, pp. 15–17). Since the banking sector continued to be dominated largely by state banks, the symbiotic relationship that had existed beforehand between them and large conglomerates continued. The banks carried the debts of the large firms to the point that, by 1993, non-performing or doubtful credits in the banks rose to exceed 22 percent of GDP, and enterprise credits amounted to another 15 percent. The banks, themselves threatened with insolvency, instead of demanding restructuring and repayment from the firms – with the painful and politically unpopular consequence of lay-offs – just rolled over the loans, and the firms, operating at a loss, appealed to the politicians for help. The macroeconomist Petr Sedlar, of the Brno Broker Group, complained as late as 1999, "Stop pumping money into the ailing industrial sectors . . . Sentimentality about companies like CKD or Skoda Plzn – giants that for decades were the engine of the national economy – is distorting policy priorities" (Patton, 1999). Somewhat later *The Prague Post* pointed out another consequence. "Even if the local banking sector wasn't hobbled, bank loans don't offer start-ups the long-term equity financing they need to optimize their chances of success" (Poston, 2000a).

From the perspective of industrial research, therefore, privatization had not only deprived the research laboratories of financial support – thus setting them at odds with state researchers – it had produced privatized firms that lacked the monies to conclude contract research with the industrial research sector, thereby undermining the government's own free enterprise industrial research policy. And it had produced a banking sector that could not serve the needs of the small high-tech firms that could have used the industrial research laboratory facilities, had loans been forthcoming. True, banks do not provide long-term equity financing for start-ups, but a healthy banking sector could have become involved, like Deutsche Bank, in financing venture capitalist operations.

The Czech government through most of the 1990s appeared, with regard to high-tech entrepreneurship, to have had its collective head in the sand. There was a small but thriving high-tech industrial sector, but the chief economist Jiri Krovat, of Investiani a Postovni Bank, noted, ". . . the government is hardly lifting a finger to help push new industries in the right direction. In this country, information technology is almost exclusively driven by the private sector. I have not seen any action by the government to support it" (Patton, 1999). Not only that, one of the interviewees, Filip Rotgeri, has added that "information technology/Silicon Valley has not been thematized by media in the late 1990s" (Rotgeri, 2002). These are somewhat astonishing statements considering that French and German ministers and media had been on a campaign during these years to raise the entrepreneurial spirit of the people, to promote entrepreneurship studies and to foster enterprise start-up processes. Perhaps the Czechs felt no need to elevate entrepreneurial spirits in general, considering the rapid growth of private firms in just a few years. But high-tech start-ups should have been different. Here are some comments from the interviewees on the subject of high-tech neglect:

Miroslava Mandiková: "The government is preoccupied with EU accession" (Mandiková, 2002).

Luboš Vávra: "The government was preoccupied in the 1990s with privatization (restitution, small-scale and large-scale privatization) and the creation of a new institutional landscape (confederation of employees, confederation of industry, trade association – Czech Trade, production cooperatives, and regional economic chambers, etc.)" (Vávra, 2002).

Jaroslav Chaloupka: "Nineteenth-century capitalism has been applied after the 'Velvet Revolution'; that means 'profit, profit, profit' is what the government aims at instead of long-term [technology] development . . . the primary concern of government is privatization, there is no strategy for development and no interest in technology development. . . . This has been reflected in the dispute between Klaus and Havel. Klaus: 'The market rules everything.' Havel: 'Visions are necessary.'" (Chaloupka, 2002a).

Pavel Komárek: "There is no innovation strategy policy in the CR since the government has been preoccupied with short-term activities (changing laws, privatization)" (Komárek, 2002b).

Lidmila Nemcová: "The principal obstacles to entrepreneurship are corruption, criminality and non-transparency of laws" (Nemcová, 2003).

These statements are interesting for what they do not say as much as what they do. Obviously, the Czech government faced a big job ending Communism in the country. That privatization along with EU entry drained its energies and distracted it and the public from high-tech concerns is understandable, if not admissible. But there is a deep cynicism, even bitterness, underlying the comments. Even Jeffrey Sachs, a consultant in the matter, admitted in 1999: "The job was without any doubt ill-done" (Chytil and Sojka, 2001, p. 14). Zdnenek Chytil and Milan Sojka state it less cryptically:

[The extraordinary burst of entrepreneurialism that accompanied the] privatization processes, with an important role for the voucher method of privatization and an insufficiently developed legal framework, together with long traditions of non-compliant predatory behaviour from the times of the Soviet-type system, created suitable conditions for predatory, protective and speculative behaviour that may remind us of the Marxian concept of the original accumulation of capital . . . Unfortunately, the Czech transformation did not try to deliberately create institutions that would strengthen motivations for productive behavior (work, entrepreneurship, investment) (p. 15).

This entrepreneurship of "original accumulation" gave Czech entrepreneurship in the 1990s a bad name.

How could the Czechs in such an historical context turn entrepreneurs into heroes? There was no bevy of Czech heroes to inspire Czech youth. How could there be, since, as Karel Mueller writes after a decade of enterprises "as far as domestic firms are concerned, no essential initiatives in the business networks for innovation have been identified" (Mueller, 2002, p. 49). There were not even enough Czech accidental heroes – those Czechs who pursued personal desires but left behind prodigious technological leaders, such as Silicon Valley's Oracle.

The imagery was entirely the reverse: Marx's version of the entrepreneur, not America's. A series of polls conducted in the early 1990s confirms as much. Lidmila Němcová reported the results at a 1995 conference on "business and ethics": "From the point of view of morality and ethics, the actual situation in Czech society was estimated as 'rather bad' by 54 percent of respondents in the first group, by 67 percent in the second and by 56 percent in the third group. By adding the classification 'very bad' to ['rather bad'] the total in the three groups becomes 71 percent, 79 percent, and 69 percent."[5] In this atmosphere it would have been out of place, if not laughable, for the government to intone the virtues of an entrepreneurial society. They already had one. Instead of introducing courses on how to start up a firm, schools needed to talk about the moral order that had to exist for positive enterprise to take place. This led Professor Němcová to conclude:

It appeared that the presentation of ethical problems to the youngest generation of students in the countries of the previous "Eastern bloc" needed to use a very broad approach because of the total lack of information on various questions of morality and ethics which are common in countries where the traditional market system has been developed and where also traditional family education, the influence of religion, the mass media and publication on appropriate ethical problems, etc. have not been suppressed.

Since a special research report in 1991 pointed out that an "absence of ethics in entrepreneurship" was very frequently mentioned to be the main obstacle to entrepreneurship, Professor Němcová started a course not on entrepreneurship but on "business ethics" at the University of Economics in Prague (Němcová, 1998, pp. 75–76).

Information age Americanization in the Czech Republic: a late and selective infiltration of high-tech entrepreneurialism

If the Americanization of Czech business education did not include entrepreneurship studies and if the government ignored the subject for

---

[5] Group I: a representative sample of individual respondents over 18 years old; Group II: representatives of Czech enterprises, members of the Union of Czech Industry; Group III: representatives of foreign countries from about twenty countries operating in the Czech Republic. Němcová, 1995, p. 1.

almost a decade, there was not much Americanization – as defined in chapter 4 – going on in these circles. But that does not mean that the Czech economy and society escaped this American influence; non-governmental agents and scientific and engineering educational elements were at work. One important step forward in technology transfer came through foreign direct investment. It amounted to about 20 percent of total investment in Czech manufacturing. Mueller notes, "The aggregate economic indicators are reporting about the high dynamics of this segment of the domestic economy" (Mueller, 2002, p. 11). These foreign firms were responsible for the direct transfer of new technology in the 1990s, which had been the special preserve of the French and the Germans in the 1970s and 1980s. The most positive example of this dynamic effect occurred in the automobile industry. The network of domestic suppliers to Skoda/Volkswagen "is an exemplary case of the positive impact of advanced foreign producers on the domestic suppliers" (Mueller, 2002, p. 50). Their diffusion of modern production methods into Czech industry is an example of a delayed, second-hand Japanization funneled through the United States.[6] The work that Volkswagen and others did in the introduction of TQM, just-in-time, continuous improvement and other production methods into their plants spilled over into their Czech operations and suppliers. The "Japanization" of manufacturing was straightforward technology transfer between firms – something to which the Czechs were accustomed. "Here," Karel Mueller concludes, "the transition to new systems of production and quality control and appropriation of advanced management techniques have progressed well" (p. 36).

Foreign firms directly transferred information technology to the Czech Republic. But, considering the importance that a start-up habitat has in the new high-tech industrial culture, the large firms could only be part of the Czech high-tech story. Since big, capital-intensive hardware producers were well established, the idea that Czech start-ups could rival them in IT had to be forgotten. But there were possibilities in the rapidly growing software industry. The Czechs, to start with, had a

[6] Professor Wildemann, who was heavily involved in the introduction of the "Japanese" production methods into Volkswagen and many other German manufacturers, notes that, since he knew no Japanese, he had learned about them primarily through production engineers on his many visits to the United States. See Locke, 1996, for Wildemann's comments about this transfer of technology.

pool of talent inherited from the Communist era. The technical university in Ostrava founded a new department of electrical engineering and computer science, and the other technical universities expanded their capacities in programming and computer science education. Charles University increased its intake of students into the faculties of mathematics and physics. Between 1989 and 1992 enrollments in computer science increased fourfold. They provided a source of ideas for start-ups and the skilled people necessary to work in them. Moreover, some computer firms, after restructuring, prospered in the market economy. With success stories and a pool of talent available, large US and foreign software firms took an interest in the Czech scene. Actors, foreign and domestic, started creating a Czech high-tech software industry almost from post-Communism's very beginning.

The spin-off survivors of old state firms were Tesla Sezam and Terosil (Fronczak, 1997). The first manufactured semiconductors, the second polished silicon wafers. Their success during the 1990s led Motorola in 1997 to acquire 57 percent of the stock of the former and 52 percent of the stock of the latter. They were absorbed into the American giant's industrial empire. Motorola, in order to strengthen these new Czech links, provided funds to Czech universities to help set up laboratories to train chip makers and to create specialized technology curricula. Other famous foreign firms made direct investments in Czech information technology. Ericsson, after it became a mobile network provider in the Czech telecommunications market, established a testing center at the Czech Technical University in Prague. IBM's world trade department for strategic outsource delivery invested $8.8 million to establish an expert center in Brno that would offer IT outsourcing services for large European firms. Because of capital scarcity, local entrepreneurs had a much more difficult time than foreign giants entering the Czech market. But there were some successes early on. APP, for example, started in July 1990 with eight people. Most of them under Communism worked for the foreign trade ministry or another large government operator. They brought to their start-up a long string of contacts with foreign computer companies, and quickly formed partnerships, working out of a small business flat. APP served the high-end computer users, banks and insurance companies, not just with software or hardware but also with systems integration products (McNally, 1992, p. 1).

The networking, often informal, could be complex. Here is an example of it. Bruce Damer's boss, Basit Hamid, who had studied computer science with a Czech émigré in Norway, had been sufficiently impressed with his friend's talent to fly to Prague shortly after the "Velvet Revolution" to recruit people for his Ventura firm, Elixir Technologies. He brought back Peter Dupal, who proved to be so valuable that the firm later hired nine more Czechs and put them to work at White Mountain. Elixir's customers, all 6,000 of them – e.g. the Bank of England, AT&T, Xerox, etc. – in seventy countries, have their bills, tax forms and accounts printed out with Elixir's Prague-generated software.

Damer had been sent to White Mountain to be chief architect by his boss, and mentor, Basit Hamid.[7] He later went to work in the faculties of mathematics and physics of Charles University, in the computer center, which operated as a basic teaching facility and an advanced research laboratory. Damer was charged with stimulating special student projects. With a Czech partner, Rudolf Kryl, who had seen a computer first in Havana in 1986, Damer started the "Prague Foundation for Informatics."

Since there had been an exodus of poorly paid professors of computer science from the universities, Damer tried to solve the teacher problem by importing videotaped lectures from Stanford University. Stanford had been videotaping lectures in computer science and affiliated courses for twenty years. The videotapes allowed students to interact with them and to be tutored in a special way. That they were in English presented no problem, since English was a prerequisite in computer science at Charles University and all the manuals and textbooks were in English. Moreover, tests showed that students who took Stanford's videotape courses performed at roughly the same level as the students who sat in regular classes. Stanford offered the tapes at a minimal cost. Moreover, Xerox Parc donated its videos of seminars held by pioneers in the computer and programming fields. Silicon Valley in this way came to Prague.

On September 22, 1993, the Prague Foundation for Informatics co-sponsored a three-day series of lectures at the faculties of mathematics and physics by William Newman and five other seminal figures in interfaces – a lecture series co-sponsored by Charles University, the Technical University, Prague, and Hewlett-Packard. Following this conference Damer packed up the computer laboratory to go to Bozi Dar in

---

[7] Damer is a Canadian who studied computer science in southern California. See Levy, 1993.

northern Bohemia, where 180 middle school teachers of computer science gathered for their annual two-week summer camp. The Prague Foundation for Informatics and Philips Corporation co-sponsored the gathering. Damer expected from these expenditures of time and effort to raise incoming student knowledge in computer sciences in just two years to "better than world class." Since the professors from the business schools interviewed for this book uniformly stated that Silicon Valley had been ignored in the 1990s, the computer scientists in the Czech Republic must have lived – to use the terminology of the French professor – in "another world."

Damer's story reveals the random nature of networking between individuals, firms and universities. Despite successful outcomes, the absence of state support made life for Czech high-tech entrepreneurs precarious. During the 1990s state subsidies to SMEs amounted to some 25 million koruna, as opposed to 400 million koruna allotted to large firms. There were no government seed and venture capital funds. Until 1997 only two or three Czech sources of venture capital existed, so Czechs had to rely on foreign capital to support their ventures. Efforts to organize non-governmental support networks at first did not help. Before 1990 there had been no innovation centers, no technology centers, no science or technology parks in the country. That year representatives from EBN (the European Business Innovation Centre Network) recommended that three BICs be set up in Czechoslovakia. Also that year newly forming technology centers, business and innovation centers and science/technology parks, in league with prominent private citizens, had formed the STPA to promote technology and innovation. Its projects aimed to turn research and development institutions into science parks. Although the European Union's "PHARE" program supported the effort, initially projects turned into real estate acquisition schemes, where established firms settled, rather than ones that created new technology-oriented ventures. There were "two results of these activities," Professor Pavel Komárek observes: "(1) We lost the idea of science parks; (2) we had no successful real projects of privatization" (Komárek, 2002a).

Because the Czech Republic possessed "Kilimanjaro-size programming talent while maintaining some of the lowest operating costs in the jungle," new ventures could prosper without governmental or nongovernmental support (Poston, 1999). Some software firms did, simply relying directly on Silicon Valley networks to survive or pleasantly perish. This happened to successful firms such as Tiny Software, which moved its headquarters to Santa Clara, California, in 1998 in order to exploit American sources in a build-up to an IPO, and to NetBeans, which Sun Microsystems bought for a hefty sum. When Silicon Valley and the general high-tech economy declined, this outlet began to disappear. This happened with the stock market collapse and the e-commerce bust. The e-commerce eclipse did not particularly hurt the Czech Republic, because there had not been that many e-commerce firms. The government's failure to support cheap access to the Internet had resulted in only 300,000 to 500,000 users, most of them students, in a country of ten million people (Poston, 2000b). Without client potential, e-retailing had not prospered. The impact that economic distress had on foreign venture capitalists had greater repercussions in the Czech Republic. When a consortium of venture capitalists – US-based Advent International Corporation, Czech fund Genesis Capital and Slovakia's Kistler Associates – withdrew its support, a promising Internet firm called Globopolis, with a staff of 140, went under (Bower and Gonderinger, 2001).

By this time, most Czech people were in pain. Whereas in the first half of the 1990s the economy had done quite well, with employment steadily under the fourth percentile, in 1997 the rate rose to 4.5 percent, in 1998 to over 7 percent and then in February 1999 to 8.87 percent. The general economic malaise led to the installation of a new left-wing government to replace the conservatives who had guided the republic through the transformation, and to policy changes that affected a broad range of issues, including innovation. Not that the new government actually devised a comprehensive policy in matters of high-tech enterprise. Mueller has written that in 2001 there was still "no distinct and coherent innovation policy document . . . no executive agency specialized in the coordination and regulation of innovation issues" (Mueller, 2002, pp. 17–18). But the economic trouble and the arrival of the new government started a process of change.

Some of it the Europeans forced on the government as part of Czech preparation for EU entry. EU policy directives worked to provide the Czech government itself with better yardsticks with which to measure innovation. Since entering the OECD in 1994, data and the method of their collection have had to conform to European and international standards. The Czech Statistical Office began to adjust its indicators to include patent statistics that now cover more than research and development organizations, information on the technological balance of payments, and data on the regional distribution of R&D resources. In cooperation with Eurostat and the OECD it introduced European indicators and surveys in addition, and began cooperation with non-governmental agencies in carrying out the work. The Council of Government for Research and Development, for example, started keeping a central registry of research and development projects. Government support to help SMEs prepare for EU entry produced a similar record-keeping effect in firms.

Government actions in favor of a high-tech habitat build-up resembled those undertaken by the French and Germans just a few years before.[8] At the end of the 1990s the state started to reform the informal networks between research community and industry that conservative government laissez-faire policies had dissolved. The ministries increased public R&D funding after 1997 to include industrial research and related activities. Grant agencies instructed their committees when funding R&D projects to assess applications according to their practical impact on manufacturing and services as well as their scientific merit, which heretofore had been the preferred – if not exclusive – criterion. They were helped in these efforts by European projects such as "Transact," which sought "to transfer existing university-based start-up support schemes, having proven their excellence, to Newly Associated Countries (NACs)." The Fraunhofer ISI and the new incubator at Crealys, near Lyon, lent their expertise in start-up networking to "Transact."[9] The government also decided to help hard-pressed start-ups in venture capital provision. In cooperation with EU authorities it started Czech Venture Partners and the Fund of Risk Capital. The former, a consulting firm, controls three venture capital funds with a capital of 1.7 billion koruna. The latter is a subsidiary of a firm funded by the Ministry of Regional Development and an EU delegation to

---

[8] Mustar and Laredo's description of the dismantling of the Colbertian state's research policies, cited extensively in chapter 5, and Karel Mueller's essay on the Czech Republic's innovation policy profile, for example, have quite similar themes: the growing importance of the EU, local government and state programs in an interactive context of locally and regionally created non-governmental agencies and institutions (University-located business innovation centers, incubators, etc.).

[9] The quote is from a "Transact" brochure, available at efrank@attempto-service.de.

the Czech Republic; EU "PHARE" funds and monies from private investors have supported it. The government pushed other familiar measures to make the habitat more friendly to start-ups: it passed laws that permit universities to invest in private enterprises, that ease patent processing and that reduce the bureaucratic red tape SMEs encounter in their development. On the demand side, the Ministry of Education, Youth and Sport and the Ministry of Culture worked out a plan in 2000 that within a year would put at least one computer with an Internet connection into every single school (Bouc, 2000).

These new programs work in concert with Czech non-governmental agencies. They, with injections of government and EU monies, have come to life. Pavel Komárek, president of the STPA and director of the Business and Innovation Center of the Czech Technical University, Prague, notes that the STPA changed its policies, after the bad beginning described above, to favor start-ups. It requires that member associations, in order to secure accreditation in the STPA, have to be involved in innovation and incubation, have links to research and technology transfer agents, educate, engage in consultation and advisory services, cooperate with regional institutions and have well-defined relations with owners, founders and operators of firms. The criteria are not about an association member's evaluation standards but its main objectives, which have to include the incubation of new technology-oriented companies. In 1995 the Ministry of Industry and Trade made these criteria its own when it began to support the creation and development of science and technology parks through its program "Park." Technology centers, BICs and science and technology parks became accepted tools for innovation in the Czech Republic. Komárek observes in his interview that now "99 percent of the members of the Czech STPA have strong relations with research and development institutions, especially the business innovation centers in Prague, Olmouc, Plzn and Ostrava" (Komárek, 2003).

Universities integrated their efforts backward into teaching and research programs as well as forward into business innovation centers. Faculties of mathematics, technical science and engineering introduced IMT programs. Although Damer's efforts in the computer center at Charles University show that this could occur in faculties of mathematics and physics at universities, the programs appeared primarily in technical universities. The construction engineering faculty at the Technical University, Prague, for instance, introduced IMT in 1998.

Before that it had offered a Master's study program "production and innovation engineering," which graduated its first students in 1997. In 1999 seventeen students finished this course. Its program is more about the transfer of technology and innovation conceptions than start-up techniques, but certain subjects cover entrepreneurship – e.g. intellectual property, patenting practices, international patenting systems, SME support systems, the legal aspects of starting up a firm, etc. (Mueller, 2002).

Innovation and start-up entrepreneurship courses are also offered in university economic and management faculties at the Technical University, Ostrava. Zdenk Mikoláš, an entrepreneurship expert, and Ladislav Ludvík, an enterprise diagnostician and valuation expert, affirm that their department has been offering entrepreneurship – as distinct from small business courses – since 1991, dealing with entrepreneurial forms at home and abroad and business diagnostics, plus a consultancy for entrepreneurs and managers (Mikoláš and Ludvík, 2003). Vojtech Korab, in the management faculty at the Technical University, Brno, relates that he started to teach small business courses in 1993 and a non-obligatory entrepreneurship course since the winter semester 1998/99 (Korab, 2002). In this course he used an American textbook translated into Czech (Hisrich and Peters, 1996). Some universities have set up programs to serve students in the faculties of engineering, technology, economics and management. In some economic and management faculties IMT lectures are part of management study, marketing or studies in informatics. The faculty of management, faculty of firm management and faculty of informatics and statistics at the University of Economics in Prague, for example, has a series of specific courses on innovation, the management of change and quality management.

Some regional universities, with both management/economics and technology/engineering faculties, set up programs that students from each can exploit. This teaching program is running at the Technical University, Brno, the regional technological faculty and faculty of management and economics in Zlín, and the University of West Bohemia in Plzn. The latter course is called "PRISMA" – Projects-Innovation-Strategies-Management – and is presented in a modular form. Again, innovation is not separated from start-up entrepreneurship in most of these programs, but for those concerned with the latter much of use is to be learned.

Within this recent educational ferment, the foreign business schools, although they stay mainly with their MBA programs, could hardly remain untouched. This change happened mostly when Czechs had partnerships with US-based management schools where entrepreneurship studies had a louder voice at home. Accordingly, the Rochester Institute of Technology has just started a course "introduction to technology management," at the US Business School, Prague. It focuses on innovation rather than IT start-ups. On the other hand, a course offered at the CMC Graduate School of Business in the spring of 2000, by the University of Calgary MBA program, offers entrepreneurship without a focus on technological innovation. Called "new venture entrepreneurship," in its syllabus the instructor, Dr. Douglas H. Pressman, specified:

As you already probably realize, MBA programs have classically focused on educating mid- and senior-level managers for already existing, larger businesses, such as the multinational corporations many CMC Calgary students have personal experience with. Entrepreneurship education is a relatively new addition to business curricula, and aims instead at training would-be creators of new enterprises.

CMC Graduate School of Business supported the attempt to create the first "project incubator for Internet-related ventures" in the Czech Republic, which, unfortunately, did not see the light of day because no appropriate manager for this incubator could be found. But the institution did not give up. CMC, with the William Davidson Institute at the University of Michigan Business School, held a two-day seminar in Prague, in May 2003, on "Entrepreneurship Development for the SME Sector.

Within the field of education in IMT, the Association of Innovative Entrepreneurship is the most influential non-governmental agency. It coordinates IMT-related programs in higher education and organizes its own part-time courses for people interested in upgrading or changing their qualifications. Its first course in the late 1990s drew management staffs from the science and technology parks. AIE actions such as establishing BICs, ministerial and EU special programs, the efforts of specially created start-up support agencies, government-sponsored venture capitalists, university faculties and local authorities have created a web of habitat networking over the past few years. The jury is still out about the effectiveness of the web. But table 6.4, reconstructed from Mueller's, gives some idea of its complexity.

Table 6.4 *Support for high-tech start-ups in the Czech Republic*

Responsible organizations	Objectives	Target public	Funding
	Support for high-tech start-ups		
Council for Quality	Realize national quality policy	Testing and control organs/firms	Public & private funds, & "PHARE"
Ministry of Industry & Trade	Support of SMEs	SMEs	Same
Ministry of Industry & Trade	"Consulting" program	SMEs	Same
Ministry of Industry & Trade, Agency for Promotion of Enterprise	BIC program	5 BICs (Ostrava, Brno, Plzen, Prague & TC AS CR)	Same
Same	RAIC program	14 centers in the country	Same
Ministry of Industry & Trade	Training & education in innovation	SMEs	Same
Ministry of Education, youth & sports program	National education	Primary, tertiary & adult education	Public
Czech-Moravian Guarantee Development Bank	Programs START & REGION	Start-up projects in lagging regions	Repayable subsidies
Same	Program MARKET	SMEs	Same
Ministry of Industry & Trade	Establish industrial zones	Municipal authorities	Subsidies for construction
Czech Innovation Relay Center	Improve competitiveness, technology transfer & diffusion of R&D	BICs SMEs	EU
Ministry of Industry & Trade	Develop industrial zones	Cities, regions & firms	EU & state funds
VC daughter firms of Regional Development Foundations	Support of start-ups	SMEs	Ministries & "PHARE"
Czech Venture Partners	Same	Domestic firms	Ministries & banks

Source: Mueller, 2002, pp. 34, 38 and 47.

Does this surge in high-tech habitat activities in the past few years amount to a belated Americanization? No, if "Americanization" has to be defined as the widespread espousal of entrepreneurship values. The Czech government does not seem to have become the public champion of entrepreneurialism. Karl Korff, before attending the Twelfth Annual Information and Communications Fair, wrote of the event's importance: "Hundreds of thousands of people will converge on this south Moravian city [Brno], the site of the largest IT fair in Eastern and Central Europe" (Korff, 2002). But, he added, "Heavy hitters, including government ministers, industry leaders and international information security experts, will hold meetings, get to know each other for the first time and cement business relationships that could affect the market. The conferences are also an opportunity to educate the average consumer, who hears bits and pieces about this technology but really isn't quite sure how it applies."

If "heavy hitters" were getting "to know each other for the first time" in October 2002, the government has not been leading as much as following the pack. Still, if ad hoc steps in habitat creation replace entrepreneurship visions and values as our criteria for Americanization, then perhaps a case can be made for it. By re-establishing the informal and formal patterns of relationships among research laboratories, firms, government and universities, the Czechs are, of course, not being Americanized but reverting to the historic patterns that had been disturbed by the Communists and the laissez-faire policies adopted by conservatives immediately after 1989. These re-established behavioral patterns pertain more to innovation through established firms and technology transfer prior to 1990. Phenomenal Silicon Valley in its second phase, however, stood for something different. It represented high-tech innovation through start-up enterprises. Since so many Czechs now work assiduously to develop and exploit a high-tech start-up habitat in their country with attributes that mirror the familiar patterns developed in the famous valley, they are, whether consciously or not, American-influenced.

7 | Conclusions and policy recommendations

THE evidence marshaled in this book supports the argument: there has been a second Americanization of management education in France, Germany and the Czech Republic. Moreover, because it reflects a new development in American academic education, entrepreneurship and – more specifically – high-tech entrepreneurship, it differs as much from the first Americanization as high-tech entrepreneurship studies and activities in the United States deviate from the management education established there after World War II.

Chapter 2 described the emergence of entrepreneurship studies in the United States as a research subject, as an educational curriculum – that is, both as academic discipline and proactive pedagogy – and as outreach programs into academia and the greater community (transversality and interdisciplinarity). Entrepreneurship studies manifested themselves in specific ways in each area. The book has not based its concept of Americanization on the degree to which other countries copied the specific forms and attributes that these studies assumed in the United States. Rather, it has established a yardstick that contains the essence of this Americanization, abstracted from the specificities of US entrepreneurship studies. One variable on the yardstick is entrepreneurial values, which had to be generally espoused for entrepreneurial research and study programs to thrive in American higher education. For Europeans to be Americanized, they had to adopt these American entrepreneurial values. This value adoption is deemed to be the important feature of Americanization – not some slavish borrowing of specific programs that might, in their specificity, be unsuited to European conditions. The second criterion added to the Americanization yardstick has to do with modes of behavior as opposed to specific forms of behavior. The specific transversal and interdisciplinary features of American entrepreneurial studies were judged to be less important than the American-like modes of behavior that Europeans adopted to foster the transversality and interdisciplinarity essential to the creation of high-tech start-up environments.

From these two perspectives – values and modes of behavior – the book has described the American influence on French, German and Czech higher education in the "information age." In general, the manifestation of American values and modes of behavior developed late in Europe – in fact, mostly in the past ten years. Comparisons are complicated by the necessity to make a distinction in the book between entrepreneurship studies and start-up activities. The former can encompass the latter, but entrepreneurship studies are an academic subject, a field of knowledge built on research into the phenomenon of "Entrepreneurship." Many individuals in each country, believing that entrepreneurship is not a field of knowledge but a practice, are deeply engaged in entrepreneurship activity. That is why the book has treated entrepreneurship studies and entrepreneurial networking separately.

Entrepreneurship studies have developed differently in each country. Preoccupied with the task of building a management education system almost from scratch, and relying on Western business schools with educational models that did not include entrepreneurship studies, Czech higher education has all but ignored entrepreneurship as a field of academic study. The Czech leadership did not praise entrepreneurship values, try to promote them in the educational system or favor the adoption of entrepreneurship studies in academic institutions. The American academic example in entrepreneurship studies has not yet been followed in the Czech Republic. The Germans reacted somewhat differently but, until quite recently, with the same effect. Experiencing Americanization after World War II, they had rejected much in management education in favor of their own educational tradition. That tradition, as explained in chapter 3, separated academic management education from business praxis, and it has shaped the introduction of entrepreneurship studies in Germany as well by opposing their adoption in academia, on the grounds of their scientific inadequacies. This has delayed and stunted the development of academic entrepreneurship studies in the country. The French hesitated to introduce entrepreneurship as a field of study in university faculties, too, but the *grandes écoles de commerce* – without any research science ethos to dampen their enthusiasm – adopted entrepreneurship studies as active pedagogy, and the universities followed, with an emphasis on the creation of an academic discipline.

Start-up networking brought in a different academic clientele in every country. Generally speaking, non-natural scientists and non-technical academics in entrepreneurship studies had very little contact with the natural scientists and engineers, and, therefore, were left out of the high-tech networking that led to actual start-ups. For their part, the natural scientists and engineers had no interest in entrepreneurship as a field of academic study and did not network with those involved in its creation. But scientists and engineers, depending on the habitats in which they operated, were involved in start-up activities. Businessmen, entrepreneurs and civil servants responded differently to entrepreneurship studies, depending on the country. Where academic research was respected, many people in praxis supported the development of entrepreneurship studies in academia. In Germany banks and businesses endowed chairs that were filled with BWL professors, while in the United States entrepreneurs funded entrepreneurship research and study centers. In France the support was less direct. Few chairs were endowed; none by successful entrepreneurs in universities, but the chambers of commerce, through the general support given to the *grandes écoles de commerce* indirectly (and sometimes directly), supported the project-oriented active pedagogy. Very little of this, however, was in high-tech enterprise. The really creative entrepreneurship/knowledge nexus occurred at those rare points that brought the heretofore separated institutions and people together; in the community-oriented high-tech habitats of Stanford and MIT, for instance, where business schools and engineering faculties cooperated, but also in the networking done in technical universities in Germany, and in the rarer instances in France – at Sophia Antipolis, for a prime example. But the presence of these nexus groups varied from country to country with regard to networking intensity, inclination and capability. The adoption of entrepreneurship studies and modes of start-up behavior in France, Germany and – especially – the Czech Republic is very much an unfinished business.

If this résumé accurately depicts the historical experience, it does not provide a basis for policy formulation. Indeed, we do not even aver that policy recommendations can be made. The introduction confronted this issue when discussing the conflict between the social scientist's and the historian's approach to knowledge. Social scientists seek to extract neutral analytical concepts from the historical records and/or economic and social theory, because they have an instrumental approach to knowledge. They want to use it to effect change. But the social scientists have failed, both on practical and theoretical grounds. There is no need to rehash the evidence that confirms this failure. Those interested can reread the introduction and the cited literature. In their stead, our approach has looked on the subject of entrepreneurship in the United States and its influence on entrepreneurship studies there and in France, Germany and the Czech Republic as a contested historical project. The goal has been simply to record the events, which are not simple, as historical specificities, unique to their time and place. There is no science of predictive model building involved.

But the introduction also stated that policy recommendations can and should be made, through historical inference, about the desirability and feasibility of developing entrepreneurship and entrepreneurship studies in Europe in the future.

Desirability

Have entrepreneurship studies a future?

The question arises because the European passion for American high-tech entrepreneurialism, recorded in chapter 1, has somewhat dampened recently. The generosity of angel investors and venture capitalists toward budding entrepreneurs has dried up, as they relearned, after the dot.com debacle, the meaning of the word "risk." And IPOs, which used to be launched without much difficulty on equity markets, have diminished in numbers. Does this signify the end of the entrepreneurial economy, and, if so, a justifiable declining interest in entrepreneurship studies and/or activities? The answer to the question is important because, depending on whether it is affirmative or negative, judgments about the future significance of the phenomena described in this book and the content of any policy recommendations they suggest would be quite different.

Since nobody can predict the future, no definitively affirmative or negative answer to the question is possible. But it is possible to prognosticate, to foretell future events by an analysis of past indications. People in Silicon Valley portray their good fortune as a series of S-curves, where a technology that runs its course is replaced by another that unfalteringly carries the economy forward, to be replaced – on *its* decline – by another technology, in a sustained process of continuous technological development. The semiconductor boom gave way after its decline to microprocessors and personal computers in the late 1970s, and they in turn to software exploitation in the mid-1980s, and then after that the Internet fostered yet more new technologies in the 1990s. This capacity for renewal has not depended on individual genius but on habitat efficacy.

Nor has it depended on stock market prosperity, for, through it all, bull and bear markets have occurred. This fact might reassure those shaken by recent stock market downturns. The disconnection between economic events and technological development has a long history. David Landes describes such a disconnection that happened over a hundred years ago.

The years from 1873 to 1896 seemed to many contemporaries a startling departure from historical experience. Prices fell unevenly, sporadically, but inexorably through crisis and boom – an average of about one-third on all commodities. It was the most drastic deflation in the memory of man. The rate of interest fell too, to the point where economic theorists began to conjure with capital so abundant as to be a free good. And profits shrank, while what were now recognized as periodic depressions seemed to drag on interminably. The economic system appeared to be running down (Landes, 1969, p. 231).

And yet Landes goes on to say that these were the years of the great technological transformation known as the Second Industrial Revolution (organic chemicals, electricals, steel, aluminum, internal combustion engines, etc.), which, particularly in Germany, progressed rapidly during the economically depressed years.

The point, based on historical precedent, is that there is no reason to believe that the era of high-tech, technologically innovative start-ups has run its course. On the contrary, Silicon Valley's experience over the past forty years suggests that it is reasonable to think that it, projected into the world, will continue, especially when markets recover. Since high-tech entrepreneurship nowadays requires the presence of a habitat, and the elements of that habitat can be identified, it behooves responsible political, educational and business leaders in the three European countries this book has studied to foster policies that enhance habitat efficacy in the promotion of high-tech start-ups. This is prudent advice, drawn from American experience. But to project this experience into the future is an act of faith – nothing more.

Should *entrepreneurship studies be emphasized?*

This question also needs to be examined, because it touches on the moral and social desirability of implementing these studies. Management education can be approached on a technical/professional level. Whether the sophisticated management and teaching that the United States exported to Europe after World War II prepared managers well for careers in corporate managerial hierarchies; whether the development of entrepreneurship studies fills an important vacuum in education at the turn of the twenty-first century that business schools have ignored – these are technical issues that have been mentioned in this study. But management education in the first and second period of Americanization has social/moral implications that exceed French, German and Czech concerns about the need for high-tech start-up entrepreneurs who could help them keep pace technologically in the information age. Educational policy decisions imply much more than protecting national economic well-being. They affect the future of a nation's moral existence.

To explain how this applies to management education, a digression needs to be made into what Locke calls American "managerialism." Western Europeans after World War II, because they had a history of class conflict rooted in propriety capitalism, sought to escape this troubled past by adopting a socially responsible market capitalism, the most distinct post-war version of which took shape in West Germany's "social market" system. Its advocates have been, and are, uneasy about the antisocial aspects of American managerial capitalism. Locke uses a heuristic device to clarify why American "managerialism" challenges Europe's social market system. He equates "managerialism" with "militarism," as defined by Alfred Vagts in 1937. In an influential book Vagts compares "militarism" to "the military way" (Vagts, 1937). The latter signifies setting a military goal and developing the most efficient organizational means to see it accomplished. "That is," Locke says, "what 'management' as applied to commercial and industrial organizations means also to firms" (Locke, 1996, p. 3). But "militarism," like "managerialism," connotes something different. As Vagts puts it, militarism presents a vast array of customs, interests, prestige, actions and thoughts associated with armies and wars and yet transcending true military purposes. Indeed, militarism is so constituted that it may hamper and defeat the purposes of the military way. Its influence is unlimited in scope. It may permeate all society and become dominant over all industry and arts . . . Militarism displays the qualities of caste and cult, authority and belief (Vagts, 1937, p. 11).

American "managerialism," Locke asserts, "has the traits of militarism. It represents 'a vast array of customs, interests, prestige, actions and thoughts associated with but nonetheless transcending the needs for the efficient running of commercial and industrial organizations." It, as it appeared in the United States, came to exhibit "the qualities of caste and cult, authority and belief. And it generated and developed into a system that defeats and hampers the purposes of management itself – that is, denies organizations the means needed to formulate and effectively reach goals" (Locke, 1996, p. 3).

Management is about efficient leadership; "managerialism" is about the privileges, status and powers of a class that, over the twentieth century, insinuated itself into American proprietary capitalism between the firm's owners (stockholders) and the firm's employees and other stakeholders. This new class holds power in non-profit and government corporations, but it is most prominent in for-profit publicly owned corporations. It is open to talent but is nonetheless a self-contained elite that distributes and redistributes top corporate jobs among its members in a well-paid game of musical chairs. Through its control over the corporations in which it is ensconced, it has lobbied Congress and state legislatures to deregulate corporate governance and eliminate laws and regulations that prohibit conflict-of-interest arrangements that restrict its latitude to exploit on a global scale. It has, through its contacts with and patronage of business and management schools and the popular media, promoted a managerial ideology that made itself the source of American prosperity. And it did this not in the interest of capitalist ownership, which extends through insurance companies and pension investment funds to a broad section of middle-class America, but primarily of itself – the top management in financial, commercial and industrial firms, who benefit from this reign of "managerialism."

Since it has the power to create its own compensation packages, it has done so without much regard for the welfare of the corporations that this managerial class heads. In "normal" times these managers' salaries were always generous, but in the boom 1990s the gap between executives' compensation and employee pay in the firms they managed became scandalous. They defended the incomes by pointing to the increasing stock valuations of their companies, which a contented but gullible stockholding public accepted at face value. But then the halcyon days of rising stock markets and expanding Silicon Valley riches disappeared. In two years the NASDAQ lost three-quarters of its value, and its high-tech imitations in Germany and France suffered a similar, or even worse, fate. In order to maintain high stock valuations, to justify the disproportionality of their rewards, managers often engaged in systematic chicanery – e.g. accounting gimmicks and offshore sham company dealings, sanctioned by auditors hired as consultants by the very firms they are auditing. Corporate fund-raisers turned to equity markets and financial institutions to leverage buyouts and promote amalgamations and/or acquisitions. The number of such deals continues to accumulate (Daimler-Chrysler, AOL-Time-Warner, Hewlett-Packard-Compaq, Enron, WorldCom., etc.). The promoters receive handsome bonuses and commissions. The work is a prime example of managerialism, since the deals are conceived of by the top executives in the interest of their caste, the members of which receive the big pay-offs. The necessary stockholder votes might be bought off, with borrowed money or through increased stock valuations, but the resulting business entity is often left saddled with huge debts, reduced liquidity and falling stock prices. And the employees, in a cost-cutting aftermath brought on by the corporate indebtedness incurred to finance the pay-offs, face benefit and pension reductions, if not redundancy.

This managerial class diligently supported the development of management studies in American and European higher education after World War II, and through it an ideology of "managerialism." But, as noted in chapter 2, because this managerialism was in temperament and training Apollonian, not Dionysian, it was not high-technology entrepreneurial. The well-paid corporate leaders of the Fortune 500 corporations were not responsible for the start-up entrepreurialism of the information age. If anything, they were blind to its possibilities, until they became obvious even to the blind. And so were the schools of management that served them.

American management in Europe has carried on a long campaign in favor of its "managerialism." The American Chamber of Commerce in Frankfurt am Main, with the support of US government officials, lobbied – if partly in vain – against co-determination in the early 1950s, and they renewed their opposition in the mid-1970s when the

SPD government under Willy Brandt extended the number of members on supervisory boards elected by a firm's employees. Some executives moved their firms' headquarters outside Germany in order to escape the control of such supervisory boards. No co-determination regimes equivalent to Germany's exist in France. A French managerial elite dominates corporate France as much as one does in the United States. But French management is imbued with a Colbertian service ethos, which rejects the relentless pursuit of profits that has come to epitomize the American executive class.

Management education has played a role in this battle over "managerialism." American schools of business and management might have projected a sophisticated research and teaching agenda into Germany and France, but they have also acted as propaganda agents for "managerialism," by preaching the ethos of management as the independent professional function of a special class, and by tacitly – if not actively – opposing all that countervails the authority and control of management in the firm: trade unions, co-determination, government regulation, employment laws, etc. French and German business education sometimes actively, but mainly inadvertently, stood in the way of this imposition of "managerialism." Although students in the *grandes écoles de commerce* generally succumbed to "managerialism," those in the *grandes écoles* of engineering (the Ecole Polytechnique, Centrale, of mines, and of bridges and roads) and in ENA imbibed an ideal of country, honor and service, which taught them to be leery of financiers and speculators. German BWL students, through their specialized education, also shunned the ethos of managerialism, to which German executives did not object since they themselves did not believe that management could be abstracted from the specificities within a business or a firm into a generalized function. The fact that German BWL professors separated themselves from praxis, in the name of *Wissenschaft*, prevented them from becoming the powerful spokesmen for the rights and prerogatives of the management class that they would have become had they fused themselves with people in praxis, as did professors in business and management schools in the United States.

In the most recent era of globalization the powerful force of American management, and its voice (management education), have intensified the attack on the obstacles that bar corporate executives from assuming the same dominance in French, German and Czech life that they have in the United States. In the 1990s Eastern Europeans turned to the successful Americans for models of management education, as the chapter on the Czechs has demonstrated, and France and Germany, in the economic doldrums, also felt increasingly obliged to look at Anglo-American forms of corporate governance to end stagnation. But high-tech start-ups and entrepreneurship studies have (perhaps ironically, since they are of American origin too) become a counterfoil to managerialism.

As discussed in chapter 1 and elsewhere in the book, Europeans have been deeply impressed by Silicon Valley and the general entrepreneurial vitality of American capitalism. They have looked upon the high-tech start-up entrepreneur as a Promethean hero, who has made the digital revolution touch almost every aspect of our daily lives. And they have also looked upon the entrepreneur's use of the high-tech habitat in a positive vein. Angel investors, venture capitalists and the university interaction with the entrepreneur are all considered to have been critical to the founding and growth of the high-tech start-ups. So have the equity markets, where stockbrokers and public relations firms floated the initial public offerings of the new high-tech firms. The habitat housed a networking process through which the firm moved from its initial conception to angel finances, to venture capitalists, to stockbrokerage and to the public relations firms that presided over the IPOs. The original entrepreneurs' share in an enterprise might have dwindled as he or she or they, to secure the necessary financing and services, had to allot larger shares of the potential returns to the much-needed investors. It was necessary to entrepreneurship; accepted as altogether socially useful management. This creative high-tech entrepreneurialism, although greatly overshadowed by the "managerialism" that has a hold on corporate America, is not to be confused with it any more than "militarism" is to be confused with "the military way."

In any appraisal of high-tech entrepreneurialism, therefore, policy makers need to distinguish clearly between high-tech entrepreneurship and entrepreneurship in general, and between high-tech entrepreneurship and "managerialism." They need to make the first distinction in order still to believe in the creative individual act. This is especially true in the former Eastern bloc countries, where, as the Czech experience typifies, entrepreneurialism became almost a synonym for predatory antisocial behavior. High-tech entrepreneurialism is different from entrepreneurialism because the former connotes an economic usefulness that the other lacks – i.e. technological progress, creative destruction notwithstanding. It is this economic benefit that gives entrepreneurship its ethical value in the United States, for people do not mind if individual fortunes are made when the community profits from an enterprise. A focus on high-tech entrepreneurship might restore the general reputation of the entrepreneur in Czech and the other ex-Communist societies.

This is true because, without this distinction, and that between high-tech entrepreneurship and "managerialism," conclusions about how to promote high-tech entrepreneurship can be confusing and contradictory. The issue of stock options can be used to make this point. Their use has been both highly praised and heavily criticized, but the evaluation depends on which of two possible perspectives is adopted. Stock options can be a device that corporate executives use to inflate their incomes beyond what are already substantial salaries. That is "managerialism." Moreover, these same corporate executives can use accounting devices (e.g. not claiming an exercised stock option on the books as a company expense) to inflate corporate profits, thereby keeping – because of these artificially inflated profits – the company's stock prices high on equity markets. The executives who then sell the stock earn a lot of money. But the manipulation can have, when revealed, an adverse effect on the market. This stock option regime, by helping to provoke a sell-off of company shares (as in the recent bear market), can enrich the top executives while impoverishing the company's ordinary stockholders. This is also "managerialism."

But a stock option regime in a high-tech start-up serves a different purpose. It is not meant to supplement already high corporate emoluments, but to constitute an "IOU" form of delayed payments for executives hired at very low salaries by a venture's cash-strapped entrepreneur. He/she will compensate these employees for the skimpy pay in early years when (and if) success crowns the start-up's efforts later. Stock options are, then, neutral instruments, so judgments about their social usefulness depend on whether they are being utilized in an entrepreneurial start-up firm or in one where well-paid executives use them to fill even further the already quite full coffers of a manipulative managerial caste. And policy that recommends the establishment of stock options must be designed to promote the one (high-tech entrepreneurship) while discouraging the other (excessively profiteering "managerialism").

The same rationale affects judgments about desirability in management education. An education that contributes to the creation of privileged power groups within society, even if the groups are ostensibly blessed with superior know-how, is socially dangerous, and less desirable than an education (in this case entrepreneurship studies and high-tech networking activity) that eulogizes the Dionysian breed of entrepreneurs, who try to embed themselves inside a habitat dynamic that has proven to be the wellspring of technological creativity and economic prosperity in the IT era. For the Czechs, moreover, the choices extend to MBA education. The Czech pre-war leadership traditions, like the German, rejected managerialism. They drew their managerial elite from specialists who joined firms at entry level and were promoted from within. If Czechs base their management recruitment on post-experience MBA generalists, the country runs the risk of saddling itself with a managerial caste.

Feasibility

Desirability is not feasibility. In other words, is it feasible to believe that an education policy that actively and successfully promotes entrepreneurship studies will result in increasing the rate of high-tech start-ups in an economy? Neither (as acknowledged in the introduction) the methodology this study employs, nor the information it has produced, can answer this question. The data examined in chapter 3 does not prove that a growth in entrepreneurship studies increases entrepreneurial activity. Certainly not in the United States, where the entrepreneurship came first and then the studies, nor in France, Germany or the Czech Republic, where, despite some encouraging results reported at the end of chapter 5, entrepreneurship studies are too recent to have had effects on praxis that are convincingly measurable. For policy makers at this stage, therefore, the promotion of entrepreneurship studies is a work in progress, which has to be conducted with the assumption under which, Professor Eliasson says, managers in the experimentally organized economy operate – "working on hunches, intuition, analogies, and with incomplete information in pursuit of their goals" (Eliasson, 1997, p. 3). If the Apollonian policy formulator is not satisfied with such justifications for actions, he has no alternatives; not in this world. And so it is the educational entrepreneur, not the educational manager, who promotes entrepreneurship studies.

This conclusion provides, in itself, policy guidelines for the implementation of entrepreneurship studies in the three European countries. It is important for entrepreneurship studies to develop as a field of knowledge, because a disciplined discussion of a subject is usually a fruitful way to develop and disseminate information about it. Since social sciences have to develop in close contact with society in order for them to have verisimilitude, high-tech entrepreneurship studies must be project-oriented and activist in their pedagogy.

In Germany this means that these studies should not be left under the control of professors of BWL. They are *Wissenschaftler* of the Apollonian school, who are suspicious of the audacious mixing of scientists and practical people that, as seen in the United States, makes entrepreneurship studies thrive. That mixing should be encouraged through programs that especially introduce natural scientists and engineers to the non-scientific and technical dimension of entrepreneurship.

In the Czech Republic the need to build a business educational system has, from the perspective of entrepreneurship studies, put people in charge who are too enamored of the scientific management education programs established in business schools in North America and Western Europe after World War II, which educate managers for insertion into bureaucratic management hierarchies. The Czech policy makers need to bring more people into the reform process from outside academia and big corporations, and to rely on foreign advisors not drawn exclusively from the circle of business school deans and management professors. They need to develop entrepreneurship studies as a separate academic discipline, but one expressed through a start-up culture that is interdisciplinary and transversal.

In France the chief problem that entrepreneurship studies face arises from the deep divisions between the engineering and non-engineering world and within management academic cultures. The answer is not to give more money and power to *commerçants*, but less. Reform should, therefore, come through the engineers in a way that will make the importance of the non-technical aspects of entrepreneurship part of their consciousness. That might be done by exposing students in the best *écoles d'ingénieur* to very successful MOT programs and high-tech start-up incubators in the United States and the rest of Europe. People in university faculties and *grandes écoles de commerce* can play a role in creating this complex, but only if they can work out a way to make themselves useful to the engineers and their clients in praxis.

References

Abegglen, J. C., and G. J. Stalk (1985) *Kaisha, the Japanese Corporation*, Basic Books, New York.

Achleitner, A.-K. (2002) telephone interview, K. E. Schöne, September 10.

Ackoff, R. L. (1977) "The future of operations research is past," *Journal of the Operational Research Society*, 30: 2, 93–104.

Albert, P. (1986) "L'entrepreneurship dans les business schools américaines," *Revue d'Enseignement et Gestion*, June, 15–21.

(2002) telephone interview, K. E. Schöne, November 26.

Albert, P., M. Bernasconi and F.-X. Boucand (1999) *L'Enseignement de l'Entrepreneuriat au CERAM: Une Histoire avec Sophia Antipolis*, transactions of the first congress of l'Académie de l'Entrepreneuriat, Pôle Universitaire Européen, Lille.

Alic, J. A., L. M. Branscomb, H. Brooks and A. B. Carter (1992) *Beyond Spin-off: Military and Commercial Technologies in a Changing World*, Harvard Business School Press, Boston.

Allègre, C., D. Strauss-Kahn and C. Pierret (1997) *Mission sur la Technologie et l'Innovation*, Ministry of Finance, Paris.

Ansoff, I. (1983) conversation with Robert R. Locke, European Institute for Advanced Studies in Management, Brussels.

Aoki, M. (1990) "Towards an economic model of the Japanese firm," *Journal of Economic Literature*: 28, 1–27.

Assises de l'Innovation (1998) *La Culture de l'Innovation et du Risque*, Ministry of Education, first round table of the Assises de l'Innovation, Paris.

Astley, W. G. (1984) "Subjectivity, sophistry, and symbolism in management science," *Journal of Management Studies*: 21, 259–72.

Autio, E., and H. J. Sapienza (2000) "Comparing process and born global perspectives in the international growth of technology-based new firms," *Frontiers of Entrepreneurial Research 2000*.

Balassa, B. (1981) "The French economy under the Fifth Republic, 1958–1978," in W. G. Andrews and S. Hoffman (eds.) *The Impact of the Fifth Republic on France*, State University of New York Press, Albany, NY, 117–38.

Barsoux, J.-L., and P. Lawrence (1990) *Management in France*, Cassell, London.

Bayer, I. (2002) telephone interview, K. E. Schöne, August 21.

Beer, H. (2000) *Hochschul-Spin-offs im Hightech-Wettbewerb: Entrepreneurship-Theorie, Education und -Support*, Kovac, Hamburg.

Bénaček, V. (1994) *Small Businesses and Private Entrepreneurship During Transition: The Case of the Czech Republic*, Center for Economic Research and Graduate Education, Charles University, Prague (published with the support of the Ford Foundation).

Beranger, J., R. Chabbal and F. Dambrine (1998) *Rapport sur la Formation Entrepreneuriale des Ingénieurs pour le Ministère de l'Economie, des Finances et de l'Industrie*, Conseil Général des Mines and Conseil Général des Technologies de l'Information, Paris.

Berne, M. (1994) *The Minitel Success*, Institut National des Télécommunications, Département Gestion, Paris.

Best, M. H. (2001) *The New Competitive Advantage: The Renewal of American Industry*, Oxford University Press, Oxford.

Birch, D. (1979) *The Job Generation Process: Program on Neighborhood and Regional Change*, MIT Press, Cambridge, MA.

Boistel, P. (2002) written answer, K. E. Schöne, November 26.

Boltanski, L. (1987) *The Making of a Class: Cadres in French Society*, Cambridge University Press, Cambridge.

Boráková, T. (2002) personal interview, K. E. Schöne, December 4, Prague.

Bouc, F. (2000) "Kids learn e-biz with the help of Czech firms," *The Prague Post*, July 12.

Bouchikhi, H. (2002) telephone interview, K. E. Schöne, November 18.

Bouvier, J. (1984) "The French banks, inflation and the economic crisis, 1919–1939," *Journal of European Economic History*, Special Issue, 13: 2, 29–80.

Bower, L., and L. Gonderinger (2001) "Globopolis bomb," *The Prague Post*, January 24.

Brinkmann, G. (1967) *Die Ausbildung von Führungskräften für die Wirtschaft*, Broschiert, Cologne.

Brinton, C. (1950) *Ideas and Men: The Story of Western Thought*, Prentice-Hall, New York.

Broder, A. (1990) "Enseignement technique et croissance économique en Allemagne et en France, 1970–74: quelques éléments en vue d'analyse approfondie," in Y. Cohen and K. Manfrass (eds.) *Frankreich-Deutschland-Forschung: Technologie und Industrielle Entwicklung im 19. und 20. Jahrhundert*, C. H. Beck, Munich.

Bygrave, W. D., and C. W. Hofer (1991) "Theorizing about entrepreneurship," *Entrepreneurship Theory and Practice*, 16: 2, 13–22.

Calás, M. B., and L. Smircich (eds.) (1997) *Postmodern Management Theory*, Ashgate Publishing, Aldershot.

Capra, F. (1982) *The Turning Point: Science, Society and the Rising Culture*, Simon and Schuster, New York.

Castells, M., and P. Hall (1994) *Technopoles of the World: The Making of Twenty-First-Century Industrial Complexes*, Routledge, London.

Certhoux, G. (2002) telephone interview, K. E. Schöne, November 26.

Chaloupka, J. (2002) personal interview, K. E. Schöne, December 5, Prague.

Chaloupka, J., and L. Kameníková (2002) personal interview, K. E. Schöne, December 6, Brno.

Chytil, Z., and M. Sojka (2001) "Ten years of economic transformation in the Czech way," in G. Gorzelak, E. Ehrlich, L. Faltan and M. Illner (eds.) *Central Europe in Transition: Toward EU Membership*, Regional Studies Association, Warsaw, 14–38.

CIDEGEF (2001) "Réflexions sur la formation à l'entrepreneuriat," *Revue Francophone de Gestion*, July, 1–15.

Clark, G. W. (2002) *History of Technogenesis*, http://www.technogenesis. org/historyoftechnogenesis.htm, 1–3.

Cohen, B. D., and D. G. Meyer (2000) "The unique characteristics of Web-based businesses: an exploratory study," *Frontiers of Entrepreneurial Research 2000*.

Colander, D. (2002) "The death of neoclassical economics," *Journal of History of Economic Thought*, 22: 2, 127–43.

Colletis, G., and J.-L. Levet (1997) *Quelles Politiques pour l'Industrie Française? Dynamiques du Système Productif: Analyse, Débats, Propositions*, Commissariat Général du Plan, Paris.

Cordonnier, M. (2002) personal interview, K. E. Schöne, December 16, Compiègne.

CPR-Group (1998) *Le Livre Blanc, "Pour la Création d'un Environnement aux Entreprises de Croissance,"* report of a private group submitted to the government, Paris.

Crespin, G., A. Schaeffer and J.-N. Tronc (1996) *Les Réseaux de la Société de l'Information*, report of the working group headed by T. Mileo, Commissariat Général du Plan, Paris.

Danjou, I. (2000) *L'Entrepreneuriat: Un Champ Fertile à la Recherche de son Unité*, Cahiers de Recherche, ESC Lille, Lille.

—— (2002) personal interview, K. E. Schöne, September 16, Lille.

Deblois, C. (2002) personal interview, K. E. Schöne, December 17, Compiègne.

Debourse, J.-P., I. Danjou and T. Verstraete (1999) *Des "Best Practices" à la Stratégie d'un Groupe – ESC Lille*, communication to the first congress of the Académie de l'Entrepreneuriat, Lille.

Degot, V. (1980) "Types of French engineers and the implementation of company policy," *International Studies of Management and Organization*, 10: 1 & 2, 165–84.

De Kerorguen, Y. (1994) "La tour de France des technopôles," *L'Entreprise*: 105, 146–55.

De Metz, A. (2002) telephone interview, K. E. Schöne, November 18.

Dilk, A. (2002) "Kulturcrash im Silicon Valley – Deutsch-amerikanische Grenzerfahrungen", *ChangeX*, www.changeX.de, 05.04.2002.

Dixon, P. (1998) "Econometrics and the science of economics," *ECONSER*, 2: 9, 1–3.

Djelic, M.-L. (1998) *Exporting the American Model: The Post-War Transformation of European Business*, Oxford University Press, Oxford.

Dorfman, R., P. A. Samuelson and R. M. Solow (eds.) (1958) *Linear Programming and Economic Analysis*, McGraw-Hill, New York.

Dowling, M. (2002a) *Prospectus: Lehrstuhl für Innovations- und Technologiemanagement*, Regensburg University.

(2002b) telephone interview, K. E. Schöne, July 16.

Drèze, J. H. (1964) "Some postwar contributions of French economists to theory and public policy," *American Economic Review*, 54: 42, 1–64.

Dubois, B. (2002) personal interview, K. E. Schöne, September 17, Lille.

Dufour, S. (2000) personal interview, R. R. Locke, April 26, San Francisco.

Dunn, P., and L. Short (2001) *An Entrepreneurship Major?* www.sbaer.uca. edu/ Research/2001/ASBE/27asbe01.htm.

Dvorák, J. (1994) "Die wirtschaftswissenschaftliche Hochschulausbildung in der CSSR," in J. Schramm (ed.) *Sozialistische Hochschulausbildung vor dem Zusammenbruch: Entwicklung Wirtschaftswissenschaftlicher Ausbildung in Ost- und Mitteleuropa*, Peter Lang, Berlin, 148–81.

Earlybird (1999) *"Earlybird/Venture Capital,"* press clippings, www. earlybird.com/en/press/clipping.

Ehrenberg, R. (1910) "Terrorismus in der Wirtschafts-Wissenschaft," in R. Ehrenberg (ed.) *Gegen den Katheder-Sozialismus*, Hobbing, Berlin, 42–132.

Eickhoff, M. (2002) telephone interview, K. E. Schöne, September 10.

Eifertsen, R. (2001) "Top entrepreneurs scorn traditional business school models," *News Release*, Washington, June 14.

Eliasson, G. (1976) *Business Economic Planning – Theory, Practice and Comparison*, Wiley & Sons, London.

(1997) *The Nature of Economic Change and Management in the Knowledge-Based Information Economy*, paper, Royal Institute of Technology, Department of Industrial Economics and Management, Stockholm.

Engwall, L., and E. Gunnarsson (eds.) (1994) *Management Studies in an Academic Context*, Uppsala University Press, Uppsala.

Engwall, L., and V. Zamagni (eds.) (1998) *Management Education in Historical Perspective*, Manchester University Press, Manchester.

Etner, F. (1978) *Les Ingénieurs-Economistes Français (1841–1950)*, dissertation for Doctorat d'Etat, University of Paris IX, Paris.

EXIST (2002) *Ergebnisse und Erfahrungen*, www.exist.de/exist/main.html.

Farrell, K. (1984) *Venture Magazine*.

Fayolle, A. (1996) *Contribution à l'Etude des Comportements Entrepreneuriaux des Ingénieurs Français*, thesis for the doctorat en sciences de gestion, University of Lyon III, Lyon.

(1999a) *L'Ingénieur-Entrepreneur Français: Contribution à la Compréhension des Comportements de Création et Reprise d'Entreprises des Ingénieurs Diplomés*, L'Harmattan, Paris.

(1999b) *L'Enseignement de l'Entrepreneuriat dans les Universités Françaises: Analyse de l'Existant et Propositions pour en Faciliter le Développement*, report prepared at the request of the Ministère de l'Education Nationale, de la Recherche et de la Technologie, EM Lyon, Lyon.

(2000) "L'enseignement de l'entrepreneuriat dans le système éducatif supérieure français: un regard sur la situation actuelle," *Gestion 2000*, 17: 3, 77–95.

(2001) *Les Enjeux du Développement de l'Enseignement de l'Entrepreneuriat en France*, report prepared at the request of the Ministère de l'Education Nationale, de la Recherche et de la Technologie, Institut National Polytechnique de Grenoble, Grenoble.

Fayolle, A. (2002a) telephone interview, K. E. Schöne, July 29.

(2002b) telephone interview, K. E. Schöne, November 11.

Fayolle, A., and C. Bruyat (2002) *Works of the Institut National Polytechnique de Grenoble and the Université Pierre Mendès-France de Grenoble*, paper delivered at the conference on Entrepreneurship Research in Europe, Valence, September 18.

Fenn, D., and M. Warshaw (2000) *The Profit Minded Professor*, May, 1–7.

Ferrary, M. (2000) personal interview, R. R. Locke, April 6, Stanford.

Florin, J., and B. Schulze (2000) "Born to go public? Founder performance in new, high-growth, technology ventures," *Frontiers of Entrepreneurial Research 2000*.

Fonrouge, C. (2002) telephone interview, K. E. Schöne, November 20.

Fores, M. (1996) "The professional as a machine: the death of each day's life," in I. Glover and M. Hughes (eds.) *The Professional Managerial Class: Contemporary British Management in Pursuer Mode*, Avesbury, Aldershot.

Fronczak, M. (1997) "Motorola and Tesal team up to renew Moravia's 'Silicon Valley,'" *The Prague Post*, June 4.

Frugier, D. (2002) personal interview, K. E. Schöne, September 16, Lille.

Fruin, M. W. (1992) *The Japanese Enterprise System: Competitive Strategies and Cooperative Structures*, Clarendon Press, Oxford.

Gallouin, J.-F. (2002) telephone interview, K. E. Schöne, November 18.

Gandois, J. (1997) *France: Le Choix de la Performance Globale*, report of the commission "Compétitivité Française", Commissariat Général du Plan, Paris.

Gartner, W. B. (1988) "'Who is an entrepreneur?' is the wrong question," *American Journal of Small Business*, 12: 4, 11–32.

Gärtner, R. (1999) "Go west, Germans," *Manager Magazin*, January, 184–90.

Gemelli, G. (ed.) (1998) *The Ford Foundation and Europe (1950s–1970s): Cross-Fertilization of Learning in Social Science and Management*, European Interuniversity Press, Brussels.

Gering, T. (2002) telephone interview, K. E. Schöne, September 10.

Giraud, P. (2002) personal interview, K. E. Schöne, September 18, Valence.

Gordon, D. M. (1994) "Chickens home to roost: from prosperity to stagnation in the postwar U.S. economy", in M. Bernstein and D. E. Adler (eds.) *Understanding American Economic Decline*, Cambridge University Press, Cambridge, 34–76.

Görisch, J., M. Kulicke, R. W. Bruns and T. Stahlecker (2002) *Studierende und Selbstständigkeit: Ergebnisse der EXIST-Studienbefragung*, an EXIST study carried out by Fraunhofer-Institut für Systemtechnik und Innovationsforschung for the BMBF, Bonn.

Gourvish, T. R., and N. Tiratsoo (eds.) (1998) *Missionaries and Managers: American Influences on European Management Education, 1945–60*, Manchester University Press, Manchester.

Guillot, B. (2002) personal interview, K. E. Schöne, September 18, Valence.

Halberstam, D. (1986) *The Reckoning*, Morrow, New York.

Hartmann, H. (1963) *Amerikanische Firmen in Deutschland: Beobachtungen über Kontraste zwischen Industriegesellschaften*, Westdeutscher Verlag, Cologne and Opladen.

HBS (2002) *Compendium on Entrepreneurship*.

Henzler, H. A., and L. Späth (1992) *Sind die Deutschen noch zu Retten?* Bertelsmann, Munich.

Hering, T. (2002) personal interview, K. E. Schöne, September 5, Dresden.

Herrigel, G. (1995) *Reconceptualizing the Source of German Industrial Power*, Cambridge University Press, New York.

Hewitt-Dundas, N. (2000) "The adoption of advanced manufacturing technology and strategic complexity," *Frontiers of Entrepreneurial Research 2000*.

Hisrich, R. D., and M. D. Peters (1996) *Založeni a Rizení Nového Podniku*, Victoria Publishing, Prague [Czech translation of R. D. Hisrich and M. D. Peters (1995) *Entrepreneurship: Starting, Developing, and Managing a New Enterprise*, McGraw-Hill, Boston].

Hofstede, G. (1980) *Culture's Consequences: International Differences in Work-related Values*, Sage, Beverly Hills.

Holland, M. (1989) *When the Machine Stopped: A Cautionary Tale from Industrial America*, Harvard Business Press, Boston.

Hope, J., and T. Hope (1997) *Competing in the Third Wave: The Ten Key Management Issues of the Information Age*, Harvard Business School Press, Boston.

Howorth, C. A., and N. Wilson (2000) "A cognitive approach to explaining technology-based venture creation," *Frontiers of Entrepreneurial Research 2000*.

Hynes, B., B. O. Cinneide, P. Byrne and A. Morgan (2000) "Technology/science parks: a proven model for technology/high-growth ventures?" *Frontiers of Entrepreneurial Research 2000*.

Jedlicková, P., M. Mandiková and I. Sládková (2002) personal interview, K. E. Schöne, December 5, Prague.

Jouandeau, A. (2002) telephone interview, K. E. Schöne, November 25.

Joyandet, A., P. Hérisson and A. Türk (1997) *L'Entrée dans la Société de l'Information*, report of information for the Sénat, Paris.

Jutta Rubach & Partner (1999) *Das Silicon Valley kommt nach Europa – So gehen High Tech-Unternehmen an die Börse*, www.rubach-pr.de.

Kagone, T., K. Kobayashi, H. Terade, K. Iwami, S. Kitamura, K. Miki and H. Kanai (1981) "Mechanistic vs. organic management systems: a comparative study of adaptive patterns of U.S. and Japanese firms," *Annals of the School of Business Administration*, Kobe University: 25, 119–41.

Kahn, G. (1999) *La Recherche et l'Innovation dans les Technologies de l'Information et de la Communication*, report of the findings of the specialist group, Commissariat Général du Plan, Paris.

Katz, J. A. (1998) *A Brief History of Tertiary Entrepreneurship Education in the United States*, OECD, Brussels.

Katz, J. A., and R. P. Green (1996) "Academic resources for entrepreneurship education," *Simulation and Gaming*, 27: 3, 365–74 [Kauffman Center for Entrepreneurial Leadership Clearinghouse for Entrepreneurship Education, www.celcee.edu].

Kenney, M., and R. Florida (1993) *Beyond Mass Production: The Japanese System and its Transfer to the US*, Oxford University Press, New York.

Kickul, J., and L. K. Gundry (2000) "Pursuing technological innovation: the role of entrepreneurial posture and opportunity and opportunity recognition among Internet firms," *Frontiers of Entrepreneurial Research 2000*.

Kieser, A. (2002a) On communication barriers between management science, consultancies and business companies, in T. Clark and R. Fincham (eds.) *The Management Advice Industry: Critical Perspectives on Consultants, Gurus and Managerial Knowledge*, Blackwell, Oxford, 206–27.

(2002b) personal interview, K. E. Schöne, May 25, Mannheim.

Kipping, M., and O. Bjarnar (eds.) (1998) *The Americanization of European Business: The Marshall Plan and the Transfer of US Management Models*, Routledge, London.

Klandt, H. (2002) personal interview, K. E. Schöne, September 20, Valence.

Klandt, H., and U. Knaup (2002) *Gründungsprofessuren 2002: Eine Studie zum Stand der Institutionalisierung der Gründungsforschung und -lehre an deutschsprachigen Hochschulen, Entrepreneurship Research*, Förderkreis Gründungs-Forschung, Cologne and Dortmund.

Komárek, P. (2002a) *Accreditation of Technology Parks – more than Ten Years' Experience in the Czech Republic*, Business Innovation Center at the Czech Technical University, Prague.

(2002b) personal interview, K. E. Schöne, December 5, Prague.

(2003) personal interview, K. E. Schöne, January 17, Prague.

Kombou, L. (1986) *Les Créateurs d'Entreprise en Aquitaine: Analyse de leurs Profils, de leurs Comportements et de leurs Evaluations des Aides Publiques pendant la Période 1977–1984*, thesis, Faculty of Management Sciences, University of Bordeaux, Bordeaux.

Korab, V. (2002) personal interview, K. E. Schöne, December 6, Brno.

Korff, K. (2000) "Czech high tech," *The Prague Post*, May 3.

(2002) "Getting wired," *The Prague Post*, September 15.

Kreim, R. (2002) personal interview, K. E. Schöne, December 3, Prague.

Krempl, S. (1999) *Dem Vermarktungs-Gen auf der Spur*, www.heise.de, 30.08.1999.

Kuisel, R. F. (1981) *Capitalism and the State in Modern France*, Cambridge University Press, Cambridge.

Laffitte, P. (1997) *Rapport sur la France et la Société de l'Information: Un Cri d'Alarme et une Croisade Nécessaire*, Sénat, Office Parlementaire d'Evaluation des Choix Scientifiques at Technologiques, Paris.

Landes, D. S. (1969) *The Unbound Prometheus: Technological Change and Industrial Development in Western Europe from 1750 to the Present*, Cambridge University Press, Cambridge.

Laredo, P., and P. Mustar (eds.) (2001) *Research and Innovation Policies in the New Global Economy: An International Comparative Analysis*, Edward Elgar, Cheltenham.

(2002) "Innovation and research policies in France (1980–2000) or the disappearance of the Colbertist State," *Research Policy*: 31, 55–72.

Lawrence, P. (1980) *Managers and Management in West Germany*, St. Martin's Press, New York.

Le Marois, H. (1985) *Contributions à la Mise en Place des Dispositifs de Soutien aux Entrepreneurs*, thesis, Faculty of Management Sciences, University of Lille, Lille.

Ledru, L. (2000) personal interview, R. R. Locke, April 4, San Francisco.

Lee, C.-M., W. Miller, M. Gong-Hancock and S. Rowan (eds.) (2000a) *The Silicon Valley Edge: A Habitat for Innovation and Entrepreneurship*, Stanford University Press, Stanford.

Lee, C.-M., W. Miller, M. Gong-Hancock and S. Rowan (2000b) "The Silicon Valley habitat," in C.-M. Lee, W. Miller, M. Gong-Hancock and S. Rowan (eds.) *The Silicon Valley Edge: A Habitat for Innovation and Entrepreneurship*, Stanford University Press, Stanford, 1–15.

Lee, M., H. Letiche, R. Crawshaw and M. Thomas (eds.) (1996) *Management Education in the New Europe*, International Thomson Business Press, London.

Lerner, J. (1990) *The Mobility of Corporate Scientists and Engineers Between Civil and Defense Activities: Evidence from the SEE Database*, Science, Technology and Public Policy Program Discussion Paper 90/102, John F. Kennedy School of Government, Cambridge, MA.

Lescat, G. (2002) telephone interview, K. E. Schöne, November 14.

Levy, A. (1993) "Bruce Damer's vision of a silicon castle," *The Prague Post*, September 1.

Linden, B. (2000) *Studienführer Mittel- und Osteuropa: Polen, Tschechische Republik, Slowakische Republik, Ungarn, Rumänien*, Bertelsmann, Bielefeld.

Locke, R. R. (1984) *The End of the Practical Man: Entrepreneurship and Higher Education in Germany, France and Great Britain, 1880–1940*, JAI Press, London.

(1985) "Business education in Germany: past systems and current practice", *Business History Review*, 49: 2, 232–53.

(1989) *Management and Higher Education since 1940: The Influence of America and Japan on West Germany, Great Britain and France*, Cambridge University Press, Cambridge.

(1996) *The Collapse of the American Management Mystique*, Oxford University Press, Oxford.

(1998a) *Factoring American Business School Education into the Revolution in Interactive Information Technology*, FNEGE.

(ed.) (1998b) *Management Education*, Ashgate Publishing, Aldershot.

(2003) "American business school education and the revolution in interactive information technology," in Paul Jeffcutt (ed.) *The Foundations of Management Knowledge*, Routledge, London, 66–82.

Lorentz, M. F. (1998) *Commerce Électronique: Une Nouvelle Donne pour les Consommateurs, les Entreprises, les Citoyens et les Pouvoirs Publiques*, report of the working group headed by M. F. Lorentz, Ministry of Finance, Paris.

Majoie, B. (1998) *Recherche et Innovation: La France dans la Compétition Mondiale*, report of the working group, Commissariat Général du Plan, Paris.

Malý, M. (2002) personal interview, K. E. Schöne, April 25, Prague.

Mancke, R. (2002) personal interview, K. E. Schöne, August 9, Leipzig.

Mandiková, M. (2002) personal interview, K. E. Schöne, December 2, Prague.

Marion, S. (2002) telephone interview, K. E. Schöne, November 25.

Marmonier, L., and R.-A. Thiétart (1988) "L'histoire, un outil pour la gestion?" *Revue Française de Gestion*: numéro spécial 70, 162–71.

Martin, F. (1997) *Cerveaux en Fuite ou en Voyages*, CNRS, French embassy, Washington, DC.

Martin-Lalande, P. (1997) *L'Internet: Un Vrai Défi pour la France*, La Documentation Française, Paris.

Masberg, M. (2003) telephone interview, K. E. Schöne, January 8.

Mason, C. M., and R. T. Harrison (2000) "Investing in technology ventures: what do business angels look for at the initial screening stage?" *Frontiers of Entrepreneurial Research 2000*.

Matusiak, K. B. (2003) *Entrepreneurship – Ein Schwachpunkt im Transformationsprozess osteuropäischer Länder?* University of Lodz, kbmat@krysia.uni.lodz.pl.

McClelland, D. C. (1964) *The Roots of Consciousness*, Nostrand, Princeton, NJ.

McCline, R. L., and S. Bhat (2000) "Empirical examination of the factors contributing to the high presence of ethnic minorities in Silicon Valley high-tech start-ups: does the classic entrepreneurship profile survive cross-cultural analysis?" *Frontiers of Entrepreneurial Research 2000*.

McCloskey, D. (1983) "The rhetoric of economics," *Journal of Economic Literature*: 21, 481–517.

McNally, B. (1992) "Czech computer company becomes a success story," *The Prague Post*, July 14.

Mertens, P. (1973) "Der gegenwärtige Stand von Forschung und Lehre in der Betriebswirtschaftslehre," *Zeitschrift für betriebswirtschaftliche Forschung, Sonderheft Bildung und Wettbewerbsfähigkeit*, 12: 18, 490–554.

Meuleau, M. (1988) *Les HEC: D'un Diplôme Marginal à la Célébrité Scolaire et Professionnelle (1881–1980)*, paper delivered at the Colloquium on History of Management, Paris, March 11–12.

Meyer, J.-B. (1999) *La Loi de Finance*, "Les personnels de la recherche" project, Sénat, Paris.

Meyer, J.-B., and M. Brown (1999) *Scientific Diasporas: A New Approach to Brain Drain*, UNESCO, New York.

Mikoláš, Z., and L. Ludvík (2003) personal interview, K. E. Schöne, January 16, Ostrava.

Miller, W. F. (2000) personal interview, R. R. Locke, April 5, Stanford.

Mortier, D. (1996) *Report on Entrepreneurial Education in France*, Coller Capital, London.

Moscovitch, E., R. DeKaser, P. Fitzgibbon and D. Fulman (1997) *MIT: The Impact of Innovation*, Boston Bank, Boston.

Moser, R. (2002) telephone interview, K. E. Schöne, August 28.

Mueller, K. (2002) *Innovation Policy Profile: Czech Republic, Innovation Policy in Six Candidate Countries: The Challenges*, report prepared for the Directorate General for Enterprise, European Commission, Charles University, Prague.

Mustar, P. (1997) "Spin-off enterprises. How French academics create hi-tech companies: the conditions for success or failure," *Science and Public Policy*: February, 17–41.

    (1998) "Partnerships, configurations and dynamics in the creation and development of SMEs by researchers," *Industry and Higher Education*: August, 217–21.

Nambisan, S. (2000) "Customer networks, entrepreneur strategy, and firm growth: insights from the software industry," *Frontiers of Entrepreneurial Research 2000*.

Nelson, J. R. (1963) "Practical applications of marginal cost pricing in the public utility field," *American Economic Review*, 53: 2, 474–81.

Němcová, L. (1995) "Conference: business and ethics," *Prague Economic Papers: Quarterly Journal of Economic Theory and Policy*, University of Economics, Prague, 2, 100–03.

    (1998) "Teaching business ethics at the University of Economics in Prague," in L. Zsolnai (ed.) *The European Difference*, Kluwer Academic Publishing, Boston.

    (2003) personal interview, K. E. Schöne, January 14, Prague.

Nguyen, J. (2000) personal interview, R. R. Locke, April 20, Redwood City.

Nonaka, I., and H. Takeuchi (1995) *The Knowledge-creating Company: How Japanese Companies Create the Dynamics of Innovation*, Oxford University Press, New York.

Nuhn, H. (1989) "Technologische Innovation und Industrielle Entwicklung – Silicon Valley, Modelle zukünftiger Regionalentwicklung?" *GR*, 41: 5, 258–65.

Oliver, N., and B. Wilkinson (1992) *The Japanization of British Industry: New Developments in the 1990s*, Blackwell, Oxford.

Operations Research Society of America (1959) *Formal Educational Offerings in Operations Research*, report of the Education Committee.

Orlinski, J. (2002a) personal interview, K. E. Schöne, September 18, Valence.

(2002b) personal interview, K. E. Schöne, December 16–18, Compiègne.

Ormerod, P. (1994) *The Death of Economics*, Faber & Faber, London.

Ouchi, W. G. (1981) *Theory Z: How American Business can Meet the Japanese Challenge*, Addison-Wesley, Reading, MA.

Ozaki, R. S. (1992) *Human Capitalism: The Japanese Enterprise System as World Model*, Penguin, New York.

Papin, R. (2002) telephone interview, K. E. Schöne, December 17.

Patton, R. (1999) "Stuck in the past," *The Prague Post*, June 9.

Peccoud, F. (2002) personal interview, K. E. Schöne, December 16, Compiègne.

Philips, D. B. (2000) "Home-based firms, e-commerce, and high-technology small firms: are they related?" *Frontiers of Entrepreneurial Research 2000*.

Pletsch, C. (1991) *Young Nietzsche: Becoming a Genius*, Free Press, New York.

Porter, M. (1990) *The Competitive Advantage of Nations*, Macmillan, New York.

(1998) "Clusters and the new economics of competition," *Harvard Business Review*: 6, 77–90.

Poston, J. (1999) "The next NetBeans," *The Prague Post*, November 10.

(2000a) "Nothing ventured," *The Prague Post*, January 26.

(2000b) "Into the Internet box," *The Prague Post*, February 16.

Prasad, V. K., and G. M. Naidu (2000) "Integration of information technology into marketing and its influence on competitive advantage of SMEs," *Frontiers of Entrepreneurial Research 2000*.

Pyke, F., and W. Sengenberger (1992) *Industrial Districts and Local Economic Regeneration*, International Institute for Labor Studies, Geneva.

Pyke, F., G. Becattini and W. Sengenberger (1990) *Industrial Districts and Inter-Firm Cooperation in Italy*, International Institute for Labor Studies, Geneva.

Raud, S. (2000) personal interview, R. R. Locke, April 4, San Francisco.

Rebouil, M. (2002) personal interview, K. E. Schöne, September 18, Valence.

Reynolds, P. D., M. Hay and S. M. Camps (2001) "2001 Executive Report," *Global Entrepreneurship Monitor*.

Reynolds, P. D., D. J. Storey and P. Westhead (1994) "Cross-national comparisons of the variation in new firm formation rates," *Regional Studies*, 28: 4, 443–56.

Rheingold, H. (1991) *Virtual Reality*, Summit Books, New York.
Ribeill, G. (1984) "Entrepreneur hier et aujourd'hui: la contribution des ingénieurs," *Culture Technique*, 12, 79–92.
Ritzer, G. (1995) *The McDonaldization of Society: An Investigation into the Changing Character of Contemporary Social Life*, Pine Forge Press, Newbury Park, CA.
Riveline, C. (1983) personal interview, R. R. Locke, September 29, Paris.
Robinson, P., and M. Haynes (1990) "Entrepreneurship education in America's major universities," *Entrepreneurship Theory & Practice*, 15: 3, 41–52.
Rogers, E. M., and K. Larsen (1986) *Silicon Valley Fieber: An der Schwelle zur High-Tech-Zivilisation*, Diogenes Taschenbuch, Berlin.
Romer, P. (1990) "Endogenous technological change," *Journal of Political Economy*, 98, 71–102.
Rosenberg, V. L., and R. Jones (1994) "Entrepreneurship scholarship in intent and use," *Frontiers of Entrepreneurship Research 1994*.
Rotgeri, F. (2002) personal interview, K. E. Schöne, December 12, Prague.
Rumpf, M. (2002) telephone interview, K. E. Schöne, September 4.
Sartre, J.-P. (1948) *Situations*, Gallimard, Paris.
Sass, S. A. (1982) *The Pragmatic Imagination: A History of the Wharton School 1881–1981*, University of Pennsylvania Press, Philadelphia.
Sawyer, O. O., and J. McGee (2000) "Strategic uncertainty and information search activities of high-technology manufacturing firms: does venture age matter?" *Frontiers of Entrepreneurial Research 2000*.
Saxenian, A. (1989) "The Cheshire cat's grin: innovation, regional development and the Cambridge case," *Economy and Society*, 18: 4, 448–77.
  (1994) *Regional Advantage, Culture and Competition in Silicon Valley and Route 128*, Harvard University Press, Cambridge, MA.
  (2000) "Networks of immigrant entrepreneurs," in C.-M. Lee, W. Miller, M. Gong-Hancock and S. Rowan (eds.) *The Silicon Valley Edge: A Habitat for Innovation and Entrepreneurship*, Stanford University Press, Stanford, 248–75.
Schade, C. (2002) personal interview, K. E. Schöne, September 11, Berlin.
Schefczyk, M. (2002) personal interview, K. E. Schöne, August 28, Dresden.
Schieb-Bienfait, N. (2002) telephone interview, K. E. Schöne, November 19.
Schlossmann, S., M. Sedlack and H. Wechsler (1987) *The 'New Look': The Ford Foundation and the Revolution in Business Education*, Graduate Management Admission Council Papers, Los Angeles.
Schmaltz, K. (1930) "German business periodicals," *The Accounting Review*: 5, 231–34.

Schmidt, K. (1986) *Der Traum vom deutschen Silicon Valley*, Verlag Moderne Industrie, Landsberg am Lech.

Schmitt, C. (2002) telephone interview, K. E. Schöne, November 19.

Schmoller, G. (1904) *Grundriß der allgemeinen Volkswirtschaftslehre*, Verlag Wirtschaft und Finanzen, Dusseldorf.

Schmude, J. (2001) "Gründungsforschung und Unternehmerausbildung an Hochschulen," *Internationales Gewerbearchiv: Zeitschrift für Klein- und Mittelunternehmen*, 49: 2, 89–104.

Schmude, J., and S. Uebelacker (2001) *Vom Studenten zum Unternehmer: Welche Hochschule bietet die besten Chancen?* Lehrstuhl für Wirtschaftsgeographie, Regensburg University, Regensburg.

—— (2002) *Gründungsausbildung in Deutschland und den USA: Eine Analyse zur Organisation und Ausrichtung von Entrepreneurship-Professuren*, Deutsche Ausgleichsbank, Bonn.

Schmude, J., and L. von Rosenstiel (1997) *Antrag zur Einrichtung eines Schwerpunktprogramms "Interdisziplinäre Gründungsforschung"*, LMU Munich, Munich.

Schumpeter, J. A. (1996) *The Theory of Economic Development*, UK Transaction Publishers, London.

Senicourt, P. (1997) *Contribution Constructiviste à la Conceptualisation, la Modélisation et l'Opérationnalisation de l'Aide à la Demarche Enterpreneuriale et la Prise des Décisions Stratégiques*, thesis for the doctorat en sciences de gestion, University of Paris IX, Paris.

—— (2002) telephone interview, K. E. Schöne, November 28.

Sérusclat, F. (1997) *Rapport sur les Techniques des Apprentissages Essentiels pour une Bonne Insertion dans la Société de l'Information*, Sénat, Office Parlementaire d'Evaluation des Choix Scientifiques et Technologiques, Paris.

Skambracks, D. (1999) *Gründungsbremse Bürokratie*, Deutsche Ausgleichsbank, Bonn and Bad Godesberg.

Smith, D. K., and R. C. Alexander (1988) *Fumbling the Future: How Xerox Invented, Then Ignored the First Personal Computer*, William Morrow and Co., New York.

Smolova, K. (2002) "Vstupenka do sveta velkeho obchodi," *Prague Tribune*, 78: 3, 18–25.

SOFARIS (1996) *SOFARIS et la Création d'Entreprise*, general delegation for the studies and for the development of SOFARIS.

Stearns, T. M., and K. R. Allen (2000) "The foundation of high-technology start-ups: the who, where, when, and why," *Frontiers of Entrepreneurial Research 2000*.

Sternberg, R. (1988) "Fünf Jahre Technologie- und Gründerzentren in der Bundesrepublik Deutschland – Erfahrungen, Empfehlungen, Perspektiven," *Geographische Zeitschrift*, 76: 3, 164–79.

Stumpf, S. A., and B. Shirley (1994) "Understanding the gaps: research-education-practice," *Frontiers of Entrepreneurship Research 1994*.

Taiichi, O. (1988) *Toyota Production System: Beyond Large-scale Production*, Productivity Press, Cambridge, MA.

Tanner, R. P., and A. G. Athos (1981) *The Art of Japanese Management: Applications for American Executives*, Simon and Schuster, New York.

Teach, R. D., and R. O. Schwartz (2000) "A temporal study of the product development management strategies in entrepreneurial technology-based firms," *Frontiers of Entrepreneurial Research 2000*.

Térouanne, D., D. Martin-Rovet and J.-B. Thibaud (1998) *L'Intéraction entre la France et les Etats-Unis en Science et Ingénierie*, CNRS, French embassy, Washington, DC.

Thurow, L. C. (ed.) (1985) *The Management Challenge: Japanese Views*, MIT Press, Cambridge, MA.

Torres, N. (2001) "Can you learn to start a business?" *Entrepreneur's Start-Up Magazine*, December, 1–4.

Trégouët, R. (1998) *Les Pyramides du Pouvoir aux Réseaux de Savoirs*, Rapport d'Information no. 331, 2 vols., La Documentation Française, Paris.

Trémembert, P., and J. Le Traon (2002) telephone interview, K. E. Schöne, November 20.

Tuunanen, M. (1997) *Finnish and U.S. Entrepreneurs' Need for Achievement: A Cross-Cultural Analysis*, Proceedings of the Academy of Entrepreneurship, Maui, Hawaii, October 14–17.

Uebelacker, S. (2002) written answer, K. E. Schöne, July 14.

Vagts, A. (1937) *A History of Militarism: Romance and Realities of a Profession*, Norton, New York.

Vávra, L. (2002) personal interview, K. E. Schöne, December 2, Prague.

Verstraete, T. (1997) *Modélisation de l'Organisation initiée par un Créateur s'inscrivant dans une Logique d'Entrepreneuriat Persistant: Les Dimensions Cognitives, Praxelogiques et Structurales de l'Organisation Entrepreneuriale*, thesis for the doctorat en sciences de gestion, University of Lille, Lille.

Vesper, K. H., and W. B. Gardner (1999) *Survey of Entrepreneurship Education*, Babson College, Center for Entrepreneurial Studies, Wellesley, MA.

Vitols, S. (2001) "Frankfurt's Neuer Markt and IPO explosion: is Germany on the road to Silicon Valley?" *Economy and Society*, 30: 4, 553–64.

Vogel, E. F. (1979) *Japan as Number One: Lessons for America*, Harvard University Press, Cambridge, MA.

Vogt, W. (1980) "Erich Schneider und die Wirtschaftstheorie," in G. Bombach and M. Tacke (eds.) *Erich Schneider 1900–1970: Gedenkband und Bibliographie*, Institut für Weltwirtschaft, Kiel, 13–48.

Volkswirt, Der – *Wirtschafts- und Finanz-Zeitung* (1965) "Betriebswirtschaftslehre, Theorie und Praxis im Streitgespräch," 19: 17, 1426–28.

Wassenberg, R. (2002) telephone interview, K. E. Schöne, August 19.

Welt, Die (1965) "Betriebswirtschaftslehre – Wohin?" July 3.

Westney, D. E. (1987) *Imitation and Innovation: The Transfer of Western Organizational Patterns to Meiji Japan*, Harvard University Press, Cambridge, MA.

Witt, P. (2002) telephone interview, K. E. Schöne, August 19.

Womack, J. P., D. Jones and D. Roos (1990) *The Machine that Changed the World*, Rawson Associates, New York.

Würth, R. (2002) written answer, K. E. Schöne, September 12.

YEO (2000) *The Spirit of Entrepreneurship*, Global Entrepreneurship Monitor.

Yolin, J.-M. (1997) *Contribution à la Réflexion sur l'Identité de l'Ingénieur et le Rôle des Ecoles des Mines*, http://cri.ensmp.fr/yolin/jmyes/ingenie.html, September 9.

Zacharakis, A., G. D. Meyer and J. O. DeCastro (1999) "National entrepreneurship assessment, United States of America," *Global Entrepreneurship Monitor*.

Zeitlin, J. (2000) "Introduction," in J. Zeitlin and G. Herrigel (eds.) *Americanization and Its Limits: Reworking US Technology and Management in Post-War Europe and Japan*, Oxford University Press, Oxford, 1–50.

Zeitlin, J., and G. Herrigel (eds.) (2000) *Americanization and Its Limits: Reworking US Technology and Management in Post-War Europe and Japan*, Oxford University Press, Oxford.

Zühlsdorff, H. (2002) written answer, K. E. Schöne, September 20.

Index

Académie de l'Entrepreneuriat 137, 138, 141
Academy of Science, and Czech research 196
Achleitner, Ann-Kristin 159
Ackoff, Russel 56
Acte de l'Entreprendre 175
Advanced Research Projects Agency ARPA 17, 19; work of 17–18
Agence Nationale Pour la Création d'Entreprises 14, 132
Albert, Philippe 119, 131–32, 136, 172, 179; "USA, Country of Entrepreneurship" 131
Allais, Maurice 93
Allègre, Claude 141
Allen, Paul 21
America, entrepreneurship studies in 51–81
American Assembly of Collegiate Schools of Business (AACBS) 193
American Business Conference 109
American Graduate School of International Management (Thunderbird) 57
Americanization 4–7, 10, 49, 66, 105–7, 108, 109, 113–15, 126, 131, 138, 152–53, 159, 160, 173–74, 183, 212; a nomenclature 4; and neutral analytical categories 7–8, 10; and France 32; and the Czech Republic 191–92, 194, 210; as contested historical project 7, 109; classical age of 6; *Fordismus* 5; Henry Ford 5; *"If Japan Can, Why Can't We"* 9; in The Czech Republic through Europe 192–94; "Japanization," 6, 10, 13, 33; mass production 5; of German entrepreneurship studies 162; Post

World War II 5; scientific management movement 4; Taylorism 4, 5; "The New Competitive Advantage" 8; translating terminology into French and German 108–9
analytically neutral production models 8, 21; see Best, Michael
angels 45, 112
Ansoff, Igor 194
ANVAR 167, 176, 177
Apollo & Dionysus, as clarifying management concepts 1, 2, 60, 61, 77, 80
Apollonian management 3, 31, 60, 122, 224
ARPANET 18
Assises de l'Innovation (Paris) 138, 169
Association of Innovative Entrepreneurship (AIE) 209
Astley, W. Grant *Subjectivity, Sophistry, and Symbolism in Management Science* 57
Augmentation Research Center 17, 18
Autio, Erkko, economist view of entrepreneurialism 19

Babson College 63, 119; Center for Entrepreneurship 71
Balassa, Bela 32
Baritault, Alain 39
Barsoux, Jean-Louis 37
Bayh-Dole Act 152
Bénacek, Vladimir 196, 197
Beranger, Chabral, and Dambrine report 138, 166, 171, 172, 173, 174; US influence 173
Berger, Gaston 95
Berger, Suzanne 47

241

Printed in the United States
By Bookmasters